Reuben Kriebel, Balthasar Heebner, Caleb Heydrick

Genealogical record of the descendents of the Schwenkfelders.

Who arrived in Pennsylvania in 1733, 1734, 1736, 1737. From the German of the

Rev. Balthasar Heebner, and from other sources.

Reuben Kriebel, Balthasar Heebner, Caleb Heydrick

Genealogical record of the descendents of the Schwenkfelders.

Who arrived in Pennsylvania in 1733, 1734, 1736, 1737. From the German of the Rev. Balthasar Heebner, and from other sources.

ISBN/EAN: 9783337724313

Printed in Europe, USA, Canada, Australia, Japan

Cover: Foto ©ninafisch / pixelio.de

More available books at **www.hansebooks.com**

OF THE DESCENDANTS OF THE

SCHWENKFELDERS,

WHO

ARRIVED IN PENNSYLVANIA IN 1733, 1734, 1736, 1737.

FROM THE GERMAN OF THE

REV. BALTHASAR HEEBNER,

AND FROM OTHER SOURCES.

BY THE REV. REUBEN KRIEBEL.

WITH

AN HISTORICAL SKETCH

BY C. HEYDRICK.

MANAYUNK:
JOSEPHUS YEAKEL, PRINTER, 4402 CRESSON ST.
1879.

PREFACE.

About four years ago a movement was inaugurated looking to the publication at some time in the not distant future of a more complete history of the Schwenkfelders than has yet appeared, and a committee charged with the collection of material for such work was appointed at the Annual Conference of the Society in October, 1875. The labors of that committee naturally turned the attention of their constituents to the subject of genealogy, and excited a very general desire for the compilation from the many existing manuscripts of a complete genealogy of the descendants of the immigrant Schwenkfelders. By common consent the superintendence of such compilation was devolved upon the undersigned, who engaged the services of Rev. Reuben Kriebel to collect and transcribe the several records in a form suitable for printing. The present volume is the result of their labors.

The Rev. Balthasar Heebner, who died at an advanced age in 1848, had prepared and kept a record of marriages, births, and deaths of those who belonged to the Society of Schwenkfelders (of which he was a minister) to within a few years of his death. This record was the most complete one extant, yet in many instances omissions occurred, which had to be supplied, partially from other manuscripts, and from other records, kept in family Bibles, etc. As Mr. Heebner kept no record of those who did not adhere to the Society, other means had to be resorted to for the necessary information. This involved considerable labor, and the compiler opened a correspondence with all from whom he could obtain any knowledge.

This correspondence extended nearly into every State of the Union. In most cases he was quite successful, yet in a few he failed to get the desired information for his purpose. This was owing to the utter indifference of some few to give their family records, and several families could not be found; yet in the whole he flatters himself that his efforts have been very successful, and must be very gratifying to the numerous descendants of those early pioneers who braved the toils and vicissitudes of the earlier settlers' life.

The record from 1846 has been supplied by the personal visits of the compiler to the descendants living in the region of country where their forefathers originally settled, and he obtained his information from authentic sources. The lists of male and female emigrants are from the original papers on file in the office of the Secretary of the Commonwealth at Harrisburg. An appendix explaining in some cases the relationship of the early immigrants, etc., is added at the end of the Record, to which the reader's attention is directed.

The historical sketch prepared by C. Heydrick, Esq., of Franklin, Pa., gives a faithful account of Caspar Schwenkfeld and his followers, and forms a very important part of the work. It is not, however, intended to take the place of the more elaborate work originally contemplated, the preparation of which, it is hoped, will, in some measure, be aided by our labors.

Those interested in getting up this work, indulge the hope that no one of the descendants will be so critical as to charge them with any dereliction of duty in not making it quite free from errors, for they issue it from the press with some diffidence, and hope that the errors may not be many.

C. HEYDRICK,
Franklin, Pa.
W. A. YEAKLE,
C. A. YEAKLE,
JOSEPH YEAKLE,
CALEB HEYDRICK,
GEO. N. HEYDRICK,
WILLIAM YEAKLE,
CHARLES YEAKLE.

FLOURTOWN, PA., July 5, 1879.

THE SCHWENKFELDERS.

AN HISTORICAL SKETCH.

BY C. HEYDRICK.

THE Schwenkfelders were so called from Caspar Schwenkfeld, a Silesian nobleman. He was born at Ossing (now Ossig), in Lübner circle, in the Principality of Liegnitz, in Lower Silesia, in 1490, was educated at Cologne, and dwelt several years at other universities, where theology early attracted his attention, and the writings of the Church Fathers became his favorite study. Quitting university life he visited many German courts, and devoted some years to the culture which, in his time, was supposed to befit his rank, qualifying himself for knighthood, and becoming, as he says in one of his epistles, a courtier. While yet a young man he entered the service of Carl, Duke of Münsterberg, a grandson of Podiebrad, the Hussite King of Bohemia, at whose court the doctrines of John Huss were received, and by none more heartily than by the young knight and courtier. They made a deep and lasting impression upon his mind, and doubtless gave direction to his future life and labors. Bodily infirmities soon unfitted him for knightly duties, and he quitted the service of the Duke of Münsterberg and became Counsellor to Frederick II., Duke of Liegnitz, whom he served in that capacity a number of years. Theology, however, had stronger attractions for him than affairs of state.

He made the acquaintance of many theologians who were drifting in the direction of the Reformation, among whom were Valentine Crautwald, Johann Sigismund Werner, and Fabian Eckel, and under the influence of such associations the impressions received at Münsterberg deepened until, as he expressed it, God touched his heart, and he withdrew from the ducal court and was chosen Canon of St. John's Church in Liegnitz. Luther had now withdrawn from the Church of Rome, and his preaching attracted Schwenkfeld's attention and inspired him with a more intense zeal for the service of the Divine Master. He was at one with Luther upon the issues which the latter had raised with the Roman Catholic Church, and could no longer hold his position in St. John's Church without violence to his conscience. He therefore renounced it to become an evangelist, and, for thirty-six years, with voice and pen, exhort men to repentance and godliness.

Although not by nature a controversialist, as his writings abundantly testify, Schwenkfeld soon came to differ with the great Reformer on several points, chief among which related to the Eucharist, to the efficacy of the Divine Word, to the human nature of Christ, and to baptism. Schwenkfeld rejected the doctrine of impanation or consubstantiation as well as that of transubstantiation, and held that Christ taught (Matt. xxvi. 26) that "such as this broken bread is to the body, so is my body to the soul, a true and real food, which nourishes, sanctifies, and delights the soul; and such as this wine is to the body, so, in its effects, is my blood to the soul, which it strengthens and refreshes;" and, as a corollary, that the impenitent, though he would eat of the bread of the Lord, could not eat the body of the Lord, but that the penitent believer did partake of *both*, not only at the sacramental altar, but elsewhere.

In respect to the second point of difference, he denied that the *external* word, which is committed to writing in the Scriptures, was endowed with the power of healing, illuminating, and renewing the mind, but ascribed this power to the Internal or Eternal Word, *i.e.*, Christ himself. (John i. 1-14; Rev. xix. 13.) He regretted that Luther, who at first was quite in accord with him, should see fit afterwards to ascribe to the written, outward, or preached word that power and efficacy which is inherent only in Christ, the Eternal Word. Luther translated Romans x. 17 : "So kommt der Glaube aus der Predigt, das Predigen aber durch das Wort Gottes"—So faith cometh by *preaching*, but *preaching* by the word of God; while Schwenkfeld followed the original closely, rendering it in the equivalent of the English translation: So then faith cometh by hearing, and hearing by the word of God.

Upon the third point of difference Schwenkfeld would not allow Christ's human nature in its exalted state to be called a creature or created substance, holding that such denomination was "infinitely below His majestic dignity, reunited, as it is in that glorious state, with the Divine Essence." He also rejected infant baptism, holding that instruction and faith should precede baptism (Acts viii. 12, 13; Mark xvi. 15, 16; Matt. xxviii. 19); and that the Sacraments of Baptism and the Lord's Supper were not intended as "a channel and means" through which the unregenerated participant could obtain salvation.

Having settled in his own mind the true meaning of the words uttered by our Lord at the institution of the sacramental feast, Schwenkfeld wrote out his views and submitted them to his friend Crautwald, who at first rejected them, and reproved him sharply for what he esteemed his heresy. Schwenkfeld, however, besought him to pray over the matter, and examine the words of the institution closely in the original tongue, declaring his conviction, in harmony with his theory of the operation of the Divine Word, that Christ had revealed the meaning to him. Crautwald finally promised to pray and think over the matter, and the result was his conversion. Speaking of this conference in one of his letters, Schwenkfeld says: "A fortnight later he (Crautwald) wrote me a Latin letter that the Lord Christ had revealed to him also the true meaning of the words."

Earnestly desiring harmony rather than polemic discussion, and hoping that an interchange of opinions would lead to an agreement with Luther, Schwenkfeld determined to seek a personal interview with him, and accordingly, in September, 1525, visited him at Wittenberg, and laid before him his views together with Crautwald's letter. Bugenhagen, Pomeranus, and Justus Jonas were present, and the conference, which continued several days, was marked by Christian courtesy. Luther was in a condescending mood and said to Schwenkfeld: "I say truly that I have been troubled with this doctrinal point for three years. Now your opinion is acceptable to me; it is very good if you can prove it. Finally, I say that your doctrinal point is not objectionable to me if you can prove it. I, also, was strongly inclined to it, and have long striven against it, and still have to strive against it."

Schwenkfeld's mission seemed to have been successful, at least so far as to justify the belief that his views would receive respectful consideration, and he parted from the reformers in friendship, and, we may well suppose, returned to his own country with a light heart. But he was doomed to disappointment. After two months Luther returned his manuscript and Crautwald's letter, and wrote him in his characteristic style, that he and Crautwald must cease to lead the people astray; that the blood of those whom they led astray would be upon their heads, and closed with these words: "Kurtzum, entwieder ihr oder wir müssen des Teufels leibeigen seyn, weil wir uns beiderseits Gottes Word rühmen"—In short, either you or we must be in the bond service of the devil, because we, on both sides, appeal to the word of God.

Troubles now began to thicken. Cut off from fellowship with the Lutherans, Schwenkfeld was none the less an object of the hatred of the Catholics. Even Ferdinand, King of Bohemia and Hungary, afterwards Emperor of Germany, whose liberality to the Protestants brought him into such disfavor at Rome that Pope Paul IV. refused to ratify his elevation to the imperial dignity, could not tolerate his teachings in respect to the Sacraments of the Lord's Supper and Baptism, misrepresented as they were by the Catholic clergy, and wrote to the Duke of Liegnitz to proceed to extreme measures for his repression—Silesia then being under the suzerainty of the Bohemian kings. But the Duke was so far in sympathy with Schwenkfeld that he had printed for the use of his own household a " Confession of Faith " drawn up by two of the latter's coworkers and most intimate friends,—Eckel and Werner,—and embodying the very doctrines which were so distasteful to the King's spiritual advisers. Moreover, a friendship, formed while Schwenkfeld was Counsellor to the Duke and never afterwards interrupted, forbade compliance with the King's command. But the Duke was powerless to protect his friend, and therefore advised him to retire from Silesia until more tolerant counsels should prevail at the royal court. He accordingly left Silesia in 1529 for a journey through Germany, but, as the sequel proved, never to return to his native land,—a circumstance which gave occasion for the story circulated by his enemies at the time, and since repeated by some German writers, that he had been expelled by the Duke at the instance of Ferdinand, a story that Schwenkfeld expressly refuted on several occasions, and which is disproved by his friendly correspondence with the Duke until the latter's death. Thenceforth he had no settled abiding-place, but moved about from city to city, defending his doctrines and faith in public conferences and discussions with the learned, and before the Magistrates at Augsburg, Nürnberg, Strasburg, Tübingen, and Ulm; often persecuted, and at least once—at Tübingen in 1535—tried for heresy, when he was so far acquitted as to be promised freedom of religious worship in private, though forbidden to speak publicly.

His life was one of unremitting labor. Besides preaching, he maintained an extensive correspondence with learned men and others of high rank throughout Germany and in Switzerland, and wrote many books and pamphlets, several editions of which were published—one in 1592, in four large quarto volumes. A spirit of deep and fervent piety pervaded his writings; and, although when controversy was forced upon him he stoutly defended his opinions upon disputed points of doctrine, he held that repentance of sin, purity of life, and humble trust in the cleansing efficacy of the blood of Christ were of infinitely more importance than subscription to dogmas and observance of the Sacraments. Hence he desired not to establish an independent church, but frequently declared, in his writings, his unwillingness to separate himself from any who loved Christ. Notwithstanding the irreconcilable differences between himself and Luther, and the harsh treatment which he had received from the latter after the Wittenberg conference, he never ceased to frankly acknowledge his obligations and express in the warmest terms his gratitude to the great reformer for the services he had rendered to him in common with all who were seeking the truth; and as late as 1543, less than three years before Luther's death, wrote him, earnestly and affectionately entreating him to examine his "Confession of Faith Concerning the Person of Christ," a work then just published, and point out his errors, if any. He died at the city of Ulm on the 10th of December, 1562, leaving a name unspotted by any charge except that of heresy, and that only in respect to the doctrines herein mentioned, and others held in common by the reformers. His opponents accorded him the praise of possessing great learning combined with modesty, meekness, piety, and a loving spirit.

Although the establishment of an independent church was a purpose never entertained by Schwenkfeld, he had, so far as successful teaching of his distinctive doctrines went, prepared the way for it. Many clergymen and noblemen and other influential and learned men in Silesia and throughout Germany, and in some localities, especially in the Principalities of Liegnitz and Jauer, almost the entire population, embraced his doctrines; and for a time his adherents enjoyed the public ministration of the Gospel in not a few of the churches where they were most numerous, not as a distinct sect, but as part of the reformed Church in its wider sense. But their prosperity was short-lived. State reasons inclined the Protestant princes to favor the larger following of Luther, and most of the evangelical pastors who adhered to Schwenkfeld's views were displaced, while but few were permitted to end their days with the churches which they served in Schwenkfeld's time, and these under admonitions to observe the Sacraments according to the Lutheran practice. Even Frederick II. of Liegnitz, whose friendship for Schwenkfeld never abated, yielded late in life to the pressure of the dominant influences in the Protestant Church, and dismissed the Court Preacher Werner for no other reason than that he continued to teach the same doctrines that the Duke approved when Schwenkfeld was near the Court. But Frederick could not entirely forget his first love, and while he lived no severity was exercised towards the people in his dominions.

After the Duke's death, however, they fared worse. That they, on the one hand, were Protestant and Evangelical, and on the other declined fellowship with the Lutherans, was enough to excite the intolerant spirit of the age, and invite persecution from all sides. Other circumstances conspired to bring them into disfavor alike with the clergy and the civil magistrates. Their rejection of infant baptism was sufficient, in the judgment of those who cared not to inquire further, to justify the charge that they were Anabaptists, and bring upon them the odium of the excesses committed by that sect but a few years before at Münster. Neither the explicit denial by Schwenkfeld in his lifetime of any sympathy with the Anabaptists, nor the blameless lives of the people, who rendered unto Cæsar the things that were Cæsar's, and strove according to their knowledge to render unto God the things that were God's, availed to free them from that charge. They were called Schwenkfelders in derision,—a name which they accepted,—and were stigmatized by almost every name that was supposed to convey a reproach. The new Duke, Frederick III., determined to stamp them out of his dominions, and issued a stringent decree against them, among other things imposing a fine of five hundred florins upon any person who should harbor an Anabaptist, by which he meant a Schwenkfelder, and later, ordered all their books to be seized and burned.

These measures had the opposite effect to that intended; the number of Schwenkfelders increased rather than diminished, but the persecutors did not gain wisdom from experience. Persecutions increased from year to year, until about 1580, when it seemed that every means that the ingenuity of man could devise was employed to coerce these people into either the Lutheran or the Catholic Church. In addition to former methods, the clergy refused to solemnize marriages until the contracting parties would partake of the Sacrament at the parochial church; men and women were dragged in chains into churches; leading men were expelled from the country; frequently when the people met at private houses for worship, as

was their custom, they were arrested and imprisoned, often in
dungeons, where many died from starvation, cold, and violent
treatment, and others contracted diseases of which they died
soon after their release; and finally large numbers were sent to
Vienna, and there condemned without trial to serve in the wars
with the Turks, or as oarsmen on Mediterranean galleys. And
so the weary years passed until the outbreak of the Thirty
Years' War necessitated conciliation, when the Schwenkfelders
accepted the horrors of that prolonged struggle as a grateful
change from the cruelties of religious persecution. But soon
after the peace of Westphalia the old persecutions were re-
newed with, if possible, increased rigor. From 1650 until 1658
they were especially severe.

Amid all these persecutions, without churches, without organization, robbed to a great extent of their religious books,
and forbidden under severe penalties to reprint those that had
been committed to the flames, the Schwenkfelders maintained
their faith and their worship in the Fatherland for more than
two centuries. The Bible was, indeed, allowed to them, and of
this they were diligent readers; and, notwithstanding the efforts
to suppress their literature, copies of Schwenkfeld's works
and the sermons and other writings of Johann Sigismund
Werner, Michael Hiller, Erasmus Weichenhan, and Christian
Hoburg were here and there preserved, and these served the
multitude who met at the houses of their possessors to hear
them read. The entire Sabbath, from morning till night, was
spent in worship and in listening to the reading of such books.

Martin John, a learned physician of Hockenau, who wrote
in the latter part of the seventeenth century, says: "Whoever
had books, read on Sundays, and the others went to hear. The
order was thus: In the morning, after each one had prayed
when he rose from his bed, they assembled and sang the morning song standing; then they prayed from a prayer-book and

sang a hymn of invocation, especially to the Holy Ghost, all standing; after that they sang sitting, then prayed, and thereupon read some sermons; then prayed again and sang a couple of hymns; after that they ate at midday; then prayed again standing and sang an invocatory hymn, after which they read quite until evening, when they prayed and sang standing. This was the order on Sunday, and when the people came together in the week-time (for spinning) they then almost always sang, and when any one wished to go home they knelt down together and prayed."

Towards the close of the seventeenth century the spirit of intolerance relaxed, and the Lutheran Church presenting her attractive side to this people, large numbers, especially of the young, were won over to her communion, and from that time the Schwenkfelders gradually decreased, until in 1718 they numbered only a few hundreds where they had formerly been counted by the thousands, and had disappeared entirely from many villages where they had once been numerous. Reduced in numbers as they now were, their conversion to the Roman Catholic faith was, nevertheless, deemed by the Jesuits an object of sufficient importance to enlist the energies of the Order in that direction, and in furtherance of such object they commenced operations about this time at the Imperial Court. It was not difficult to persuade Charles VI. that the treaty of Westphalia in its interdiction of religious persecution did not protect the Schwenkfelders. An order to the government at Liegnitz to send in an official report of that people and their creed was therefore readily obtained, and in obedience thereto some of the leading men were summoned to appear at Liegnitz on the 19th of May, 1718, where they were questioned and required to hand in a written declaration or confession of their faith and some of their doctrinal and devotional books. Next, the Lutheran pastors at Harpersdorf and Neudorf were required to furnish lists of the Schwenkfelders in their respective parishes.

These proceedings were followed in December, 1719, by the appearance of two Jesuit priests bearing a "Legitimation," issued by the Superior Magistracy at Breslau, in the name and by command of the Emperor, accrediting them as missionaries for the conversion of the Schwenkfelders, in the following words:

"The Roman Emperor, also King in Germany, Spain, Hungary, and Bohemia, by his acting Privy Counsellor, Director, Chancellor, and Counsellors at the Royal Superior Domain in the Duchy of Upper and Lower Silesia.

"Offers first his courteous services, amity, and all blessings to the royal offices and domains, as also to the magistrates, rulers, and officers, and to all lower jurisdictions, and others. And whereas his Imperial Majesty, our most gracious master, by virtue of a most gracious rescript issued unto the Royal Superior Domain on the 18th day of September last, has graciously declared in what manner a mission should be established for the conversion of the Schwenkfelders living in the Principalities of Schweidnitz, Jauer, and Liegnitz, and has most graciously thought proper to appoint for this purpose two priests from the Jesuit Society, namely, the worthy P. P. Johann Milahn and Carolum Regent, and has furthermore graciously commanded that the Superior Domain should provide said *Patres Missionarios* with letters patent so that they might not be impeded in their beneficial undertaking, therefore all the magistrates, rulers, and other inhabitants, of whatever standing, office, or condition, are accordingly enjoined not to molest in any way those *Patres Missionarios*, nor to impede them in their ecclesiastical functions *quo quo modo*, under avoidance of severe animadversion, but moreover they are commanded to render them readily all possible assistance and help, and thus not to give cause for any complaint. In executing hereby the most gracious command of his Imperial Majesty we have no doubt of your acting in accordance therewith.

    "Hans Anton Count Schafgotsch (L. S.), ex consilio Reg. Cur.
    "Franz Carl Count Cottulinsky, Duc. Silesiæ.
    "M. J. Aglo von Wiesenstein, etc."
"Breslau, the 9th of October, 1719."

The royal government at Liegnitz added to this Legitimation of the Superior Magistracy, the following:

"All the hereinbefore named dominions, especially those at Harpersdorf, Armeuruh, and Hockenau, where within the Principality of Liegnitz the most Schwenkfelders are living and dwelling, and all the inhabitants of the precinct of Goldberg, are hereby strictly directed, ordered, and commanded not to hinder the above-named two *Patres Soc. Jesu* in this mission charge conferred upon them by his Maj., not even under the pretence that they are overreaching the missionary object; but much less subject them to anything unbecoming or troublesome, but moreover to manifest to them with readiness all necessary assistance. By all of which ye shall show your proper regard, etc.

"W., COUNT OF WURBEN, Governor-General.
"LIEGNITZ, the 15th day of December, 1719."

At first the missionaries required only the men to attend their services, and sought to win them by expounding the doctrines of the Catholic Church, and attempting to refute those of the Schwenkfelders. But in the latter they found no easy task. To the end that they might know what they had to refute, they demanded answers in writing to a number of questions. These were cheerfully given, and at considerable length; every proposition being supported by abundant citations of Scripture and from the Church Fathers. Finding the people so strongly fortified in their religious opinions, and so apt to defend them, the missionaries became irritated and threatened to adopt harsher methods after the close of the year 1720. Accordingly, early in the year 1721, it was announced that the women and children must be brought to the missionaries for instruction in the Catholic religion; and an imperial edict to this effect was exhibited.

There was now consternation among the people. So long as only men of mature judgment were required to hear the instructions of the missionaries, they feared nothing, but they could not endure the subjection of their tender offspring to teachings and influences which they regarded as pernicious. They therefore, on the 5th of May, 1721, dispatched three deputies—Christopher Hoffmann, Balthasar Hoffmann, and Balthasar Hoffrichter—to Vienna to sue for toleration. These deputies were graciously received by the Emperor, and remained at the Court five years, during which time they presented no less than seventeen memorials to the Emperor in person at audiences granted for that purpose, setting forth the persecutions suffered by their people at the hands of the missionaries and of the magistrates at the instigation of the missionaries, and praying for toleration and protection. But notwithstanding the Emperor's uniform kindness of manner at these audiences, and that he ordered a cessation of violence until further consideration, matters constantly grew worse in Silesia.

When parents refused to present their children for instruction, they were imprisoned; women were placed in the stocks and compelled to lie in cold rooms in the winter without so much as straw under them; and when imprisonment failed to bring the people with their children to the missionary services, fines and extortions were added. Marriages were forbidden unless the parties would promise to rear their offspring in the Catholic faith, and when young people went into other countries to be married, they were imprisoned for that on their return. The dead were not allowed Christian burial in the churchyards where their ancestors of the same faith for many generations slept, but were required to be interred in cattle-ways, and sorrowing friends were forbidden to follow the remains of loved ones to these ignominious resting-places. Hundreds of Schwenkfelders were so buried at Harpersdorf, Laugenneudorf, and Lauterseifen during the twenty years that the mission was maintained. The missionaries claimed guardianship of all orphan children of Schwenkfelders, and thus the last hours of the dying were embittered by the thought that their children must be educated in a faith that they themselves abhorred. And to prevent escape from the horrible situation in which they were placed, the people were forbidden to sell their property or, under any pretext, leave the country, and severe penalties were denounced against any person who should assist a Schwenkfelder to escape by purchasing his property, or otherwise.

The deputies made a final appeal to the Emperor for mercy on the 28th of July, 1725. That appeal was answered by the publication—in September—of the following decree:

"CHARLES THE SIXTH.

"DEAR FAITHFUL: We received your obedient report of March 20th, of this year, by which you have informed us of the condition of the ecclesiastical mission appointed for the conversion of those Schwenkfelder *Sectariorum* sojourning at several places in our Duchy of Silesia. As we now most graciously desire a better progress of the mission, we therefore provide:

"*Primo*, most graciously to wit: That the mission henceforth exercise all their power to accomplish the work of conversion with profit and good effect. And likewise

"*Secundo*, that all watchful oversight of the mock preachers and *Seductores* from the authority of the country, and especially from those missionaries, be kept as heretofore commanded, and in case of any trespass at once to arrest the guilty and to punish them *in terrorem alior*, and to report to us aggravating occurrences if thought proper, and also we desire that the same may be understood concerning those Schwenkfelder inhabitants and housekeepers who permit Schwenkfelder *conventicula* in their houses, or who are leaders or instigators to persistence in those heretical errors. In such a manner that they shall be arrested as soon as the same shall be sufficiently apparent, brought here and their names entered. So it shall

"*Tertio*, not only be a settled matter that the Schwenkfelder books of instruction shall be hunted up and taken away, as also no less

"*Quarto*, that the children of the Schwenkfelders shall be brought to preaching and catechizing, and also the *adulti Sectarii* themselves shall be held to the presence and hearing thereof, and those who without good cause absent themselves, shall at the first occurrence be charged with a money fine in proportion to their circumstances; for the second time it shall be doubled; upon further *renitenz* to the contrary they shall be punished according to the nature of the case with arrest or *opere publico:* and further the Schwenkfelder congregations in their submissive requests to be tolerated in their confession of faith in future, are once for all refused, and they shall never hereafter venture to present any new supplications; and he it in all seriousness announced to all the respective jurisdictions and public authorities that the missionary fathers shall by nothing, and in no way or manner, be hindered, but upon their call shall receive all necessary assistance with all force and effect. Also to report to us, from time to time, all future occurrences by and through our royal Bohemian Court Bureau. Herein let our will be executed.

"Decreed at Vienna, the 30th of July, 1725.

"CHARLES,
"Ad mandatum,
"Joh. Christoph Jordan.

"FERD. COMES VINSKY,
"Ris Bohœmiæ Sup Cancellarius.
"To the Royal Superior Magistracy
"in Silesia.
"Presented the 19th of August, 1725.
"The foregoing copy was taken from the original, with the same carefully compared and found to agree with the same in every particular, which is hereby attested by deliberately attaching thereto the great royal official seal.
"So done at the Royal Castle in Jauer, the 19th of September, 1725.

"L. S."

The missionaries now bent all their energies to the accomplishment of the work in hand, and to the full exercised with the utmost rigor the powers granted to them, and were aided therein by the civil magistrates even to patrolling the highways to prevent the escape of any of the doomed people. Thus was this unhappy people shut up to the choice of either apostasy, or continued endurance of the ever-increasing miseries of their situation, or flight. The first was to the true Schwenkfelder simply impossible; the second was too horrible to be contemplated. They therefore resolved to escape from the country at all hazards.

The exodus commenced in the month of February, 1726. During that month and the months of March, April, and May following, upwards of one hundred and seventy families escaped by night from Harpersdorf, Armenruh, and Hockenau, and fled on foot to Upper Lusatia, then a part of the Electorate of Saxony, and found shelter at Wirsa near Greissenberg, Görlitz, Hennersdorf near Görlitz, Berthelsdorf, and Herrnhut. In consequence of the prohibition of sales of property by Schwenkfelders, and the police regulations to prevent emigration, they were obliged to leave all their property behind except what they could carry upon their backs or upon wheelbarrows. Consequently the less provident, who had laid up little or no money, found themselves in great destitution amongst strangers. They were, however, hospitably received, and treated with much consideration by the Senate of Görlitz, and by Count Zinzendorf, at Berthelsdorf and Herrnhut, and soon after their arrival assistance came to them unexpectedly from theretofore unknown friends in Holland. They lived here in a state of uncertainty as to the future for eight years.

The assistance received from Holland led to a correspondence with the Dutch benefactors, who strongly advised emigration to Pennsylvania. Some, however, began to purchase homes in Lusatia, and it is doubtful whether all would not have settled there permanently had not subsequent events proved the advice of the Hollanders to have been both timely and wise. In the spring of 1733 Count Zinzendorf informed them that they would be tolerated no longer in Lusatia, and referred them to the superior magistrate at Bautzen for the reasons. It was ascertained that application had been made for their enforced return to Silesia. They were, however, permitted to remain until the next spring.

Soon after Count Zinzendorf's announcement that protection would be withdrawn, two families emigrated to Pennsylvania, arriving at Philadelphia on the 18th of September (O. S.), 1733. Their report of the country, and the advice of the friends in Holland, determined about forty families to follow them Their first care was to proceed orderly and obtain the permission of the sovereign to whom they proposed to transfer their allegiance. This secured, they set out in April, 1734, for Altona, in Denmark, where they arrived on the 17th of May. On their arrival at Altona, they found preparations made for their reception, and were most hospitably entertained until the 28th, when they embarked on three small vessels for Haarlem, arriving at the latter place on the 6th of June. Here they were received with open arms, and overwhelmed with kindness by their benefactors of former years.

The disinterested kindness of a mercantile house in Haarlem, composed of three brothers, Abraham, Isaac, and John Von Byuschanse, deserves more than a passing notice here. Their attentions to the strangers were not limited to seeing that there were no actual wants unsupplied; they strove by personal attentions to make the stay of the party in Haarlem enjoyable. The little ones especially came in for a full share of their kindly offices. Part of the contribution sent to Görlitz in 1726 for the relief of the destitute remained unexpended, and those having it in charge offered to return it to the donors, there being no further need of such assistance. The Messrs. Von Byuschanse would not listen to the offer, but directed the fund to be expended for the benefit of the poorer people when they should arrive in Pennsylvania. And not content with all that they had done, they insisted upon providing at their own expense a vessel for the transportation of the whole company to Philadelphia, and defraying the entire expense of the voyage. This noble benefaction was bread cast upon the waters. The descendants and successors in the business of the Messrs. Von Byuschanse met with reverses in the year 1790. Information of this fact coming to the Schwenkfelders in Pennsylvania, they, in grateful remembrance of the kindness shown to their own ancestors and to some of themselves in childhood more than half a century before, raised a considerable sum of money, and sent it to the relief of the distressed house.

The emigrants remained at Haarlem, enjoying the munificent hospitality of the Messrs. Von Byuschanse, until the 19th of June, when they proceeded to Rotterdam, and there embarked for Pennsylvania on an English ship, the St. Andrew, which had been chartered for them by their large-hearted friends, and touching at Plymouth, England, arrived at Philadelphia on the 22d of September (N. S.), 1734. On the next day all male persons over the age of sixteen years proceeded to the Statehouse, and there subscribed a pledge of allegiance to George II., King of Great Britain, and his successors, and of fidelity to the proprietor of the province. They spent the 24th in thanksgiving to Almighty God for delivering them out of the hands of their persecutors, for raising up friends in the times of their greatest need, and for leading them into a land of freedom, where they might worship Him unmolested by civil or ecclesiastical power. This day, the 24th of September, was thenceforth set apart to be observed by them and their descendants, through all time, as a day of Thanksgiving commemorative of the Divine goodness manifested in their deliverance from the persecutions of the Fatherland. To this day it is so observed.

The little band who had passed through so many trials together were now to separate. Some settled within the present limits of the city of Philadelphia, in the neighborhood of Chestnut Hill; others in the now counties of Montgomery, Berks, and Lehigh, there to convert the wilderness into happy homes, that in many instances have been enjoyed by their descendants till this day. It is needless to dwell on the hardships and privations of the first few years. They were such as were the common lot of all the early settlers of Pennsylvania, mitigated by the remembrance of what had been exchanged for them.

Dispersed as the people were, they nevertheless remained one in faith and in the bonds of mutual sympathy and love, and promptly set up the worship of Almighty God in their new home. They were without a pastor, but fortunately not without a man qualified by many gifts and graces to fill the sacred office. That man was George Weis. He had been selected on the eve of departure from Lusatia to "give instruction to the children, and render such other spiritual services as might be required," and had conducted the thanksgiving services on arrival in this country and perhaps other services, and having proved acceptable, was, in December, 1734, elected by the "house fathers" to the pastoral office. He served with great acceptance till his death, in 1740, when he was succeeded by Rev. Balthasar Hoffman.

It was natural to expect that the remaining Schwenkfelders would follow their emigrant brethren as rapidly as circumstances would admit. Such, however, was not the case. The very violence of the missionaries worked its own temporary cure, and for a time the necessity for flight was removed. Says Kadelbach :* " The respective local rulers, lords of the soil, saw with indignation the expatriation of their most active and peaceful subjects, and the decline of the prosperity of their communities." Thus was an influential public opinion awakened against the missionaries, not so much, indeed, by the outrageous cruelty of their methods, as by its effects on the public prosperity; but it was none the less potent, and its pressure was felt in a quarter where it was least expected to be respected. The same author says : " Even the Catholic clergy of the surrounding country declared themselves by no means in accord with the behavior of the missionaries, and were greatly dissatisfied with this sort of conversion." Of course this meant a change of tactics, and the Schwenkfelders had comparative rest for a few years.

---

* Ausführliche Geschichte Caspar Schwenkfelds und der Schwenkfelder in Schlesien, der Ober Lausitz und Amerika, Lauban, 1860.

About the close of the year 1735, however, the old methods of conversion were revived, and in the following year a number of families fled into Saxony, whence one family came to Pennsylvania the same year, and four others in 1737. Again there was anxiety about the loss of subjects, and, whether in consequence of representations by the local governments or of other promptings, an imperial order was issued temporarily suspending the exercise of the extraordinary powers of the missionaries, and directing a searching investigation of their conduct; and again there was comparative exemption from persecution.

But whatever steadiness of purpose Charles VI. manifested in the general administration of the affairs of the empire, his conduct towards the Schwenkfelders had always been characterized by fickleness. Each spasmodic exhibition of a tolerant disposition had been followed by a more intolerant decree from the Imperial Court, and it was too late now when, nearing the end of his career, he was engaged in securing guarantees of the inviolability, after his death, of the Pragmatic Sanction, to expect more firmness in his good intentions towards this people than he had before shown. The next spring a decree was published to the effect that the "Schwenkfelder heresy" must be trodden out, and its adherents coerced into the Catholic Church within one year. But it was a vain decree. The hour of final deliverance and, in some measure, of retribution, was approaching. Within the year appointed for the extermination of the Schwenkfelders Charles had paid the debt of nature, and Frederick the Great had vindicated his better title to Silesia, under the agreement of mutual succession made two centuries before between his ancestor, the Elector of Brandenburg, and the Duke of Liegnitz, and had proclaimed religious freedom in the long-misgoverned principalities.

Frederick was not content to merely put a stop to religious persecutions. Damage had been sustained by the country in the loss of valued subjects, and great wrongs had been done to individuals. He desired to repair the former and was willing to redress the latter even at the expense of the royal treasury. For that purpose he issued an edict in 1742 which reflects the highest honor upon himself, and, when the insignificance of their numbers is considered, pays a flattering tribute to the worth of the exiled Schwenkfelders. As exhibiting the estimation in which the ancestors of those whose names are contained in the following pages were held, and at the same time as a happy contrast to the before-recited decree of Charles VI., that edict is here presented *in extenso:*

" Edict to provide for the re-establishment of the so-called Schwenkfelders in Silesia and other provinces of his Royal Majesty; De dato Selowitz the 8th of March, 1742.

" We, Frederick, by the Grace of God, King of Prussia, Margrave of Brandenburg, Arch Chamberlain, and Elector of the Holy Roman Empire, etc., etc.

" Be it known to all to whom these presents may come: Whereas we do hold nothing to be so contrary to Nature, Reason, and Principles of the Christian Religion as the forcing of the subjects' consciences, and persecuting them about any erroneous doctrines which do not concern the fundamental principles of the Christian Religion. We have, therefore, most graciously resolved that the so-called Schwenkfelders, who were exiled through an imprudent zeal for Religion, to the irreparable damage of commerce and of the country, be recalled into our Sovereign Duchy of Lower Silesia. We have, therefore, thought fit by these presents to assure all those who possess the said doctrine, upon our Royal word that they shall and may safely return not only into our Sovereign Duchy of Lower Silesia, but also into all our provinces, peaceably to live and trade there, since we not only do receive them into our special protection, but also will give them all necessary supplies for the promotion of their commerce. And all those who, several years ago, were deprived of their habitations and estates in our country of Silesia, shall be reinstated without any compensation in case those estates are not paid for by the new possessors. Such as will settle in our villages shall have farms assigned to them, and care shall be taken to provide them employment, and those who choose to live in towns shall, besides several ordinary

Free years, have places assigned them gratis for the building of their houses, for which purposes they need only apply to our Military and Domainen Chambers.

"We do therefore command our Superior Colleges of Justice and Finance, as also all mediate Princes, Lords, Magistrates, etc., carefully to observe the same.

"In Witness whereof we have signed this present Edict with our own hand, and caused our Royal Seal to be affixed.

"Done at Selowitz, March 8th, 1742.

[L. S.] "FREDERICK,
"V. COCCEJI. "Per C. v. MUNCHON."

Much as they loved the Fatherland in spite of the cruel wrongs which they and their ancestors for two centuries had suffered, none of the Schwenkfelders in Pennsylvania availed themselves of the royal invitation to return to their former homes. They had become attached to the government under which they had for eight years enjoyed absolute freedom and a measure of prosperity that promised better things in the future than restoration of their estates in Silesia. They had come here to stay, and had laid foundations which they were loath to abandon. They had acquired permanent homes; they had established and thus far maintained public worship; remembering the words of Christ: For ye have the poor with you always, and whensoever ye will, ye may do them good; they had established a Poor Fund, which, increasing with increased prosperity, has, for nearly a century and a half, satisfied every call upon it from within their communion and scattered its blessings outside; and they had established a School Fund which supplied every want intended to be supplied by the system of public instruction established by the State many years later. In short, they had taken root in the soil of Pennsylvania.

For many years they could not be said to have had an organization as a church. Indeed, the want of an organization was not felt while there were but few families, and they widely separated. But after the death of their second pastor, Rev. Balthasar Hoffman, in 1775, with increased membership, the necessity for an organization was recognized and soon received attention. Christopher Schultz, a man of great learning, ability, and zeal, and withal peculiarly fitted for the special work before him, was now, after fervent prayer for the divine guidance therein, called to the pastoral office. He addressed himself to the work of organization, and prepared a constitution or system of church government which was formally adopted on the 17th of August, 1782. For administrative purposes two districts were created, known as the "Upper District" and the "Lower District." It was provided that each district should elect a president, three elders, two trustees, and a treasurer of the School Fund, and a treasurer of the Poor Fund. Two congregations or individual churches were then organized, one in each district.

The duties of the elders are to see that church order is strictly observed, and to examine all matters in dispute between members and, if possible, adjust the same. One elder is elected every year in each district for the term of three years, and no elder can be re-elected until at least one year after the expiration of his last term. After the adoption of the common school system of the State the name of the School Fund was changed to "Literary Fund," and the fund itself devoted to literary purposes, and the duties of the officers of the Fund were correspondingly modified. The duties of the other officers are sufficiently indicated by their titles. The members on their part are enjoined to pay their debts without legal proceedings, and to "live quiet, virtuous, peaceable, Christian lives according to the will of Christ in all meekness and lowliness as the quiet in the land, and to be true and faithful in their spiritual as well as their temporal calling."

Owing to the dispersion of the members and the consequent impracticability of assembling any considerable numbers at any one point, no church edifices were erected until the year 1789. In that year a church was erected in the upper district, and soon after one in the lower. At later periods two more churches were built in each district, making six in all. Until these accommodations were provided, divine service was held at private houses, as it had been in the Fatherland, and in the absence of the pastor was conducted by one of the members. The service was opened with singing and prayer. The Gospel lesson for the day was then read, and sometimes expounded, after which a sermon from Weichenhan's, Werner's, or Hiller's Postille was read, followed by singing and prayer. While there was but a single pastor, there were a number of members who acceptably led meetings for worship and performed much of the pastoral work. At later periods the ministry was increased, until there are now three active ministers in each district.

The religious training and education of their children was from an early period regarded by the Schwenkfelders as a matter of prime importance. The exact date of the establishment of Kinder Lehr cannot now be ascertained, but the first appointment of George Weis before he was called to the full work of the ministry proves that the institution was brought to this country from Germany, and when the immigrants devoted, as they did, every alternate Sabbath to the instruction of the youth by catechetical lectures, it was evidently no new thing. Rev. Christopher Schultz gave an impetus to this department of church-work by his untiring labors therein, and by an excellent Catechism which he prepared for the instruction of children. The solicitude of the church for the children is shown in a ceremony originated in this country. As soon as conveniently may be after the birth of a child it is brought into church and the minister prays for its happiness and prosperity, and admonishes its parents to "bring it up in the nurture and admonition of the Lord according to the will of God." This service is sometimes performed at the home of the parents.

The literature of the Schwenkfelders is almost exclusively in the German language. Their printed works are mainly those hereinbefore incidentally mentioned, to which may be added the Erläuterung, etc., published in 1771, and of which a second edition appeared in 1830; and a work by the venerated Schultz, entitled "A Compendium of Christian Faith." But a large and valuable portion of their literature is yet in manuscript, being in part the writings of cotemporaries of Schwenkfeld and of others of the next century. A single volume appeared in an English dress in 1858, containing Schwenkfeld's "Heavenly Balm and Divine Physician," and "Threefold Life of Man," translated by the Rev. F. R. Anspach, D.D.

LISTS OF SCHWENKFELDERS WHO ARRIVED IN PENNSYLVANIA IN 1733, 1734, ETC., AT PHILADELPHIA.

September Eighteenth, 1733, O. S.

JOHANN KLEMM.
GOTLOB KLEMM.*
BALTHASER KRAUSS.
GEORGE SCHOLTZE.
DAVID SCHOLTZE.

September Twelfth, 1734, O. S.

CHRISTOPHER WIEGNER.
GEORG HÜBNER.
GEORGE KRIBEL.
BALTZER JÄCKEL.
CASPAR KRIBEL.
GEORG ANDERS.
ABRAHAM JÄCKEL.
GEORG REINWALD, JR.
HANS WIEGNER.
BALTZAR JÄCKEL, JR.
GEORG WIEGNER.
GEORG JÄCKEL.
HANS HENRICH JÄCKEL.
MELCHIOR MENTZEL.
GEORG MENTZEL.
GEORG WIESS.
CASPAR HEYDRICH.
GEORG SCHOLTZ.
CHRISTOPH WIEGNER.
GEORG SCHOLTZ.
CASPAR JOHN.
FREDERICK SCHÖPPS.
DAVID SCHUBERT.
MELCHIOR NEUMAN.
TOBIAS HERTTERANFFT.
BALTHASER HEYDRICH.
CHRISTOPH NEUMAN.
CASPAR JÄCKEL.
MELCHIOR HÜBNER.
CHRISTOPH SCHUBERT.
MELCHIOR KRIBEL, SR.
BALTHASER HOFFMAN.
MELCHIOR KRIBEL, JR.
GEORG HOFFMAN, SR.
BALTHASER HOFFMAN, JR.
JEREMIAS JÄCKEL.
CHRISTOPH JÄCKEL.
GREGORIUS MEISTHER.
CHRISTOPH REINWALD.
GEORG ANDERS.
DAVID SEIBR.
CHRISTOPH SEIBR.
GEORG HEYDRICH.
GEORG DRESCHER.
MELCHIOR MEISTHER.
BALTHASER ANDERS.
MATTHIAS JÄCKEL.
CHRISTOPHER JÄCKEL.
GREGORIUS SCHOLTZE.
DAVID MEISTHER.
CHRISTOPHER DRESCHER, JR.
MELCHIOR SCHOLTZE.
CHRISTOPHER SCHOLTZE.
HANS HUBNER.

Sick upon their arrival.

CHRISTOPHER KRIBEL.
DAVID HÜBNER.
DAVID JÄCKEL.
ANDREAS WARMER.
GEORGE REINWALD.

---

* Tradition has it that the Klemms were Schwenkfelders, but this needs confirmation.

LIST OF SCHWENKFELDERS.   xxxi

Under Sixteen Years of Age.

DAVID NEUMAN.
ABRAHAM WIEGNER.
GEORG WIEGNER.
CASPAR SEIBB.
ABRAHAM HEYDRICH.
GEORGE ANDERS.
MELCHIOR HÜBNER.
DAVID SCHUBERT.
ABRAHAM HERTTERANFFT.
FREDERICK DRESHER.*
CHRISTOPHER KRIBEL.

CHRISTOPHER HÜBNER.
DAVID SCHUBERT.
GEORG KRIBEL.
CHRISTOPHER HOFFMAN.
CHRISTOPHER REINWALD.
MELCHIOR WIEGNER.
CHRISTOPHER MEISTHER.
BALTHASAR JÄCKEL.
GEORG HERTTERANFFT.
MELCHIOR HERTTERANFFT.
CHRISTOPHER HEYDRICH.

Females who arrived September Twelfth, 1734, O. S.

MARIA HÜBNER.
MARIA KRIBEL.
SUSANNA KRIBEL.
ANNA KRIBEL.
MARIA KRIBEL.
ROSINA KRIBEL.
MARIA HÜBNER.
ROSINA KRIEBEL.
REGINA JÄCKEL.
ANNA JÄCKEL.
SUSANNA JÄCKEL.
MARIA JÄCKEL.
ROSINA JÄCKEL.
BARBARA SCHUBERT.
ANNA MARIA SCHUBERT.
SUSANNA SCHUBERT.
MARIA KRIBEL.
SUSANNA KRIBEL.
MARIA ANDERS.
URSULA HOFFMAN.
ANNA HOFFMAN.
ROSINA HOFFMAN.
ANNA KRIBEL.
URSULA HOFFMAN.
MARIA JÄCKEL.
SUSANNA JÄCKEL.
ROSINA HEYDRICH.
SUSANNA NEUMAN.
ROSINA JÄCKEL.

MARIA JÄCKEL.
REGINA JÄCKEL.
SUSANNA SCHOLTZE.
ROSINA JÄCKEL.
BARBARA HOFFMAN.
SUSANNA HOFFMAN.
BARBARA REINEWALD.
SUSANNA REINEWALD.
ANNA WIEGNER.
MARIA WIEGNER.
ROSINA WIEGNER.
SUSANNA JÄCKEL.
MARIA MEISTHER.
ANNA MEISTHER.
MARIA MEISTHER.
SUSANNA REINEWALD.
BARBARA REINEWALD.
SUSANNA JÄCKEL.
URSULA MENTZEL.
BARBARA MENTZEL.
ANNA MENTZEL.
BARBARA MENTZEL.
MARIA NEUMAN.
ANNA WARMER.
BARBARA HERTTERANFFT.
MARIA HERTTERANFFT.
ROSINA HERTTERANFFT.
ANNA WIESS.
EVA HEYDRICH.

---

* It is supposed he was a Schwenkfelder, but what became of him after his arrival is not known.

URSULA ANDERS.
JUDITH SEIBB.
ROSINA SCHOLTZE.
SUSANNA SCHOLTZE.
ROSINA SCHOLTZE.
EVA MEISTHER.
ANNA SCHOLTZE.
SUSANNA SCHOLTZE.
MARIA SCHOLTZE.
BARBARA SCHOLTZE,
SUSANNA WIEGNER,
SUSANNA WIEGNER.
MARIA WIEGNER.

ROSINA WIEGNER.
REGINA JÄCKEL.
ANNA MEISTHER.
MARIA DRESCHER.
ROSINA DRESCHER.
MARIA DRESCHER.
REGINA MEISTHER.
ANNA ANDERS.
MARIA HÜBNER.
ANNA HÜBNER.
SUSANNA SCHUBERT.
ANNA ANDERS.

In all 184 persons of the Society of Schwenkfelders settled in Pennsylvania in 1734, of which number 81 were males and 83 females. Copied from the list preserved in the office of the Secretary of the Commonwealth at Harrisburg, and indorsed by John Steadman, Captain of the ship St. Andrew.

June 28, 1735, O. S.

MELCHIOR SCHOLTZE.

October 19, 1736, O. S.

ABRAHAM BEYER, or BAER.
ROSINA BEYER (wife).
ANNA ROSINA BEYER.
ANNA MARIA BEYER.

ABRAHAM BEYER.
ANDREW BEYER.
GEORGE BEYER.
SUSANNA BEYER.

September 26, 1737, O. S.

CHRISTOPH KRAUSS.
MELCHIOR KRAUSS.
MARIA KRAUSS (widow).
ANNA WAGNER (widow).
CHRISTOPH WAGNER.

CHRISTOPH HÜBNER.
ABRAHAM WAGNER.
SUSANNA WAGNER.
MELCHIOR WAGNER.
ANNA WAGNER (widow).

DAVID WAGNER or WAGENER.

NOTE.—The names of Scholtze, Hübner, Kriebel, Jäckel, Meisther, Seibb, and Hertteranfft, have undergone considerable change since the arrival of the emigrants in this country, and are now generally written Schultz, Heebner, Kriebel or Krieble, Yeakle or Yeakel, Meschter or Master, Seipt, and Hartranft.

GENEALOGICAL RECORD.

GEORGE WEISS, the first minister of the society of Schwenkfelders in America, came to Pennsylvania, in 1734, with the colony, and settled in Lower Salford, then Philadelphia County. He was born in Harpersdorf, Lower Silesia, in Germany, in 1687. In 1720, when the Roman missionaries appeared in Silesia to convert the followers of Schwenkfeld to the Roman Catholic faith, George Weiss was selected on the part of the latter to write their confession of faith, or reply to the written questions of the missionaries. How well he performed this important task may be seen by reference to the "Erläuterung," page 85, and also page 341.* But the more these missionaries were worsted in argument, the more they had recourse to force ; the result is well known. Weiss with his wife and other friends fled the country by night in the month of April, 1726, leaving their properties in the hands of their persecutors; came to Herrnhut in Saxony on the 5th of May. During his eight years' stay at Herrnhut he followed weaving and teaching. We do know that Rev. Christopher Schultz, Sr., then quite a young lad, came to Weiss for instruction in languages, and that the warmest friendship and attachment existed

---

* "Erläuterung fur Caspar Schwenkfeld und die Zugethanen, Seiner Lehre." Printed in Tauer by Mullorn in 1771.

between teacher and pupil during the remaining years of Weiss's lifetime. In a historical manuscript written by Rev. Baltzer Hoffman, 1750, compiled by Christopher Hoffman, 1771, we find that our pilgrim fathers on the eve of their departure for America appointed Weiss as a kind of leader or teacher in spiritual things for adults, as well as catechist for the young, there and on shipboard, which appointment he accepted and carried out ; and that about a year and a quarter after arriving in America (December 9, 1735) Weiss was formally appointed the first Schwenkfelder minister of the Gospel and catechist in this country, and that he officiated in that capacity in an acceptable manner up to the time of his death, which occurred on his farm on Skippack Creek, in Lower Salford, Montgomery County, on the 11th of March, 1740, in the fifty-third year of his age. His body lays buried at the meetinghouse near by, where a handsome stone has been erected to his memory. Rev. B. Hoffman writes that Weiss was married in 1715 to Anna Meschter, of Langenneudorf; that they had one child, a son, who died when about a year old ; that he also had a brother and a sister who both died young in Silesia; that shortly after their arrival in America he also lost his wife by death, and had her buried in the "Pilgrims' Cemetery" at Philadelphia. Thus Weiss himself was the only remnant left of the family this side of the grave, and having the spiritual welfare of his disorganized and scattered flock at heart, he labored for them in season and out of season; but in time he became considerably disappointed in seeing no better results, and finding so much lukewarmness and worldly-mindedness, etc., that during a spell of sickness which befell him in 1739, he was on the point of relinquishing his ministerial labors altogether; but with returning health, God gave him increased courage, and he kept on laboring in his Master's cause until within a few days of his unlooked for and early death.

On the 3d of March, 1740, he was at Goshenhoppen, where in the evening he for the last time met and instructed his catechumens; and on the following morning, although in feeble health, and only six days before his death, he preached for the last time to his congregated friends. A synopsis of Weiss's remarks on these occasions is given by Hoffman at the close of his interesting Manuscripts.

Weiss was an example of unaffected piety, simplicity, and fidelity, well versed in spiritual knowledge, earnest and impressive in his ministrations. He was a worthy son of the venerable Casper Weiss, who, when quite old and weak in body, was called before the notorious Neander and compelled to stand in the latter's study for six long hours to give an account of his faith. See "Erläuterung," page 54, also page 59.

George (Scholtze) Schultz and his wife Anna, maiden name (Huebner) Heebner, came in 1733 to Pennsylvania, with their children:
  Melchior, died March 3, 1764.
  George.
  David.
  George Schultz died February 22, 1754, aged 80 years.
  Anna, widow of G. S., died October 17, 1756, aged 76 years.

Anna Krauss, widow, came in 1733 to Pennsylvania, with her son,
  Balthasar Krauss.

Anna Krauss, widow, died January 14, 1755, aged 81 years.

Balthasar Anders and his wife, Anna Hoffrichter, came in 1734 to Pennsylvania, with one child:
George, born, 1733, in Germany.
Anna, born April 8, 1736.
Abraham, born April 1, 1739.
Balthasar Anders was by trade a shoemaker, and lived in Towamencin Township, Montgomery County, Pennsylvania, upon the property now owned by George Anders, and there followed his trade until his death, which occurred May 25, 1754, aged 56 years. His wife died March 29, 1784, aged 83 years and 9 months.

His mother, who came with him to this country, was buried September 30, 1734, in Philadelphia, eight days after their arrival.

George Anders and his wife Maria came in 1734 to Pennsylvania; had one child:
Maria, born April 25, 1738.
George Anders died August 4, 1738.
Maria, his widow, died November 7, 1757.

George (Drescher) Dresher and his wife Maria came in 1734 to Pennsylvania, with their children:
Christoph.
Maria.
Rosina.
Maria, wife of G. D., died March 18, 1762.
George Drescher died March 3, 1774.

George Anders, brother of Balthasar, page 4, came to Pennsylvania in 1734, and died March 14, 1794, aged 83 years.

Tobias Hartranft and his wife Barbara, maiden name (Jaeckel) Yeakle, came in 1734 to Pennsylvania, with their children:
George.
Abraham.
Melchior.
Maria.
Rosina.
Tobias Hartranft died October 4, 1758, aged 74 years.
Barbara, wife of T. H., died February 15, 1764.
Governor John F. Hartranft is the sixth in descent from this Tobias.

Regina (Jaeckel) Yeakle, widow of Christopher, and sister of David and Christopher Heebner, see below, came to Pennsylvania in 1734, with her only son,
Christopher.
R. Y. died April 4, 1758, aged 65 years and 5 months; her husband died in Germany previous to her emigration.

Balthasar Hoffman, son of Christopher Hoffman, came to Pennsylvania in 1734, with his three children:
Anna.
Rosina.
Christopher, born in 1728.
Among the Schwenkfelders who arrived in Pennsylvania in the year 1734, Balthasar Hoffman,* who settled in Lower Salford Township, was one of the most eminent. He was born in Harpersdorf, Principality of Lieg-

---

* This sketch of the life of the Rev. Balthasar Hoffman was written by his son Christopher in German in 1777, and translated by Abraham H. Cassel for the forthcoming work of M. Auge, Esq., "The Prominent Men of Montgomery County, Pa." The compiler of this work cheerfully acknowledges the courtesy of Mr. Auge in allowing him to make use of this memoir.

nitz, in Silesia, Austria. By his own testimony he was born of "worthy poor and lowly parents," and was first reared to the trade of a weaver, occasionally working as a day laborer in the summer. He early embraced the religious principles of Caspar Schwenkfeld. He was tall in stature, lean in person, and "after his fiftieth year wore an entire white head." From his earliest youth he seems to have been very industrious and desirous of acquiring truth. By assiduous labor he soon gained a knowledge of Latin, Greek, and Hebrew, and by help of good books set himself to study the Sacred Scriptures, for which his knowledge of the languages gave him great facilities. He was very diligent in acquainting himself with Christian teachings around him, and especially of those promulgated by Caspar Schwenkfeld.

In 1719 the Reformation had made great progress in Silesia, and the Catholic Church in 1721 sent a mission to convert the people back to the old faith, at first laboring with them mildly, but soon after committing great acts of violence. The persecuted people in 1721, therefore, resolved to send an embassy to the Emperor, to implore toleration. Of this body Balthasar was one. During this effort, which lasted five years, Hoffman delivered no less than seventeen memorials to the royal ruler. At last, however, in 1726, the mission turned the heart of the sovereign still more against the reformed people, so that Balthasar dared not show himself by day, but had to return by night, taking with him to Ober Lausitz his wife and two daughters. Even there he was not safe, but fled again with his gray-haired father from Vienna by way of Prague to Lausitz, and obtained the protection of Count Zinzendorf. Here he resided eight years, during which time a son was born to him. As tolerance was not even here assured he, with many others, concluded to emigrate to Pennsylvania, where William Penn had promised religious freedom to all. This resolution was formed in 1734, and on September 22 of the same year, with his wife and family, "under the guidance of the good Lord they arrived at Philadelphia, and offered praise to God for his graciousness to them." He was especially grateful that no evil had befallen them on the way, and further that kind friends in Holland had sent himself over free and without cost to him. He did not remain in the city, but removed to the country, "where, too, the grace of God provided for him and his." During all this time he continued a diligent Bible reader and Christian teacher to those around him. Here he freely worshipped God according to the dictates of conscience.

Upon the death of the Rev. George Weiss, the first minister of the Schwenkfelders in America, in 1740, Hoffman was chosen to officiate in his stead. Not being constitutionally strong in body, he several times withdrew, especially in 1749, when he became afflicted on his breast and debilitated in his power of speech and of singing. Still, demands were made upon him, particularly for outdoor services, as catechizing the children; but by the help of God he labored till the weight of years made it impossible. Nor did he ever tire in his many duties. His Sabbath forenoons, afternoons, or evenings, were employed in writing, reading, and singing. He left many letters and writings on Holy Scripture and Christian teachings, prompted by the questions of others as well as of his own conception, thus at once rendering service to his brethren in time to come. He also left hymns. Of these writ-

ings we have a catalogue. "To him idleness and the want of truth were of great moment, seeing how God's gift of freedom was misapplied."
The closing years of Balthasar Hoffman's life were spent in a small room, spinning; yet daily would he read, write, sing, and pray. And as he had long been blessed with bodily health, so God protected him against much and severe sickness in his last days. Gradually, however, his sanctified spirit was loosened from its earthly tabernacle, and nature sank year by year, till December 21, 1774, when he was attacked with vertigo and increasing debility, and on July 11, 1775, in his 89th year, he passed peacefully away. His wife, Ursula, died May 15, 1767, aged 80 years, and both lie buried in the Schwenkfelder burying-ground belonging to the congregation in Lower Salford. Balthasar Hoffman and wife left three children, Anna, Rosina, and Christopher, who succeeded his father as minister of the society; his children were all born in Europe. All three were married, but the son left no issue. There are descendants of the daughters, however, to the fifth and sixth generations.
He remained an acceptable minister of the Schwenkfelders from the death of Weiss in 1740 until the time of his death. He resided on a tract of land by the east side of Skippack Creek, two miles west of Franconia village, now owned by Henry Derstine. He was a man of eminent wisdom and piety, and left behind him a catalogue of his writings, embracing fifty-eight tracts, all on theology and practical religion, besides eighty-three letters on various kindred topics.
Christopher Hoffman, the father of Balthasar, died in Saxony, under the protection of Count Zinzendorf; he,

together with his son Balthasar and Balthasar Hoffrichter, constituted the embassy to the court of Charles VI, at Vienna.

David (Huebner) Heebner and his wife Maria came in 1734 to Pennsylvania. Their children were:
Christoph.
Susanna.
Rosanna, born May 9, 1738.
George, born June 21, 1744.
David Heebner died December 27, 1784.
Maria, widow of D. H., died June 11, 1793.

David Yeakel came to Pennsylvania in 1734, and was on the sick list when he landed at Philadelphia. No record of the time of his death can be found, nor of his wife; it is supposed that he was a widower when he arrived with his children, six sons and two daughters, namely:
Christopher.
Abraham.
Balthasar.
Jeremias.
Hans Heinrich.
Caspar.
Susanna, married George Weigner.
Rosina.

Maria Meschter, sister of Gregorius and Melchior, page 12, died May 4, 1769, aged 80 years, single.

Balthasar Heydrick and his wife Rosina came in 1734 to Pennsylvania. Their children were:
Christopher, died December 28, 1756.
George, born September 22, 1737.
Rosina, wife of B. H., died October 23, 1738.

Balthasar Heydrick married second time Maria, daughter of Christoph Hoffrichter, May 15, 1741. Children:
Abraham, born November 5, 1742.
Susanna, born October 5, 1745.
Melchior, born October 23, 1747; died October 19, 1777.
Balthasar, born December 29, 1750.
Maria, wife of B. H., died January 10, 1753.
Balthasar Heydrick died January 12, 1753.
It is supposed that he lived in Frederick Township, as in the appraisements of his personal effects it is so stated.

Abraham Yeakel and his wife Maria came in 1734 to Pennsylvania. Their children were:
Balthasar, born August 19, 1736.
Hans, born January 1, 1739.
Susanna.
Rosina.
Elizabeth.
Abraham Yeakel died January 12, 1762.
Maria, widow of A. Y., died January 2, 1781.

Frederick Schoeps came in 1734 to Pennsylvania, and died March 28, 1762. He never married.

Regina Yeakel, widow of Balthasar Yeakel, came in 1734 to Pennsylvania, with her children:
George.
Susanna.
Anna, died January 1, 1771.
Maria, died September 25, 1784.
Rosina, born September 14, 1720.
Regina Yeakel, widow, died August 9, 1747.

George Heydrick and his wife Eve came in 1734 to Pennsylvania.
George Heydrick died September 5, 1765.
Eve, widow of G. H., died January 4, 1776. No issue.

Caspar Heydrick and his wife Eve came in 1734 to Pennsylvania.
Eve, wife of C. H., died December 9, 1742.
Caspar Heydrick died April 13, 1761, aged 80 years. No issue.

Christoph Kriebel and his wife Maria came in 1734 to Pennsylvania, with their children:
George.
Susanna, died January 30, 1740.
Christoph.
Anna.
Maria.
Rosina, died February 23, 1750.
Maria, wife of C. K., died April 11, 1738.
Christoph Kriebel died May 14, 1741.

Caspar Kriebel and his wife Susanna came in 1734 to Pennsylvania. Their children were:
George, born November 3, 1732, in Saxony, Europe.
Abraham, born October 8, 1736, in Pennsylvania.
Susanna, wife of C. K., died April 17, 1769.
Caspar Kriebel died February 16, 1771; he lived in Towamencin, upon the property of his descendant, Abm. K. Kriebel, which he owned.

Melchior Kriebel and his wife Anna, daughter of Christopher Drescher, came in 1734 to Pennsylvania. Their children were:
David, born March 14, 1736.

Susanna, born October 28, 1739.
Rosanna, born December 31, 1742. Died January 17, 1743.
Melchior, born May 26, 1746.
Rosina, born September 4, 1751. Died December 26, 1820.
Anna, wife of M. K., died December 26, 1789, aged 79 years.
Melchior Kriebel died February 14, 1790, aged 80 years and 2 weeks. The property of Abm. Rittenhouse in Towamencin was his residence. He was a brother of the above Caspar.

Melchior Meschter and his wife Regina came in 1734 to Pennsylvania. Their children were:
George, died August 1, 1801.
Susanna, born April 16, 1739.
Maria, born April 26, 1742.
Christopher, born December 17, 1746.
Regina, wife of M. M., died December 14, 1773.
Melchior Meschter died October 5, 1776.

George Reinewald and his wife Susanna came in 1734 to Pennsylvania, with their children:
Christoph.
Susanna.
George Reinewald died July 10, 1755.
Susanna, widow of G. R., died January 17, 1781, over 80 years of age.

Christoph Reinewald and his wife Susanna came in 1734 to Pennsylvania. Their children were:
Balthasar.
Christoph, born March 6, 1737.
David, born March 13, 1739.

Abraham, born November 4, 1740. Died July 30, 1745.
Melchior, born March 21, 1744.
Susanna, born July 10, 1749.
Susanna, wife of C. R., died July 23, 1749.
Christoph Reinewald died January 14, 1770.

Gregorius Schultz and his wife Rosina Yeakel came in 1734 to Pennsylvania. Their children were:
Susanna.
George, died August 17, 1751.
Rosina.
Anna, born November 10, 1738.
Maria, born February 28, 1741. Died December 18, 1779.
David, born September 3, 1743.
Rosina, wife of G. S., died March 31, 1769.
G. S. died May 9, 1772.
Gregorius Schultz was a son-in-law of David Yeakel, page 9, and upon his arrival in Pennsylvania he went to Macungie, in Lehigh County, then Bucks, where he located upon the Jordan Creek in company with his brothers-in-law, Balthasar and Hans Heinrich Yeakle, but after some years returned to Upper Hanover, then Philadelphia County, and purchased a large tract of land upon which he lived the remainder of his life. The Yeakles returned a short time previously.

Mathias Yeakle and his wife Rosina Ott came in 1734 to Pennsylvania, with their children:
Maria, died July 14, 1752.
Regina, died July 4, 1758; married a Lutheran minister, September 30, 1754.
Mathias Yeakle died September 20, 1756.

Rosina, widow of M. Y., died in December, 1759.
Tobias Hartranft, page 5, was his brother-in-law.

Caspar John came in 1734 to Pennsylvania, and died July 16, 1747. Was not married.

Susanna Schultz, maiden name Dieterich, and widow of Balthasar Schultz, came in 1734 to Pennsylvania, with her children:
    George, born about Candlemas, 1710.
    Susanna.
    Maria.
    Barbara.
Susanna Schultz, widow, died February 23, 1765.
Balthasar died in Saxony, Germany, in 1727, in the 47th year of his age. He was a son of Mathias.

Hans Heebner and his wife Maria came in 1734 to Pennsylvania, with their children:
    Hans.
    Melchior.
    Anna.
Hans Heebner died September 17, 1754, in the 70th year of his age.

Christoph Schubert, brother of David, and his wife Barbara came in 1734 to Pennsylvania, with their children:
    David, died in January, 1768.
    Susanna.
    Anna Maria.
Barbara, wife of C. S., died January 1, 1768.
Christoph Schubert died June 4, 1769.

David (Seibb) Seipt and his wife Judith came in 1734
to Pennsylvania, with their children:
Christoph.
Caspar.
David Seipt died November 24, 1765.
Judith, widow of D. S., died September 13, 1775.

Susanna Wiegner, widow, maiden name Seipt, came in
1734 to Pennsylvania, with her children:
Abraham.
George.
Rosina, died September 14, 1800.
Susanna Wiegner, widow, died September 18, 1755.

Barbara Reinewald, widow, came in 1734 to Pennsylvania. Died March 17, 1740.

Barbara Reinewald came in 1734 to Pennsylvania.
Died August 24, 1775, unmarried, aged 85 years.

Gregorius Meschter and his wife Maria Krauss came in
1734 to Pennsylvania. Their children were:
Christoph, born in June, 1734, on the Atlantic Ocean.
Maria, born December 21, 1736.
Melchior, born June 28, 1740.
Susanna, born September 25, 1742.
Baltzer, born October 1, 1745. Died August, 2, 1809.
Anna, born May 29, 1748.
George, born April 18, 1750.
Maria, wife of G. M., died November 10, 1756.
Gregorius Meschter died December 16, 1775, in the
71st year of his age.

Hans Wiegner and his wife, Anna Reinewald, came in
1734 to Pennsylvania, with their children:
  Melchior, died single.
  Susanna.
Hans Wiegner died November 23, 1767, aged 77 years.
Anna, widow of H. W., died February 22, 1785, aged 85.

Eve Meschter, widow, maiden name Yeakel, came in
1734 to Pennsylvania, with her children:
  David.
  Rosina.
  Anna Maria.
Eve Meschter, widow, died April 8, 1752.

Melchior Neuman and his wife Maria came in 1734 to
Pennsylvania. Had no issue.
M. N. died April 28, 1745.
M., widow of M. N., died December 24, 1744.

Christoph Neuman and his wife Susanna Muchmer came
in 1734 to Pennsylvania, with their children:
  David.
  Rosina.
S., wife of C. N., died March 27, 1760.
C. N. died September 10, 1768. He lived in Gwynedd,
near the present village of West Point.

George Mentzel and his wife Ursula came in 1734 to
Pennsylvania. No issue.
G. M. died August 1, 1744.
W., widow of G. M., died January 29, 1754.

Melchior Mentzel and his wife Anna Groh came in
1734 to Pennsylvania. No issue.
M. M. died September 6, 1755.
A., widow of M. M., died February 10, 1758, at the
age of 76 years.

Melchior Wiegner and his wife Rosina came in 1734 to Pennsylvania. Child,
  George, died January 25, 1776.
  M. W. died July 29, 1766, aged 66 years.
  R., widow of M. W., died December 29, 1772.

Susanna Wiegner, widow of Adam Wiegner, came in 1734 to Pennsylvania. Children:
  Christoph, died June 3, 1746.
  Rosina, died July 13, 1756.
  S. W. died February 10, 1752; her husband died in Germany.

Andreas Warmer came in 1734 to Pennsylvania, and married Susanna Wiegner November 15, 1738. No issue.
  S. W., wife of A. W., died July 29, 1757, aged about 43 years.
  A. W. died January 28, 1786, aged 81 years.

Abraham Beyer and his wife Rosina Yeakel came in 1736 to Pennsylvania, with their children:
  Abraham.
  Andrew.
  Anna Rosina.
  Anna Maria.
  A. B. lived in Worcester, then Philadelphia County, and died October 30, 1754, aged 64 years.
  R. B., widow of A. B., died July 30, 1770, at the age of 71 years.

Anna Wagner, widow of Melchior Wagner, maiden name Yeakel, came in 1737 to Pennsylvania, with her children:
  Abraham.
  Melchior.

Susanna.

A. W., widow of M. W., died March 16, 1749.
She resided with her children in Worcester Township.

Anna Wagner, or Wagener (widow), came to Pennsylvania in 1737 and settled in Worcester Township, Philadelphia, now Montgomery, with her two sons, viz.:
Christopher, born November 15, 1727.
David, born May 24, 1737.
A. W. died January 2, 1790.

Christoph Heebner and his wife Maria Yeakel came in 1737 to Pennsylvania, with their son,
Hans Christopher.
C. H. died September 26, 1763, aged 74 years.
M. H., widow of C. H., died July 10, 1768, aged 76 years.

Maria Krauss, widow, maiden name Beyer, came in 1737 to Pennsylvania with her sons:
Melchior, died September 16, 1779.
Christoph.
M. K., widow, died March 12, 1768.

Hans Heinrich Yeakel, son of David Yeakel (page 9), married Susanna Heydrick, A. D. 1735. Had issue:
Jeremias, born April 9, 1736.
George, born November 19, 1738.
Balthasar, born 1740.
Melchior, born February 25, 1742.
Susanna, born February 1, 1744.
Maria, born October 2, 1748.
Anna, born May 30, 1752.
H. H. Y. died December 21, 1781, aged 74 years.

S. Y., widow of H. H. Y., died September 23, 1793, aged 84 years.

Hans Heinrich Yeakel became a large landowner in the Hosensack Valley, in Lower Milford Township, now Lehigh County, Pa. He purchased what was then known as the Hamilton tract, containing about 500 acres of excellent farm land, which at his death he divided among his sons. His descendants became quite numerous, and much of his property is still owned by them. He had gone with his brother-in-law, Gregorius Schultz, to the Jordan in Lehigh County, but the location being too much exposed, on account of Indian depredations, he returned in a short time afterwards and settled permanently in the Hosensack.

Balthasar Krauss, son of Anna Krauss, widow (page 3), married Susanna Hoffman January 16, 1736. Had issue:

 Rosina, born April 10, 1737.
 Susanna, born August 29, 1738.
 Barbara, born July 22, 1742.
 Balthasar, born November 28, 1743.
 Maria, born July 17, 1750.
B. K. died February 25, 1774, aged 68 years.
S. K., widow of B. K., died April 14, 1791.

David Meschter, son of Eve Meschter, widow (page 16), married Ursula, sister of Baltzer Anders (page 4), March 2, 1736. No issue.
D. M. died March 31, 1785.
U. M., widow of D. M., died April 14, 1793, aged 88 years.

George Schultz, son of Susanna and Balthasar Schultz (page 14), married Anna, daughter of Rev. Balthasar Hoffman (page 5), May 3, 1737. Their children were:

    Susanna, born August 5, 1740.
    Balthasar, born April 23, 1744.
    Christoph, born October 7, 1746.
    Ursula, born November 2, 1749. Died July 4, 1750.
    Gregory, born February 24, 1753.
    Eve, born January 31, 1756.

G. S. died March 21, 1784, aged 74 years.

A. S., widow of G. S., died January 16, 1796, aged 84 years.

He was a farmer and resided in Upper Hanover Township, Montgomery County, where his descendants are quite numerous.

Balthasar Yeakel, son of David Yeakel (page 9), married Barbara Warmer November 24, 1737. Had issue:

    Susanna, born March 19, 1739. Died September 7, 1808.
    Anna, born June 25, 1743.
    David, born December 29, 1744. Died March 2, 1756.
    George, born February 20, 1746. Died August 5, 1751.
    Caspar, born January 6, 1748.
    Rosina, born December 13, 1752.

B. Y. died January 28, 1762.

B. Y., widow of B. Y., died February 25, 1808.

George Heebner came in 1734 to Pennsylvania, and married Rosina Kriebel November 22, 1738. Had one child,
  Melchior, born July 2, 1742. Died December 21, 1744.
R. H., wife of G. H., died July 25, 1745.
George Heebner married, second time, Susanna, daughter of Balthasar and Susanna Schultz (page 14), May 16, 1749. No issue.
S. H., wife of G. H., died November 2, 1772.
G. H. died November 3, 1773.

Christoph Wiegner came in 1734 to Pennsylvania, and married Anna Schultz November 18, 1739. Their children were:
  Susanna, born August 5, 1740.
  Anna, born July 8, 1742.
  Christoph, born February 29, 1744. Died November 7, 1783.
  Maria, born December 9, 1745.
  Rosina, born May 28, 1749. Died April 29, 1835.
  Andreas, born August 1, 1751. Died August 27, 1758.
  Daniel, born July 31, 1755.
C. W. died December 24, 1777, aged 65 years.
A. W., widow of C. W., died June 26, 1789, aged 75 years.

David Schubert came in 1734 to Pennsylvania, and married Anna Krauss April 29, 1740. Their children were:
  Susanna, died August 5, 1756.
  Maria, born December 21, 1742.
  Rosina, born May 28, 1745.
  Melchior, born July 9, 1747.

Anna, born November 27, 1749.
Barbara, born January 16, 1755.
D. S. died October 24, 1774.
A. S., widow of D. S., died August 13, 1778.

George Kriebel came in 1734 to Pennsylvania, and married Susanna, daughter of Balthasar and Regina Yeakel (page 5), November 25, 1740. They had issue:
George, born July 11, 1744.
Andrew, born September 17, 1748.
Susanna, wife of G. K., died September 14, 1775, aged 61 years.
G. K. died September 2, 1778, aged 63 years.

Melchior Schultz, son of Melchior Schultz, brother of Rev. Christopher (page 24), married Anna Maria, daughter of Melchior Meschter (page 9), February 13, 1741. No issue.
A. M., wife of M. S., died July 2, 1742.
He married, second wife, Maria, daughter of Tobias Hartranft (page 5), April 29, 1746. No issue.
M. S. died September 1, 1787.
M., widow of M. S., died December 9, 1799.

George Yeakel, son of Balthasar Yeakel, came in 1734 to Pennsylvania, and married Susanna, daughter of Anna and Melchior Wagner, May 12, 1741.
Had issue, Rosina, born February 9, 1742. Died March 10, 1743.
Susanna, wife of G. Y., died June 16, 1742.
G. Y. died July 24, 1742.

Christopher Seipt, son of David Seipt (page 15), married Rosanna, daughter of Balthasar Hoffman (page 5), November 16, 1742. One child,
Susanna, born May 7, 1745.

C. S. died May 8, 1748.
The widow afterwards married Christopher Yeakel.

Christopher Yeakle, son of Regina and Christopher Yeakle (page 5), married Maria, daughter of Susanna and Balthasar Schultz (page 14), August 9, 1743. Their children were:
Susanna, born October 8, 1744.
Maria, born September 21, 1747.
Regina, born October 1, 1749.
Abraham, born March 14, 1752.
Anna, born July 16, 1755.
Christopher, born October 7, 1757.
Maria, wife of C. Y., died March 4, 1807, aged 89 years.
C. Y. died January 3, 1810, aged 91 years and 9 months.
Christopher Yeakle was about 18 years of age when he came to Pennsylvania with his mother in 1734; his father died in Germany. He apprenticed himself to a cooper, and continued during life to follow his trade. He built the log-house in 1743 (yet standing, 1879) at Cresheim, Germantown Township, Philadelphia, which was his dwelling until nearly the Revolution, when he purchased the property on the summit of Chestnut Hill, now owned by his granddaughter, and died there at a very advanced age. By his industrious and frugal habits he died possessed of considerable property. His descendants are quite numerous in Philadelphia and in Montgomery County, Pennsylvania.

George Schultz, son of Melchior Schultz, brother of Rev. Christopher (page 24), married Maria, daughter of Abraham Yeakel, January 31, 1744. Their children were:

Abraham, born March 23, 1747.
Melchior, born March 25, 1756.
G. S. died October 30, 1776, aged 65 years.
Maria, widow of G. S., died December 13, 1797, aged 79 years.

Christopher Dresher, son of George Dresher (page 4), married Anna, daughter of Christopher Kriebel (page 11), June 19, 1744. Their children were:
George, born October 13, 1746.
Rosina, born November 8, 1748. Died January 31, 1749.
Abraham, born May 14, 1750.
Susanna, born August 7, 1753. Died August 30, 1780.
Maria, born October 9, 1757. Died January 4, 1758.
C. D. died August 2, 1770, aged 52 years.
Anna, widow of C. D., died July 4, 1786.

Christopher Schultz, son of Melchior Schultz, married Rosina, daughter of Regina and Balthasar Yeakel (page 5), October 9, 1744. They had issue:
Regina, born April 10, 1749.
Andrew, born January 29, 1753.
David, born April 10, 1757.
Susanna, born December 15, 1759.
C. S. died May 9, 1789, aged 71 years 1 month and 13 days.
Rosina, widow of C. S., died January 27, 1800.
This was the Rev. Christopher Schultz,* Sr., born at

---

* Mathias Schultz was born A.D. 1612 on a Sunday (Invocavit). Lived through the "thirty years war." Died A.D. 1682 in the seventieth year of his age at Lower Harpersdorf, Dukedom Liegnitz, Silesia. His son, Melchior Schultz, is said to have been born A.D. 1647, and died on a Sunday (Invocavit), A.D. 1708 in the sixty-first year of his age. And his son, also called

Lower Harpersdorf, Dukedom Liegnitz, Silesia, March 26, 1718. He was the youngest son of Melchior Schultz (who was born in 1680); had two brothers, George and Melchior. In the spring of 1726, owing to religious persecutions then prevailing, this family and other friends left their homes and possessions and fled the country by night, came to Berthelsdorf, in Saxony, May 1. Here young Christopher was employed as a shepherd boy, and also learned the weaver's trade, besides being occupied with spinning and other work. He evinced a great desire for books and learning, the means to obtain which not being at hand he was granted whatever time he could gain by extra exertions; this inducement was irresistible, and no doubt marks the beginning of a new era in the lad's career. He now performed his allotted work in two-thirds of the ordinary time, thus gaining two days per week, during which he would hasten to his kind friend and teacher, Rev. George Weiss, to study languages. In these studies he advanced with astonishing alacrity; before he was ten years of age he had acquired a pretty general knowledge of the Latin, and also knew the rudiments of the Greek and Hebrew languages. After enjoying comparative liberty and quiet under the kind protection of Count Zinzendorf for nearly eight years, the important question again arose whether the family and their religious friends should *leave the country or their faith*, and by the aid of Him in whom they believed and whom they served, it was again decided in the right way; but both parents went to rest

---

Melchior Schultz, was born June 26, 1680, and died February 15, 1734, in the fifty-fourth year of his age at Berthelsdorf, Saxony, about two months before the then contemplated emigration. The last-named Melchior Schultz was the father of George, Melchior, and Christopher Schultz.

in death shortly before the then contemplated emigration to America.

The three orphan boys, George, Melchior, and Christopher, joining some forty Schwenkfelder families, forever turned their backs upon their native land, embarked for Philadelphia, where, after a tedious voyage of about five months, they arrived September 22, 1734. Young Christopher kept a diary ("Reise Beschreibung"), which is found in print in the "Erläuterung," of which book he also was the chief compiler, and which gives a brief history of the persecutions which befell Schwenkfeld and his followers in Silesia, and an impartial exposition of the doctrinal points upon which they and their opponents differed, etc.

At a comparatively early period Christopher Schultz was looked to as a leading spirit among the Schwenkfelders, and was chosen as their Gospel minister, in which capacity he served faithfully and efficiently to the end of his life.

He was the chief organizer of the Schwenkfelders into a formal religious body or congregation, composing their present catechism, collating their hymn-book, writing their constitution (Grund Regeln), and a "Compendium" of religious doctrines of faith of 600 octavo pages—an excellent work, eminently catholic, and, like the catechism, everywhere substantiated by Bible truths and references.

For many years, up to the end of the American Revolution, Father Schultz kept up a correspondence with friends left in Germany; copies of some of his letters and of those written in reply (all in German manuscript) are still at hand. Father Schultz lived in stirring times and he experienced a great deal. At the age of eight years we find him with the family fleeing the country at night. A year and more thereafter we find him employed as a shepherd boy near Berthelsdorf, in Saxony, book in hand, translating from Latin into German extracts from the "Zehen Haupt Verfolgungen Der Ersten Christen." At the age of sixteen he was on the British ship St. Andrew, a close observer and recorder of the events of a five months' voyage to the land of Penn. At the age of eighteen we find him and his two brothers in a dense wood forty-two miles north of Philadelphia, two miles west of what is now the borough of East Greenville, selecting a site for their future home, which they found at a spring where the bear and deer at first seemed inclined to dispute possession. Here, in 1736, with the assistance of Melchior Neuman, carpenter, they commenced felling the tall oaks, rolling them on a scaffold over a trench, *sawed them by hand into three-inch plank*, whereof the outside walls of their capacious two-story house was constructed. Wagon-wheels were made of the same article, horse collars skilfully plaited of straw, traces of hemp, grubbing hoe preceded the plough with wooden mould-board; no saw-mill was within reach, no grist-mill within fifteen miles. For clothing the Schultz's raised their own flax and wool, spun it with the aid *of a single spindle* (without wheel or machinery of any kind), erected a weavers' loom, wove the yarn into cloth. When the supply exceeded the wants they took it to Philadelphia, and, on one occasion, sold it to the Governor of the Province at eight shillings per yard. The Governor spoke very highly of their linen, which encouraged them not a little.

The three brothers lived together in peace and harmony, and at the end of about ten years, under the blessings of Providence, they had considerably extended their landed domains, increased their flocks, and filled their coffers, so that the question which once engaged the attention of Abraham and Lot, at their parting, now agitated the minds of the Schultz brothers. The result was, Melchior and Christopher sold out to their elder brother George; the former went about three miles north, bought a farm there; Christopher, having married in 1744, now bought and settled on what is at present the fine farm of his great-grandson, Henry S. Schultz, near Clayton, Berks County. Here he lived to the end of his life. Let us here take a short retrospective glance at the situation of our plundered and persecuted Pilgrim fathers in their temporary home in Saxony, which certainly was not one of ease and comfort, and the family of Melchior Schultz was no exception to this; and when death came, removing a kind father and a loving mother, the three orphan boys must have felt like lambs cut off from the flock and left alone in the wilderness. There was yet one way left for them; their united bleatings could be heard by the ever-listening ear of the Good Shepherd on high. But we were going to say, situated as they then were, a liberal school education was out of the question. In this dilemma they may have taken the advice of St. James, 1:5. Be this as it may, in Christopher Schultz we find a learned man with very little schooling. His marvellous memory, and all his mental and spiritual faculties, were of the highest order, and he was an industrious and attentive reader. Among the early Fathers of the Church St. Augustine seems to have been one of his principal favorites. Among the German reformers of a later day, Schwenkfeld was pre-eminently so.

Chistopher Schultz, as already indicated, was gifted with a good judgment, with wisdom to discern right and fortitude to defend and execute it; owing to this he was frequently called upon to settle differences. He had a mild but convincing way of telling the reprobate, "Thou art the man." In his ministrations and writings he endeavored to give the true spiritual sense of the Scriptures; his chief aim and end being the glorification of God and the well-being of man.

He could work on his farm, or at the loom, exercise deeds of kindness, courtesy, and condescension, without compromising his never failing dignity. His life motto was "SOLI DEO GLORIA." (To God alone the honor.) We have no evidence that this motto ever appeared on the walls of his study, but his works prove that they were inscribed in his heart. Among the early records of Berks County, we find the last will and testament of Christopher Schultz; it is a model of its kind, is dated the 24th day of October, A.D. 1788, and is witnessed by his friends, Abraham Schultz, Gregory Schultz, and George Kriebel; in it the testator, among other things, disposes of about 800 acres of land in Berks, Montgomery, and Northumberland counties, Pa., embracing two of the finest farms in Eastern Berks; one of them, late that of his brother Melchior, however, had been bought by the testator for and in the name of his son Andrew. His family, all of whom survived him, consisted of his wife Rosina, a daughter of Baltzer Yeakel, and four children, Regina, Andrew, David, and Susanna.

It might be asked: How is it that the once fatherless, motherless shepherd and weaver-boy of Berthelsdorf had so much property at his disposal? See Matt. 19 : 29.

Or,

"Es gilt dem Hoechsten allesgleich
Den Reichen arm und kleinzumachen,
Den Armen aber gross und reich."

Father Schultz died on the 9th of May, 1789, aged 71 years, 1 month, 13 days; the immediate cause of his death was apoplexy, although he had been indisposed some time previous to the attack.

His last words, barely audible to the family, were:
"A little while, and ye shall not see me, and again a little while and ye shall see me, because I go to the Father."

The Rev. Chistopher Hoffman, of Skippack, preached the funeral sermon, taking for his text the words of St. Paul, 2 Timothy 4: 7-8: I have fought a good fight, I have finished my course, I have kept the faith, etc.

This sermon, fully written out and remaining in the family, has lost nothing of interest on account of its great age.

David Schultz, son of George Schultz (page 3), married Anna Rosina, daughter of Abraham Beyer (page 17), October 29, 1745. No issue.

A. R., wife of D. S., died June 13, 1750.

David Schultz married, second time, June 27, 1758. Had issue:

    Magdalena, born November 6, 1759.

    Anna,
    Anna Maria, } twins, born in 1762.

D. S. died April 25, 1797.

He lived in Upper Hanover Township, then Philadelphia County, where he followed surveying and conveyancing. His first wife, Anna Rosina, was killed while he was absent from home, on the night of the 13th of June, 1750, by a German servant in his employ, whom he had shortly before procured from shipboard. The murderer was apprehended and taken before court, tried, and convicted October 22, 1750, in Philadelphia, and was hung on the 14th of November following.

Hans Christopher Heebner, son of Christopher Heebner (page 18), married Barbara, daughter of Susanna and Balthasar Schultz (page 14), October 21, 1746. Their children were:
    Rosanna, born December 9, 1747.
    Susanna, born April 12, 1750.
    Elizabeth, born June 24, 1752. Died October 7, 1796.
    Isaac, born August 1, 1754. Died June 19, 1776.
    Job, born September 4, 1757. Died July 24, 1781.
    Abraham, born February 29, 1760.
    Barbara, wife of H. C. H., died January 26, 1786, aged 65½ years.
    H. C. H., died January 30, 1804, aged 82 years. He resided in Worcester Township, where Henry H. Heebner now lives.

Abraham Hartranft, son of Tobias Hartranft (page 5), married Susanna, daughter of Christopher Schubert (page 14), November 3, 1747. Their children were.
    Christopher, born October 5, 1748.
    Abraham, born April 2, 1750.
    Barbara, born December 20, 1751.
    John, born April 21, 1753.
    William, born November 23, 1754.
    1 Leonard, born April 17, 1757. Died August 25, 1758.

2 Leonard, born November 6, 1759.
Maria, born December 23, 1761.
Susanna, wife of A. H., died April 12, 1762.
A. H. died December 12, 1766.

Barbara Hartranft, daughter of Abraham Hartranft (see above), married Godfrey Hamled May 10, 1774. No further record.

Anna Yeakel, daughter of Balthasar Yeakel, and sister of the wife of the Rev. Christopher Schultz (page 24), died January 1, 1771, in the 60th year of her age. Single.

Christopher Kriebel, son of Christopher Kriebel (page 11), married Maria, daughter of George Dresher (page 4), August 10, 1748. Their children were:
Abraham, born March 30, 1750.
Rosina, born October 2, 1751.
Jeremiah, born January 26, 1755.
Anna, born November 25, 1758.
Susanna, born May 11, 1762. Died January 5, 1795.
Maria, wife of C. K., died December 30, 1772, aged 49 years.
C. K., died December 31, 1800, aged 80 years.

Abraham Yeakel came in 1734 to Pennsylvania, and married Anna Maria, daughter of Abraham Beyer (page 17), October 19, 1748. Their children were:
Susanna, born October 10, 1750.
Anna Rosina, born November 5, 1752.
Abraham, born May 14, 1755. Died January 12, 1783.

Maria, born March 12, 1758. Died September 17, 1839.
George, born March 4, 1761. Died 19 days after birth.
David, born March 26, 1762.
Anna, born September 19, 1764. Died November 13, 1798.
A. Y. died October 26, 1768.
Anna Maria, widow, of A. Y., died April 9, 1802, aged 81 years, 5 months, 5 days. She married, second time, Peter Gerhard, the second of that name in this record.

Abraham Wagner, son of Anna and Melchior Wagner (page 17), married Maria, daughter of Christopher Kriebel (page 11), April 6, 1749. Had no issue.
Maria, wife of A. W., died March 19, 1760.
A. W. was a physician, and died May 5, 1763, in the 49th year of his age.

Melchior Wagner, son of Anna and Melchior Wagner (page 17), married Gertrude Steyer.
Their children were:
 Susanna, born June 4, 1750.
 David, born January, 1752.
 Jacob, born September 13, 1754.
 Abraham, born 1756. Died March 19, 1760.
 Anna, born August 6, 1757.
M. W. died October 22, 1784. He lived in Worcester Township.
Gertrude, widow of M. W., died March 4, 1798.

George Wiegner, son of Susanna Wiegner, widow (page 15), married Susanna, daughter of David Yeakel (page 9), April 13, 1749. Their children were:
 Esther, born October 9, 1751.

Susanna, born October 3, 1754.
Rosina, born March 1, 1759.
G. W. died April 8, 1784, aged 62 years.
Susanna, widow of G. W., died November 16, 1790.

Christopher Krauss, son of Maria (Beyer) Krauss, widow (page 18), married Susanna, daughter of Gregorius Schultz (page 13), May 15, 1750. They had issue:
Maria, born March 13, 1751.
Susanna, born January 11, 1753. Died November 16, 1818.
Rosanna, born September 14, 1754. Died September 16, 1777.
Elizabeth, born August 28, 1756.
Jeremiah, born October 28, 1758.
Regina, born December 14, 1760. Died April 11, 1823.
Anna, born February 7, 1763. Died August 3, 1847.
Catharine, born March 18, 1765. Died December 15, 1792.
Eve, born March 19, 1767. Died August 18, 1846.
Helena, born June 17, 1769. Died January 22, 1773.
David, born December 29, 1771.
Magdalena, born December 20, 1774. Died June 29, 1834.
C. K. died October 23, 1795, aged 75 years, 5 months.
Susanna, widow of C. K., died June 21, 1797.

Abraham Wiegner, son of Susanna Wiegner, widow (page 15), married Susanna, daughter of Abraham Yeakel (page 10), May 31, 1750. Their children were:
Maria, born May 27, 1751.
Sarah, born June 5, 1753. Died August 8, 1758.

Rosina, born February 7, 1755.
Susanna, born July 25, 1757. Died August 19, 1788.
Abraham, born September 25, 1760.
John, born July 9, 1765.
A. W. died March 13, 1781, aged 62 years.
Susanna, widow of A. W., died January 28, 1812, aged 83 years and 1 month.

Abraham Beyer, Jr., son of Abraham Beyer (page 17), married November 8, 1750. He had children:
Hans, born October 23, 1752.
Jacob, born December 6, 1755.
Susanna, born June 3, 1758.
Esther, born May 26, 1760.
Abraham, born March 10, 1762.
A. B., Jr., died March 6, 1796, aged 74 years.

Caspar Scipt, son of David Seipt (page 15), married Rosina, daughter of Abraham Yeakel (page 10), November 27, 1750. Their children were:
Elizabeth, born November 21, 1751. Died March 5, 1849.
Maria, born November 2, 1754. Died August 25, 1757.
David, born July 26, 1757. Died February 9, 1816.
Susanna, born January 1, 1762.
Rosina, born February 9, 1764.
Abraham, born October 1, 1766.
Regina, born March 15, 1772. Died March 6, 1841.
Caspar Scipt died December 11, 1773, aged 48.
Rosina, widow of C. S., died July 16, 1820, aged 90.

David Wagener, son of Anna Wagener (page 18), married Susanna Umstead, and had issue, as follows:
    Deborah, married Adam Deshler.
    Elizabeth, married Jacob Mixsell.
    Mary, married Christian Butz.
    John, died in Allentown, Pa.
    Abraham, died in Philadelphia.
    Daniel, born 1766.
    David, born 1771.
D. W. was born May 24, 1736, and died May 9, 1796, and his wife died April 22, 1810.

David Wagener having in 1773 purchased a tract of land from the Penns situated on the Bushkill Creek, near Easton, made it the place of his permanent residence.

His tombstone contains this inscription: "Beneath "this marble are deposited the remains of David "Wagener, Esq., late of the borough of Easton, one "of the Associate Judges of Northampton County, "born in Silesia in Germany, May 24, A.D. 1736, "and departed this life May 9, 1796, aged 59 years, "11 months, and 15 days."

Christopher Yeakel, son of David Yeakel (page 9), married Rosina, widow of Christopher Seipt (page 22), and daughter of Balthasar Hoffman (page 5), May 30, 1751. Had issue:
    Jacob, born January 9, 1753.
    Salome, born October 24, 1762.
Rosina, wife of C. Y., died June 14, 1788, aged 70 years.
C. Y. died July 1, 1800.

Melchior Hartranft, son of Tobias Hartranft (page 5), married January 3, 1753. Had issue:
    Catharine, born December 2, 1753.

Maria, born April 6, 1755. Died January 5, 1759.
Maria, born August 12, 1759.
M. H. died November 3, 1760, aged 34 years.

Christopher Hoffman, son of Rev. Balthasar Hoffman (page 5), married Rosanna, daughter of George Dresher (page 4), May 17, 1753. Had no issue.
Rosanna, wife of C. H., died July 3, 1794, aged 70 years and 9 months.
C. H. died January 29, 1804, aged 76 years. He was a minister of the society of Schwenkfelders, and was an acceptable and faithful divine.

Christopher Wagner, son of Anna Wagner, widow (page 17), married Susanna, daughter of David Heebner (page 9), November 26, 1754. Their children were:
    Sarah, born February 11, 1756.
    Salome, born August 28, 1761.
    Christina, born February 17, 1764.
    Infant daughter, born December 18, 1767. Died January 1, 1768.
C. W. died November 29, 1810, aged 83 years, less 2 weeks.
Susanna, widow of C. W., died June 2, 1817, aged 82 years, 8 months.

Jeremiah Yeakel, son of David Yeakel (page 9), married —— Wolf; had issue as follows:
    Christiana, born 1748.
    Susan, married William Getman.
    Anna Maria.
    Charlotte.
    Isaac.
    Juliann, died single.

Catharine, } born, married Conrad Wolf.
Salome, } born, died September 4, 1762.
J. Y. died February 22, 1763, and his wife December, 1761, shortly after giving birth to twins.

George Hartranft, son of Tobias (page 5), married, and had issue:
  First child, named Rosina.
  Second child, born June 23, 1752.
  G. H. died November 11, 1759, and his wife died October 6, 1797.

Heinrich (Schneider) Snyder, born August 3, 1729, in Germany, arrived in Pennsylvania August 30, 1749, joined the society of Schwenkfelders, and married Rosina, daughter of Christopher Neuman (page 16), 1756. He settled in Gwynedd Township, Philadelphia, now Montgomery County, Pennsylvania. They had children:
  Rosina, born March 8, 1757.
  George, born 1758.
  Christopher, born January 12, 1761.
  Henry, born November 22, 1762.
  Christian, born November, 1764.
  Abraham, } twins, born July 23, 1769.
  Isaac, }
  Susanna, born 1772.
  John, born ——.
  Regina, born ——. Died 2 weeks old.
H. S. died April 3, 1779, aged 67 years.
R., his widow, died March 16, 1804, aged 67 years.

George Anders, son of Balthasar (page 4), married Barbara Diehl February 14, 1757. Their children were:
  Rosina, born December 24, 1757.

GENEALOGICAL RECORD. 39

Abraham, born April 1, 1759.
Susanna, born November 30, 1760.
Andrew, born July 16, 1763.
Anna, born March 15, 1766.
George, born June 29, 1768.
John, born August, 1770.
G. A. died October 28, 1803, aged 66 years.
Barbara, his widow, died January 28, 1812, aged 81 years, 1 month, 3 days.

Christopher Heebner, son of David Heebner (page 9), married Susanna, daughter of Hans Wiegner (page 16), May 3, 1757. Their children were:
    Melchior, born November 16, 1759. Died May 10, 1781.
    John, born July 12, 1761. Died March 10, 1824.
    Sarah, born April 21, 1763. Died January 12, 1833.
    Abraham, born December 28, 1766. Died November 25, 1846.
    Christopher, born May 11, 1770.
    Susanna, born October 1, 1773. Died August 13, 1777.
    David, born September 19, 1778. Died May 19, 1783.
Susanna, wife of C. H., died January 17, 1814, aged 76 years.
C. H. died August 21, 1827, aged 80 years.

David Neuman, son of Christopher Neuman (page 16), married December, 1757, to whom unknown. Their children were:
    Christopher, born November 20, 1758.
    Rosina, born December 29, 1759.

Abraham, born June, 1761.
D. N. died September 18, 1775.
His wife died February 4, 1802.

Peter Gerhard, a native of Germany, born in 1736, married Susanna, daughter of Christopher Seipt (page 22). Their children were:
Daughter, born October 2, 1759. Died October 15, 1759.
Daughter, born September 26, 1766. Died same day.
Jacob, born October 27, 1767.
Magdalena, born August 31, 1768.
Anna, born January 17, 1772.
Matthias, born February 20, 1777.
P. G. died May 20, 1791, aged 55 years.
Susanna, his widow, died January 9, 1822.

Christopher Reinewald, son of George Reinewald (page 12), married Rosina, daughter of David Heebner (page 9), April 4, 1758. One child,
Susanna, born August 12, 1759. Died July 15, 1762.
C. R. died September 10, 1759.

Andrew Beyer, son of Abraham Beyer (page 17), married Philipina Weyand November 7, 1758. Their children were:
Susanna, born August 2, 1759. Died June 4, 1764.
Abraham, born October 8, 1760.
Jacob, born February 14, 1762.
Wendel, born December 9, 1763. Died December 17, 1779.
Daniel, born November 6, 1765.
Rosanna, born April 27, 1769.

Andrew, born ———.
David, born ———.
Anna Maria, born ———.
Andrew Beyer died April 19, 1773, aged nearly 40 years.

George Kriebel, son of Caspar Kriebel (page 11), married Anna, daughter of Balthasar Anders (page 4), October 11, 1758. Their children were:
Abraham, born May 26, 1760.
Susanna, born July 1, 1761.
Jacob, born February 12, 1764.
Anna, born November 20, 1766.
G. K. died December 1, 1805, aged 73 years, 1 month, 22 days.
Anna, his widow, died June 4, 1822, aged 86 years, 2 months, less 4 days.
This is the Rev. George Kriebel who resided in Lower Milford, Lehigh County; was well educated; in his younger days taught school, and was many years a minister of the society of Schwenkfelders, which position he filled acceptably. He was frequently engaged as a conveyancer and in settling differences in his vicinity. He lived on the property owned now, 1879, by a man of the name of Brey.

George Heydrick, son of Balthasar Heydrick (page 9), married Rosina, daughter of Balthasar Krauss (page 19), June 17, 1760. Their children were:
Susanna, born June 10, 1761.
Balthasar, born November 13, 1765. Died February 4, 1846.
Eve, born January 17, 1767.
Rosina, born February 9, 1773. Died March 15, 1773.

George, born March 14, 1775.
G. H. died January 29, 1824, aged 86 years, 4 months.
Rosina, his widow, died October 29, 1828, aged 91 years, 6 months.
G. Heydrick was a shoemaker by trade, and farmer likewise; lived and owned the place where Samuel Heydrick now resides, in Lower Salford Township.

Balthasar Yeakel, son of Abraham Yeakel (page 10), married Rosina, widow of Christoph Reinewald (page 40), and daughter of David Heebner (page 9), October 7, 1760. Their children were:
  Esther, born July 28, 1761.
  Maria, born January 16, 1763. Died January 28, 1765.
  Catharine, born August 11, 1764.
  Abraham, born May 24, 1767.
B. Y. died April 18, 1789.
Rosina, his widow, died February 9, 1819, aged 80 years, 10 months.

David Kriebel, son of Melchior (page 11), married Susanna, daughter of George Reinewald (page 12), June 16, 1761. Their children were:
  Christopher, born April 19, 1762.
  Abraham, born May 30, 1764.
  1 Melchior, born December 3, 1765. Died January 1, 1767.
  2 Melchior, born March 25, 1768. Died May 3, 1769.
  Rosina, born June 12, 1772.
Susanna, wife of D. K., died June 16, 1780.
David Kriebel married, second time, Rosina, daughter

of Abraham Wiegner (page 35), May 17, 1781. Their children were:
Susanna, born December 6, 1782.
Daniel, born September 11, 1784. Died September 18, 1786.
John, born February 16, 1787. Died October 27, 1796.
Maria, born November 2, 1788. Died August 29, 1830.
Catharine, born December 17, 1790. Died April 20, 1796.
Jacob, born January 4, 1795. Died January 22, 1839.
D. K. died September 26, 1815, aged 79 years, 6 months.
Rosina, his widow, died April 20, 1834, aged 79 years.

Balthasar Yeakle, son of Hans Heinrich Yeakel (page 18), married Susanna, daughter of Balthasar Krauss (page 19), August 25, 1761. Their children were:
Rosina, born July 28, 1762.
Sarah, born April 17, 1765. Died May 28, 1833.
Barbara, born November 22, 1766.
David, born April 6, 1770.
Andrew, born March 1, 1774.
Susanna, born October 29, 1775. Died February 1, 1795.
B. Y. died October 12, 1797, aged 64 years. He was blind the last 28 years of his life.
Susanna, his widow, died February 15, 1820, aged 81 years, 5 months, 14 days.

Christopher Reinewald, son of Christopher Reinewald (page 12), married Maria, daughter of Melchior Meschter (page 12), April 21, 1762. Their children were:

David, born April 24, 1763.
Susanna, born August 17, 1765.
Rosina, born September 29, 1767. Died February 17, 1847.
1 Christopher, born January 24, 1770. Died February 27, 1770.
Maria, born January 9, 1771.
Regina, born May 4, 1773.
2 Christopher, born April 7, 1775. Died September 26, 1828.
Magdalena, } twins, born June 23, 1777.
Catharine,
Died August 10, 1846.
Died November 4, 1843.
Abraham, born January 26, 1780.
Elizabeth, born July 29, 1782.
Anna, born April 24, 1787.
C. R. died December 13, 1814, aged 77 years, 9 months.
Maria, his widow, died February 10, 1826, aged 83 years.

Abraham Kriebel, son of Caspar Kriebel (page 11), married Susanna, daughter of George Schultz (page 20), May 13, 1762. Their children were:
Christian, born February 4, 1764. Died October 12, 1812.
Andrew, born October 5, 1765.
A. K. died January 30, 1801, aged 64 years, 3 months, 26 days.
Susanna, his widow, died October 10, 1820.
He inherited the farm where he lived and died, at the Schwenkfelder meeting-house, now occupied by his great-grandson, in Towamencin Township.

Hans or John Yeakel, son of Abraham Yeakel (page 10), married Anna, daughter of Christopher Wiegner (page 21), May 27, 1762. Their children were:
    Maria, born April 24, 1763. Died March 14, 1764.
    Regina, born December 17, 1764. Died April 15, 1812.
    Christopher, born August 8, 1766. Died January 14, 1769.
    Joseph, born March 14, 1768. Died October 22, 1836.
    Magdalena, born December 24, 1769. Died January 2, 1832.
    Jacob, born August 14, 1771.
    Christian, born January 4, 1774.
    Anna, born January 14, 1776. Died single and aged.
    Abraham, born August 1, 1777.
    John, born March 3, 1783. Died single and blind.
    J. Y. died December 9, 1801, aged 62 years, 6 months, 1 day. Lived in Lower Salford.
    Anna, his widow, died March 30, 1822, aged 79 years, 10 months, 20 days.

Jeremiah Yeakel, son of Hans Heinrich Yeakel (page 18), married Susanna, daughter of Christopher Wiegner (page 21), June 16, 1763. Their children were:
    Salome, born April 27, 1764.
    Lydia, born March 4, 1766.
    Catharine, born June 11, 1768.
    Maria, born August 22, 1770.
    Helena, born September 29, 1772. Died November 19, 1859.
    John, born November 15, 1774.
    Rosina, born June 10, 1777.

Anna, born October 20, 1780.

J. Y. died after 1800. He lived in Hosensack, where Anthony Schultz resides.

Susanna, his widow, died February 10, 1818, aged 77 years, 8 months, 15 days.

Balthasar Reinewald, son of Christopher Reinewald (page 7), married Elizabeth, daughter of Abraham Yeakel (page 10), November 24, 1763. Their children were:

Regina, born November 28, 1764.

Sarah, born May 26, 1768.

Elizabeth, wife of B. R., died June 26, 1801, aged 66 years, 4 months, 3 days.

B. R. died in February, 1818, aged 82 years, 11 months.

Abraham Anders, son of Balthasar Anders (page 4), married Susanna, daughter of Melchior Kriebel (page 11), November 25, 1765. Their children were:

Benjamin, born November 30, 1766.

Rosanna, born July 19, 1769. Died December 24, 1853.

Abraham, born June 2, 1774.

Anna, born April 13, 1780.

Susanna, wife of A. A., died March 28, 1813, aged 73 years, 5 months.

A. A. died April 19, 1819, aged 80 years, 6 days.

Christopher Meschter, son of Gregorius Meschter (page 15), married Christina, daughter of Jeremiah Yeakel (page 37), May 7, 1766. Their children were:

Susanna, born February 20, 1767. Died May 2, 1767.

Maria, born March 10, 1768. Died October 18, 1769.
David, born September 13, 1769. Died December 20, 1774.
Christina, born December 24, 1771. Died December 2, 1775.
George, born 1774. Died January 2, 1775.
Regina, born September 26, 1776.
Christopher, born March 13, 1778.
Magdalena, born June 17, 1780.
John, born June 22, 1783.
Isaac, born January 23, 1787.

This Christopher Meschter lived in Chester County, somewhere opposite Pottstown, and his descendants changed their name to Master, as will appear further on in the Record.

Abraham Heydrick, son of Balthasar Heydrick (page 9), married Susanna, daughter of Christopher Yeakle (page 23), May 4, 1767. Their children were:
Sarah, born September 25, 1768.
Christopher, born April 7, 1770.
Susanna, born August 5, 1773.
Regina, born December 25, 1775.
Abraham, born May 18, 1779.
Maria, born February 20, 1781.
A. H. died August 30, 1826, aged 83 years, 9 months, 25 days.
Susanna, widow of A. H., died September 18, 1834, aged 90 years.
After his marriage he settled and kept a store, and farmed at the foot of Chestnut Hill, in Springfield Township, where Charles Heydrick now lives.

Melchior Reinewald, son of Christopher Reinewald (page 12), married Maria, daughter of George Anders (page 4), May 5, 1767. No issue.
Maria, wife of M. R., died July 11, 1768.
Melchior Reinewald married, second time, Rosanna, daughter of Henry Snyder (page 25), April 5, 1785. Their children were:
    Henry, born August 25, 1791. Died February 4, 1799.
    Lydia, born August 27, 1793. Died.
    Jonas, born July 20, 1796.
M. R. died December 2, 1812, aged 68 years, 8 months.
Rosanna, widow of M. R., died November 8, 1843, aged 86 years.

George Yeakel, son of Hans Heinrich Yeakel (page 18), married Rosina, daughter of David Schubert (page 21), May 5, 1768. Their children were:
    Anna, born November 20, 1769.
    Abraham, born March 31, 1772. Died 1836.
    Maria, born April 4, 1776.
    Jacob, born June 6, 1778.
    George, born August 19, 1782.
Rosina, wife of G. Y., died January 25, 1799, aged 53 years, 9 months.
G. Y. was drowned June 1, 1812, in attempting to cross the Hosensack Creek on a log. He lived on the farm that Daniel S. Yeakel now owns.

Balthasar Schultz, son of George Schultz (page 20), married Anna, daughter of Balthasar Yeakel (page 20), November 24th, 1768. They had issue:
    Barbara, born November 13, 1769.
    George, born June 28, 1771.

GENEALOGICAL RECORD. 49

Andrew, born August 18, 1773.
Eve, born June 23, 1775.
Matthias, born February 20, 1777.
David, born November 23, 1779.
Susanna, born August 14, 1782.
Rosina, born May 11, 1785.
Anna, wife of B. S., died September 8, 1799.
B. S. lived in Upper Hanover, on the Hosensack Creek, on the fine farm now owned by his grandson, Reuben Schultz, and died there April 12, 1813, aged 69 years.

———

George Heebner, son of David Heebner (page 9), married Susanna, daughter of Balthasar Heydrick (page 9), April 26, 1769. They had issue:
  Balthasar, born June 12, 1770.
Susanna, wife of G. H., died June 19, 1770.
George Heebner married, second time, Anna, daughter of David Shubert (page 21), November 21, 1771. They had issue:
  Maria, born April 28, 1773.
  Salome, born October 18, 1774. Died March 31, 1776.
  Regina, born January 13, 1777.
  Henry, born December 1, 1778.
  Barbara, born March 13, 1780. Died May 16, 1786.
  Catharine, born July 17, 1782. Died May 14, 1786.
G. H. died August 18, 1783, aged 39 years, 2 months.
Anna, widow of G. H., died August 23, 1784, aged 35.

———

Balthasar Krauss, son of Balthasar Krauss (page 19), married Susanna, daughter of H. Heinrich Yeakel (page 18), June 14, 1769. Their children were:
  John, born March 1, 1770.

4

Andrew, born June 21, 1771.

Balthasar, born November 10, 1772. Died August 26, 1779.

Regina, born February 24, 1775. Died January 18, 1807.

Helena, born October 31, 1776.

Rosanna, born September 30, 1780. Married —— Hunsberger.

George, born February 23, 1783.

Lydia, born July 31, 1786.

B. K. died October 14, 1805, aged 61 years, 16 days.

Susanna, widow of B. K., died January 8, 1820, aged 75 years, 11 months, and 8 days.

George Dresher, son of Christopher Dresher (page 24), married Maria, daughter of Christopher Yeakle (page 23), October 23, 1770. Their children were:

Christopher, born August 8, 1771.

Samuel, born November 6, 1773.

Maria, born January 17, 1779.

G. D. died October 17, 1822, aged 76 years.

Maria, widow of G. D., died September 23, 1823, aged 76 years.

Melchior Yeakel, son of Hans Heinrich Yeakel (page 18), married Regina, daughter of Christopher Schultz (page 24), November 15, 1770. Their children were:

Rosina, born October 29, 1771.

Solomon, born October 17, 1773.

Christopher, born August 31, 1775.

Susanna, born November 4, 1777.

Christina, born February 14, 1780.

Daniel, born November 23, 1781.

Maria, born February 11, 1784.

Isaac, born June 7, 1786. Died January 26, 1805.
Catharine, born March 14, 1789.
Regina, wife of M. Y., died November 2, 1821, aged 72 years, 5 months, and 19 days.
M. Y. died May 18, 1831, aged 89 years, 2 months, and 6 days.

George Urfer, son of Michael Urffer, was born in Alsace, in Germany, July 20, 1735, and came to Pennsylvania August 24, 1765, and married Barbara, daughter of Balthasar Krauss (page 19), December 10, 1770. They had issue:
    Susanna, born November 30, 1771.
    Maria, born March 5, 1774.
    Catharine, born January 7, 1776.
    David, born October 1, 1777.
    Michael, born June 28, 1779.
    Gertrude, born March 25, 1781.
    Balthasar, born May 26, 1783.
    Barbara, born March 17, 1785.
G. U. died May 5, 1794. He lived where the borough of East Greenville now stands. This borough and part of Pennsburg is built upon his land.
Barbara, his widow, died November 24, 1821.

Christopher Schultz, son of George Schultz (page 20), married Maria, daughter of Hans Heinrich Yeakel (page 18), April 25, 1771. They had issue:
    John, born March 11, 1772.
    Jacob, born June 17, 1774.
    Susanna, born October 29, 1775.
    Samuel, born February 24, 1778.
    George, Caspar, } twins, born December 20, 1781.
    Anna, born April 29, 1785.

C. S. died September 10, 1830, aged 84 years. Resided in Upper Hanover, Montgomery County, Pa. Maria, his widow, died August 20, 1832, aged 84 years, less 45 days.

Andrew Kriebel, son of George Kriebel (page 22), married Susannah, daughter of Abraham Yeakel (page 32), May 16, 1771. Their children were:
  Rosanna, born September 24, 1773. Married Daniel Diehl, in 1818, and died 1836.
  Abraham, born September 27, 1774.
  Samuel, born June 13, 1776.
  George, born October 2, 1778. Died May 20, 1779.
  Regina, born June 25, 1780.
  David, born July 19, 1783.
  Sophia, born November 1, 1785.
  Salome, born December 9, 1787.
  Israel, born September 14, 1790.
Susannah, wife of A. K., died April 22, 1808, aged 57 years, 5 months, 14 days.
A. K. died April 17, 1830, aged 81 years, 7 months.

Abraham Schultz, son of George Schultz (page 23), married Regina, daughter of Christopher Yeakle (page 23), October 24, 1771. Their children were:
  Benjamin, born July 20, 1772. Died March 20, 1802.
  Adam, born September 20, 1775.
  Isaac, born March 4, 1778.
  Abraham, born February 18, 1781. Died March 23, 1802.
  Frederick, born August 10, 1784. Died December 17, 1794.
  Joseph, born January 22, 1787.
  Melchior, born June 23, 1789.

A. S. died December 25, 1822, aged 76 years, 8 months. Regina, his widow, died November 9, 1826, aged 77 years, 1 month, 8 days.

Abraham Schultz, the eldest son of George Schultz, was born in Upper Hanover, March 23, 1747. In his youth, after some brief school instruction, he became, not only a great lover of books and literature, but an industrious reader, and being gifted with a comprehensive mind and retentive memory, he soon acquired a good deal of general knowledge, of which he made good use through life. He was a member of the religious society of Schwenkfelders, and served them in the capacity of trustee, school-inspector, teacher, and catechist, and the community in which he lived as scrivener and counsellor, and in the year 1796 was elected a member of the General Assembly of the State from Montgomery County.

He died nearly 76 years of age. Among some papers left at his demise there were a few letters written by him that are quite interesting. One of them, dated June 14, 1783, to Chr. Groh, J. F. Heintze, Jeremiah Heydrick, and others, in Germany, giving an account of the then existing situation of the followers of Schwenkfeld in this country, and how they fared during the troublous times of the "Revolution;" giving also some of the incidents, effects, and consequences of the war then just closed.

Another letter, to his young friend Dr. Christopher Heydrick, who was then about entering upon the practice of his profession. The letter is full of sound sense and good advice, and is still carefully treasured up by the doctor's worthy descendants in Western Pennsylvania.

Another, written in 1820, in reply to a request of Pastor Plitt, editor of the "Americanische Ansichten," constitutes a short defence of Schwenkfeld against the unwarrantable attacks of some German historians and other perverters of truth; also a brief account of the ministers, places of worship, schools, etc., of the followers of Schwenkfeld in America.

David Schultz, son of Gregory Schultz (page 13), married Catharine, daughter of Melchior Hartranft (page 36), October 6, 1772. They had issue:
    Sarah, born November 3, 1773. Died Feburary 3, 1775.
    Christina, born September 29, 1775.
    Magdalena, born April 4, 1778. Died April 4, 1802.
    Maria, born February 13, 1781. Died January 22, 1809.
    Julianna, born April 22, 1784.
    Gabriel, born January 28, 1789.
Catharine, wife of D. S., died August 27, 1804, aged 51 years.
D. S. died January 25, 1810, aged 66 years, 6 months, and 3 days. He was a farmer, and lived in Upper Hanover, Montgomery County, Pa.

George Kriebel, son of George Kriebel (page 22), married Esther, daughter of George Wiegner (page 33), October 15, 1772. Their children were:
    1 Christopher, born September 27, 1774. Died June 2, 1779.
    George, born July 28, 1777. Died May 28, 1779.
    2 Christopher, born October 8, 1779.
    Susanna, born November 11, 1782. Died February 15, 1789.

George Kriebel was killed while cleaning out his well. A stone fell from the top and struck his head, from the effects of which he died instantly. This occurred September 14, 1792. Esther, his widow, died February 13, 1816, aged 64 years, 4 months and 4 days.

Melchior Kriebel, son of Melchior Kriebel (page 11), married Rosina, daughter of Hans Christopher Heebner (page 30), October 28, 1772, and had issue,

    Susanna, born May 1, 1775. Died June 18, 1775.

Rosina, wife of M. K., died May 22, 1775, aged 28 years.

Melchior Kriebel married, second time, Barbara, daughter of David Schubert (page 21), November 25, 1779, and had issue:

    Sarah, born October 6, 1780.
    Anna, born February 19, 1782. Died August 26, 1794.
    Solomon, born November 3, 1783.
    John, born June 15, 1785.
    David, born April 22, 1787.
    Job, born October 15, 1788.
    Melchior, born May 3, 1790.
    Hannah, born September 16, 1791.
    Samuel, born February 22, 1795.

Barbara, wife of M. K., died October 9, 1803, aged 48 years, 4 months.

M. K. died December 13, 1833, aged 87 years, 6 months, 17 days. He was many years a minister of the Schwenkfelders, and lived in Gwynedd, where Abraham Rittenhouse now resides.

Christopher Meschter, son of Melchior Meschter (page 12), married Rosina, daughter of Christopher Kriebel (page 32), October 21, 1773. Their children were:
Maria, born July 6, 1775.
Jeremiah, born August 27, 1777.
Christopher, born July 21, 1779.
Regina, born May 10, 1781.
Catharine, born May 3, 1783. Died in February 1837.
David, born October 18, 1786.
Hannah, born July 13, 1789. Married John Wasser. Have no further record.
C. M. died May 4, 1797, aged over 53 years.
Rosina, his widow, died September 19, 1823, aged 72 years, 28 days.

Melchior Meschter, son of Gregory Meschter (page 15), married Anna Maria Zoller, widow, and daughter of Jeremiah Yeakle (page 37), November 20, 1774. Their children were:
George, born April 14, 1775.
Rosina, born September 13, 1776.
Barbara, born August 14, 1778.
David, born October 10, 1780. Died October 24, 1793.
M. M. died October 21, 1793.

Melchior Schubert, son of David Schubert (page 21), married Maria, daughter of Christopher Krauss (page 34), May 30, 1775. Their children were:
Susanna, born April 17, 1776. Married Michael Miller.
Sarah, born January 18, 1778.
David, born December 31, 1779.

Anna, born September 23, 1781.
Christopher, born November 18, 1783.
Regina, born August 18, 1785.
Hannah, born December 9, 1788.
Sophia, born July 17, 1791.
M. S. died December 24, 1831, aged 84 years, 5 months, 15 days.
Maria Schubert died December 13, 1849.

Balthasar Meschter, son of Gregory Meschter (page 15), married Magdalena Getman. Their children were:
Susanna, born July 21, 1777. Died.
Abraham, died.
David, died.
George, died.
John, died.
Jacob.
Maria, born April 12, 1787.
Elizabeth. Married Andrew Kuhns.
Magdalena.
B. M. died August 3, 1809, aged 63.
Magdalena, widow of B. M., died October 4, 1846, aged 86 years, 1 month.

Caspar Yeakel, son of Balthasar Yeakel (page 20), married Anna, daughter of Christopher Yeakle (page 23), August 10, 1775. Their children were:
Balthasar, born October 11, 1777. Died October 26, 1778.
Maria, born May 25, 1779.
Jeremiah, born August 11, 1781.
Esther, born May 24, 1783.
Regina, born February 6, 1785.
Elizabeth, born December 9, 1786.

Susannah, born August 21, 1788.
Abraham, born August 28, 1790.
Benjamin, born August 16, 1793. Died September 2, 1796.
Anna, born June 7, 1798.
C. Y. died July 11, 1804, aged 56 years.
Anna, his widow, died May 11, 1837, aged 81 years, 10 months.

Abraham Yeakle, son of Christopher Yeakle (page 23), married Sarah, daughter of Christopher Wagner (page 37), October 10, 1776. Had issue:
Isaac, born November 9, 1777.
Samuel, born February 26, 1779. Died March 5, 1779.
Jacob, born September 29, 1780.
Susannah, born November 11, 1782.
Maria, born September 4, 1784.
Christopher, born May 21, 1787. Died July 10, 1813.
Sarah, wife of A. Y., died May 28, 1833.
A. Y. died June 17, 1841. He lived in Springfield, Montgomery County, and owned the farm now occupied by Daniel Yeakel, his grandson.

Matthias Gerhard married Maria, daughter of Balthasar Krauss (page 19), November 14, 1776. No issue:
Maria, wife of M. G., died September 10, 1777.
Matthias Gerhard married, second time, Anna, daughter of Hans Heinrich Yeakel (page 18), February 11, 1779. Had issue:
Christopher, born June 5, 1780.
Daniel, born September 15, 1781.
Jacob, born August 5, 1784.

Maria, born January 18, 1787. Died March 23, 1788.
Sarah, born October 16, 1788.
Magdalena, } twins, born April 12, 1791.
Salome,
Susannah, born June 26, 1794.

The death record of Matthias Gerhard's cannot be found, and is consequently omitted.

Andrew Schultz, son of Rev. Christopher Schultz (page 24), married Charlotte, daughter of Jeremiah Yeakel (page 37), November 21, 1776. Had issue:

Christopher, born October 12, 1777.
Susannah, born December 13, 1778.
Regina, born August 1, 1780.
Esther, born March 14, 1783.
Maria, born October 4, 1784.
Christina, born August 22, 1787.
Henry, born July 3, 1793.

A. S. died February 5, 1802, aged 49 years, 6 days.
Charlotte, his widow, died February 11, 1825.

Gregory Schultz, son of George Schultz (page 20), married Rosina, daughter of Balthasar Yeakel (page 20), May 1, 1777. Their children were:

Son, born July 27, 1778. Dead.
Susannah, born May 1, 1780.
Maria, born May 25, 1783. Died November 15, 1787
Barbara, born May 22, 1785. Died May 6, 1808.
Daniel, born July 2, 1788.
Eve, born May 3, 1791.

Rosina, wife of G. S., died December 22, 1819, aged 67 years, 9 days.

G. S. died February 25, 1827, aged 74 years, less 4 weeks.

Abraham Dresher, son of Christopher Dresher (page 24), married Eve, daughter of George Schultz (page 20), May 15, 1777. Their children were:
  Daniel, born March 4, 1778. Died March 6, 1778.
  Anna, born April 27, 1779.
  Susannah, born July 29, 1781.
  Regina, born February 13, 1783. Died September 23, 1804.
  Abraham, born April 20, 1785. Died May 7, 1786.
Eve, wife of A. D., died April 6, 1786, aged 35 years, 10 months, 6 days.
Abraham Dresher married, second time, Susannah, daughter of Caspar Seipt (page 35), May 22, 1787. Their children were:
  George, born July 20, 1788. Died October 6, 1788.
  Jacob, born May 13, 1790.
A. D. died July 30, 1811, aged 61 years, 2 months, 15 days.
Susannah, his widow, died January 21, 1840, aged 78 years, 20 days.

Abraham Beyer, son of Andrew Beyer (page 40), married Catharine Rickerd. Children:
  Elizabeth, born 1780.
  John, born July 18, 1783.
  Ann, born June 1, 1786.
  Catharine, born January 9, 1790.
  Henry, born June 7, 1792.
  Abraham, born November 26, 1796.
  Mary, born March 16, 1798.
  A. B. died August 8, 1832.

Abraham Kriebel, son of Christopher Kriebel (page 32), married Rosina, daughter of George Hartranft (page 38), February 12, 1778. Children:
    Isaac, born February 5, 1779.
    Christina, born December 24, 1780.
    Maria, born April 26, 1788. Died December 22, 1808.
    Susannah, born August 24, 1796.
    Rosina, wife of A. K., died November 14, 1814.
    A. K. died December 16, 1818, aged 68 years, 6 months, 12 days.

Jacob Yeakel, son of Christopher Yeakel (page 36), married Susannah, daughter of Christopher Schultz (page 24), May 7, 1778. Children:
    Magdalena, born February 20, 1779. Died, December 21, 1828.
    Rosina, born July 4, 1780.
    Daniel, born September 7, 1781. Died October 5, 1781.
    Regina, born October 19, 1782. Died June 28, 1783.
    Christopher, born September 4, 1784.
    Andrew, born June 7, 1786.
    Carl, born June 21, 1788.
    Christina, born March 30, 1790.
    Sarah, born February 8, 1795.
J. Y. was a farmer in Upper Hanover, and died there February 17, 1819, aged 66 years, 1 month, 8 days, and his widow died June 28, 1829, aged 70 years.

Leonard Hartranft, son of Abraham Hartranft (page 31), married Christiana Moyer, and had issue, as follows:
    Jacob, born May 9th, 1780. Died 1862. Married Mary Geiger.

Rebecca, born   , married John Beideman.

Leonard, born about 1782.

Maria, born December 16, 1784, married John Fox.

Susanna, born October 31, 1786, married Andrew Maurer, and died 1861.

John, born September 2, 1788, married Bucher.

David, born October 31, 1789, married twice; descendants living in Montgomery County.

Anthony, born March 24, 1791. Died young and unmarried.

Margaretha, born February 23d, 1793, married Conrad Rhoads.

Henry, born February 9th, 1795, married Ann Gresh; children living in Berks County and Philadelphia.

Catarina, born   , married James Coates.

Amos, born April 3d, 1799, married Mary Habenstein; descendants in Schuylkill County, Pa.

Sarah, born June 21st, 1801, married Jacob Gilbert.

William, born July 14th, 1803.

Christina, born September 14th, 1807, married Jacob Lutz, and died May, 1863; 7 children.

Leonard Hartranft, Sr., lived in Montgomery, Philadelphia, and Tamaqua, Schuylkill County, where he died, July 24, 1841, aged 81 years, 8 months, and 18 days.

Jeremiah Kriebel, son of Christopher Kriebel (page 32), married Anna Rosina, daughter of Abraham Yeakel (page 32), November 11, 1779, and had issue:

Benjamin, born September 16, 1780.

Anna, born June 26, 1782.

Joseph, born March 6, 1786.

Andrew, born January 8, 1789. Died May 4, 1789.
Susannah, born March 14, 1791. Died November 5, 1793.
Samuel, born August 26, 1796.
Anna Rosina, wife of J. K., died May 20, 1808, aged 55 years, 6 months, and 2 days.
J. K. died March 8, 1842, aged 87 years, 1 month, and 20 days; was a resident of Lower Salford Township.

George Snyder, son of Henry Snyder (page 38), married Rosanna, daughter of George Anders (page 38), April 13, 1780, and had issue,
 Abraham, born April 3, 1781. Died April 12, 1781.
Rosanna, wife of G. S., died November 6, 1781, aged 23 years, 10 months, and 18 days.
George Snyder married, second time, Susannah, daughter of George Wiegner (page 33), April 25, 1784. Had issue:
 Rosanna, born September 13, 1785.
 Abraham, born October 30, 1787. Died March 8, 1789.
 Susannah, born April 18, 1789.
G. S. died July 28, 1832, aged 74 years.
S., his widow, died April 15, 1833, aged 78 years.

Jacob Seibert, born February 28, 1755, married Anna, daughter of Gregory Meschter (page 15), 1781. Had issue:
 Abraham, born April 18, 1782.
 Christopher, born March 10, 1785. Died May 17, 1864.
 Daniel, born October 6, 1787.

David, born January 9, 1790.
J. S. died September 26, 1823.
Anna, his widow, died May 17, 1833.

David Schultz, son of Rev. Christopher Schultz (page 24), married Anna, daughter of Christopher Kriebel (page 32), May 17, 1781. Children:
Susannah, born May 7, 1782.
Andrew, born October 4, 1784.
William, born November 11, 1786.
Rosina, born September 1, 1788.
Christopher K., born August 29, 1790.
Philip, born June 6, 1793. Died October 25, 1817
Maria, born July 8, 1795.
Jeremiah, born June 7, 1797.
Christina, born January 15, 1799.
Regina, born February 23, 1801.
Anna, wife of D. S., died December 4, 1831, aged 73 years.
D. S. died August 4, 1833, aged 76 years. He resided in Hereford, Berks County, Pa., immediately adjoining the Schwenkfelder Meeting-House.

Melchior Schultz, son of George Schultz (page 23), married Salome, daughter of Christopher Wagner (page 37), November 29, 1781. Their children were:
Christina, born September 29, 1782.
Regina, born November 10, 1783.
Maria, born August 21, 1785.
Henry W., born December 3, 1788.
Sarah, born January 11, 1792.
Frederick } twins, born June 28, 1795.
Susannah, } Susannah died April 25, 1848.

Rosina, born January 15, 1798.
M. S. died June 11, 1826, aged 70 years, 2 months, 15 days.
Salome, his widow, died January 27, 1835, aged 73 years, 5 months.
This is the Rev. Melchior Schultz who very acceptably filled the position of minister of the Society of Schwenkfelders for quite a long time. He was a farmer by occupation likewise. He lived in Worcester Township, and owned the farm lately in possession of his son Melchior, deceased.

Jacob Beyer, son of Andrew Beyer (page 40), married Rachael Metz. Children:
Catharine, born September 14, 1783.
Andrew, born July 24, 1785.
Christianna, born October 20, 1787.
Joseph, born November 17, 1789.
Margaret, born April 13, 1794.
Rachel, born February 12, 1796.
Jacob, born April 19, 1798.
Mary, born July 4, 1800.
John, born October 17, 1802. Died July 2, 1832.
Elizabeth, born January 5, 1806.
J. B. died August 23, 1846.
Rachel, widow of J. B., was born July 26, 1763. Died July 5, 1855.

Christopher Snyder, son of Henry Snyder (page 38), married Susannah, daughter of George Heydrick (page 41), April 18, 1782. Had no issue.
Susannah, wife of C. S., died August 20, 1801, aged 40 years, 2 months, 10 days.
Christopher Snyder married, second time, Maria,

daughter of Christopher Meschter (page 56). Had no issue.

C. S. died August 2, 1810, aged 49 years, 6 months, 2 days.

Maria, his widow, died October 7, 1833, aged 57 years, 3 months, 1 day.

Christopher Yeakle, son of Christopher Yeakle (page 23), married Susannah, daughter of Rev. George Kriebel (page 41), June 6, 1782. Their children were:
  Lydia, born March 8, 1783.
  Agnes, born August 31, 1785.
  Daniel, born November 4, 1786. Died May 28, 1788.
  Anna, born July 18, 1789.
  Sarah, born July 16, 1791.
  George, born July 19, 1793. Died November 8, 1794.
  Rebecca, born November 3, 1795.
  Samuel, born August 25, 1798.

Susannah, wife of C. Y., died April 24, 1830, aged 68 years, 9 months, and 3 days.

C. Y. died July 10, 1843, aged 85 years, 9 months, and 9 days. He lived and died on the place inherited from his father, now owned by his daughter Rebecca, on Chestnut Hill, Philadelphia.

Abraham Kriebel, son of Rev. George Kriebel (page 41), married Salome, daughter of Christopher Yeakel (page 36), April 29, 1784. Their children were:
  Benjamin, born January 22, 1785.
  Lydia, born September 22, 1786.
  Daniel, born September 14, 1788. Died May 1, 1869.

Jacob, born September 13, 1790.
Anthony, born August 16, 1792.
Jonathan, born May 5, 1795.
Sophia, born April 30, 1797.
Anna, born July 1, 1799.
Samuel, born July 26, 1801.
Susannah, born April 16, 1804.
Rachel, born July 7, 1808.

A. K. died September 2, 1814, aged 54 years, 4 months. and 2 days. He owned and lived on the farm now in possession of Joel Yeakel, in the Hosensack.

Salome, his widow, died November 14, 1815, aged 53 years, 3 months, and 21 days.

Abraham Anders, son of George Anders (page 38), married Esther, daughter of Balthasar Yeakel (page 42), May 27, 1784. One child,

Catharine, born August 18, 1785.

Esther, wife of A. A., died July 2, 1826, aged 65 years less 26 days.

A. A. died March 23, 1839, aged 80 years, less 8 days.

Christopher Kriebel, son of David Kriebel (page 42), married Susannah, daughter of Abraham Wiegner (page 34), August 17, 1784. No issue.

Susannah, wife of C. K., died June 26, 1793, aged 35 years, 11 months.

Christopher Kriebel married, second time, Rosina, daughter of Caspar Scipt (page 35), October 30, 1794. Children:

Benjamin, born October 11, 1795.
Elizabeth, born April 1, 1798. Died.
Lydia, born March 12, 1801.
Regina, born January 3, 1804.

Abigail.

Rosina, wife of C. K., died September 19, 1816, aged 52 years, 7 months.

C. K. died January 18, 1845, aged 82 years, 9 months, 1 day.

Henry Snyder, son of Henry Snyder (page 38), married Regina, daughter of Balthasar Reinewald (page 46), May 10, 1785. Their children were:
- Joseph, born September 17, 1786.
- Abraham, } twins, born July 23, 1789.
- Isaac,
- Job, born November 11, 1793.
- Regina, born December 8, 1795. Died December 15, 1795.
- Elizabeth, born November 28, 1798. Died.

Regina, wife of H. S., died November 5, 1825, aged 61 years.

H. S. died April 2, 1836, aged 73 years, 4 months.

Daniel Wagener, son of David Wagener (page 36), married Eve, daughter of John Opp, February 13, 1785, and had issue:
- Mary, born April 30, 1786, married Philip Mixsell, and left issue.
- Susanna, born May 30, 1788, married Joseph Burke, and left issue.
- Jacob, born December 10, 1790.
- David D., born October 11, 1792.
- John O., born May 17, 1800, was a physician by profession, and never married. He died June 9, 1829.

Daniel Wagener died in Easton on the 24th of May, 1842. He pursued the occupation of a merchant.

He became also the owner of a large number of mills, three of which were erected under his own supervision, one as early as 1792. He was a man of sound judgment and great decision of character, and amassed a large estate. He was an Associate Judge of Northampton County for about forty-two years, and it is said that in that time no bond was ever taken in court the sureties to which proved insufficient to pay it.

Christopher Neuman, son of David Neuman (page 39), married Rosina, daughter of George Wiegner (page 33), May 11, 1786. They had issue:
  Samuel, born June 23, 1790.
  George, born October 2, 1794. Died April 24, 1815.
Rosina, wife of C. N., died December 18, 1819, aged 60 years, 11 months, 16 days.
C. N. died April 18, 1833, aged 75 years.

Andrew Anders, son of George Anders (page 38), married Sarah, daughter of Balthasar Reinewald (page 46), September 6, 1787. They had issue:
  Anna, born August 15, 1789. Died March 3, 1802.
  Joseph, born January 22, 1793.
  Elizabeth, born November 5, 1795.
A. A. died August 10, 1832, aged 69 years, 24 days.
Sarah, his widow, died August 20, 1841, aged 73 years, 23 days.

David Yeakel, son of Abraham Yeakel (page 32), married Anna, daughter of Rev. George Kriebel (page 41), November 29, 1787. They had issue:
  Salome, born August 22, 1788.
  Abraham, born December 10, 1789. Died November 5, 1793.
  Maria, born December 4, 1791, married Hains.

Susannah, } twins, born December 24, 1793.
Jacob,

George, born August 29, 1795.

David, born May 26, 1797.

Ephraim, born March 23, 1799. Died September 25, 1853.

Anna, born May 12, 1801.

Rosanna, born October 21, 1803. Married Jacob Wiegner.

D. Y. died April 15, 1820, aged 58 years, 10 days. He lived in Milford, Bucks County.

Anna, his widow, died February 14, 1841, aged 74 years, 2 months, 25 days.

Balthasar Heydrick, son of Balthasar (page 9), married, wife's name unknown. Children:

George, married twice, second wife Sarah Flew. He left two children, Henry and Mary.

Mary, died unmarried.

Catharine, married George Cress. Had issue: Reuben and Amelia.

He married, second time, Elizabeth Nungesser, and by her had issue:

Abraham, who died single.

Isaac, born July 25, 1796.

Samuel, born April 10, 1798.

Elizabeth, married David Toole. Issue: David, Edward, Amelia, and Sarah.

Ann, married Henry Baum, and had one daughter, Mary.

Susan.

B. H. died December 19, 1831, aged 12 days less than 81 years. He lived in Flourtown, Montgomery Co., Pa., and was a Captain in the Revolution.

His second wife was born March 7, 1751. Died February 19, 1841.

Abraham Kriebel, son of David Kriebel (page 42), married Eve, daughter of George Heydrick (page 41), April 17, 1788. Their children were:
  Sophia, born January 18, 1789.
  Rosina, born March 26, 1790.
  George, born July 4, 1791.
  Joseph, born September 30, 1799.
Eve, wife of A. K., died October 23, 1826, aged 59 years, 9 months, 6 days.
A. K. died February 10, 1831, aged 66 years, 8 months, 13 days.

Isaac Yeakle, son of Jeremiah Yeakle (page 37), married Susannah, daughter of George Anders (page 38), April 24, 1788. Their children were:
  Sabina, born April 6, 1789.
  Anthony, born November 10, 1790. Died December 22, 1795.
  Charlotte, born November 11, 1792.
  Hannah, born June 12, 1796. Died January 26, 1818.
  Susannah, born February 21, 1800.
  Augustus, born January 13, 1803.
I. Y. died February 5, 1830, aged 75 years, 4 months. Susannah, his widow, died February 14, 1853, aged 92 years, 2 months, 16 days.

Jacob Kriebel, son of Rev. George Kriebel (page 41), married Lydia, daughter of Jeremiah Yeakle (page 45), May 29, 1788. Their children were:
  Christina, born February 24, 1789.

Andrew, born November 28, 1790. Died October 31, 1793.
Anna, born May 14, 1792. Died April 4, 1861.
Abraham, born January 9, 1794.
Catharine, born October 25, 1795.
Jacob, born November 24, 1797.
George, born February 1, 1800. Died April 10, 1821.
Lydia, wife of J. K., died February 8, 1838, aged 72 years, less 23 days.
J. K. died June 18, 1847, aged 83 years, 4 months, 6 days.

Christian Snyder, son of Henry Snyder (page 38), married Susannah, daughter of Christopher Reinewald (page 43), November 4, 1788. They had issue:
Catharine, born November 9, 1789.
Andrew, born February 17, 1792.
Henry, born March 21, 1794.
Maria, born August 1, 1796.
Susannah, born May 16, 1799. Died.
George, born August 27, 1801. Died single.
Abraham, born September 24, 1804.
Regina, born September 25, 1807.
C. S. died April 22, 1841, aged 76 years, 6 months.
Susannah, his widow, died April 28, 1848.

Abraham Heebner, son of H. Christopher Heebner (page 31), married Christina, daughter of Christopher Wagner (page 37), May 11, 1790. Their children were:
Isaac, born June 16, 1791. Died September 28, 1823.
Jacob, born June 19, 1793.
Sarah, born September 24, 1794. Died.

Susannah, born January 5, 1797. Died.
Deborah, born June 28, 1799.
Abraham, born November 19, 1802.
David, born February 5, 1805. Died October 12, 1823.
Maria, born August 16, 1807. Died October 14, 1868.
Christina, wife of A. H., died April 18, 1830, aged 66 years, 8 weeks.
A. H. died December 26, 1838, aged 78 years, 10 months, less 4 days.

Edmund Flinn, native of Ireland, married Maria, daughter of Christopher Wiegner (page 21), October 7, 1790. Had no issue.
Maria, wife of E. F., died January 18, 1832, aged 86 years, 6 months, 18 days.
E. F. died December 24, 1836, aged 81. He left by will a portion of his estate to the charity fund of the Schwenkfelder Society.

Abraham Heebner, son of Christopher Heebner (page 39), married Catharine, daughter of Matthias Rittenhouse, December 1, 1791. Their children were:
Sarah, born November 20, 1792.
Hannah, born October 1, 1794.
Christopher, born January 17, 1797. Died January 25, 1797.
John, born January 15, 1798. Died same day.
Joseph, born April 9, 1799.
Susannah, born July 25, 1801.
Catharine, born January 5, 1804.
Rebecca, born July 9, 1806.
Mary, born August 27, 1808.

Elizabeth, born March 23, 1811.
A. H. died November 25, 1846. He lived on the farm now occupied by Henry L. Heebner in Norriton. Catharine, his widow, died September 27, 1851.

Jacob Frey, born June 15, 1760, married Susanna, daughter of George Urffer (page 51), left no issue.
J. F. died January 39, 1852. He lived in Greenville, Montgomery County, Pa.

Christopher Heebner, Sr., son of Christopher Heebner (page 39), married Susannah Smith, January, 1792. Children:
    David, born November 13, 1792.
    Sarah, born February 21, 1795.
    Margaret, born December 25, 1796.
    Abraham, born December 14, 1799.
    John, born January 19, 1802.
    Susannah, born June 22, 1804.
    Christopher, born June 11, 1809.
    Ann, born December 19, 1811.
    Myra, born November 1, 1815.
Susannah, first wife, died June 17, 1816, she was born in 1773. He afterwards married Hannah Tompson, March, 1819. No issue.
C. H. died August 21, 1827, aged 58 years, and his widow died January 6, 1859, aged 84 years.

Christopher Heydrick, son of Abraham Heydrick (page 47), married Mary Care, April 13, 1793. Had issue:
    Harriet, born June 11, 1795, married N. P. Hood, and died December 5, 1873.
    Caroline, born January 27, 1797.

Charles H., born March 5, 1799.
Chr. H. died February 9, 1856.

Dr. Christopher Heydrick was born in Springfield Township, Philadelphia County (now Montgomery), April 7, 1770. In his youth, after having fitted himself by a thorough course of education, he studied the science of medicine under the instruction of the celebrated Dr. Benjamin Say, of Philadelphia, and in 1792, at the age of 22 years, graduated with high honors at the University of Pennsylvania. Six years afterwards, in 1798, he was elected a member of the Philadelphia Society of Medicine, and during the same year, and for some time afterwards, he held the position of Physician to the Philadelphia Hospital. In 1815 he was elcted Resident Member of the Cabinet of Sciences in Philadelphia, an honor which has been conferred upon few, and those the most learned and scientific men in the country.

Having been engaged in the practice of medicine, and with much success, at Chestnut Hill, Philadelphia, and in the city of Philadelphia, from 1792 until 1819, he at the latter date removed to the borough of Mercer, in Mercer County, Pennsylvania. He resided in this place several years, and had a very successful and lucrative practice in his profession. But from his youth having a passion for agriculture, he determined to abandon his profession and enjoy for the remainder of his life his favorite pursuit, and having this object in view, he removed from Mercer to a farm in the valley of French Creek, Venango County, where he continued to reside until the day of his death. During the last ten or twelve years of his life he was afflicted with blindness.

Dr. Heydrick, after a long and eventful life, died February 9, 1856, in the 86th year of his age.

George Anders, son of George Anders (page 38), married Catharine, daughter of Balthasar Yeakel (page 42), May 2, 1793. Their children were:
Esther, born March 1, 1794.
Edith, born March 27, 1795. Died April 6, 1853.
Abraham, born July 26, 1796.
George, born March 5, 1798.
Anthony, born September 19, 1799.
Daughter, born May 4, 1803. Died same day.
G. A. died August 11, 1849.
Catharine, his widow, died October 22, 1850, aged 86 years, 2 months, 11 days.

Andrew Kriebel, son of Abraham Kriebel (page 44), married Maria, daughter of George Heebner (page 49), October 31, 1793. Their children were:
Lydia, born October 1, 1794.
*Daniel, born April 1, 1796. Died February 27, 1855.
George, born October 3, 1797.
Hannah, born August 8, 1799.
Abraham, born August 21, 1802.
Susannah, born June 20, 1804.
Sophia, born June 27, 1809.
A. K. died October 15, 1853, aged 88 years, 10 days.
Maria, his widow, died September 22, 1857, aged 84 years, 4 months, 24 days.

Abraham Wiegner, son of Abraham Wiegner (page 34),

---

* Daniel Kriebel was a minister of the Schwenkfelder Society. He never married.

married Susanna, daughter of Henry Snyder (page
38), May 1, 1794. They had issue:
  Elizabeth, born April 1, 1795. Married Samuel
    Smith.
  Sarah, born November 3, 1796. Married Henry
    Ruth.
  Maria, born April 17, 1799. Married John Souder.
  Anna, born February 10, 1801. Died December
    28, 1827.
  Christopher, born January 12, 1803.
  Joseph, born November 30, 1804.
  Abraham, born November 16, 1806.
  Susanna, born December 6, 1808.
  Sophia, born March 3, 1811. Married Jesse Krupp.
  Edith, born July 24, 1814. Married Antrim Hom-
    sher.
A. W. died December 6, 1824, aged 64 years, 2 months,
11 days.
Susanna, his wife, died May 20, 1834, aged 62 years.

Abraham Yeakle, son of Balthasar Yeakle (page 42),
married Sarah, daughter of Abraham Heydrick (page
47), May 8, 1794. They had issue:
  Abigail, born February 10, 1795.
  Susannah, born April 26, 1797.
  Regina, born June 2, 1800. Died same day.
  Abraham, born July 16, 1803.
A. Y. died December 13, 1812, aged 45 years, 6 months,
19 days. Lived in Hatfield Township.
Sarah, his widow, died March 31, 1825, aged 56 years,
6 months.

Balthasar Heebner, son of George Heebner (page 49),
married Susannah, daughter of Christopher Schultz
(page 51), May 20, 1794. They had children:

George, born July 22, 1795. Died April 10, 1796.
Daughter, born January 7, 1796. Died two days old.
Anthony S., born November 23, 1798.
Anna, born August 9, 1800.
Maria, born October 26, 1803. Died September 10, 1815.
Catharine, born October 12, 1806.
David S., born June 25, 1810.
Lydia, born September 8, 1812.

Susannah, wife of B. H., died March 22, 1848, aged 72 years, 4 months, 18 days.

B. H. died April 29, 1848, aged 77 years, 10 months, 21 days. He lived in Worcester Township, Montgomery County, Pa., and owned the farm lately purchased by Abraham Anders, Sr. He was a minister of the Schwenkfelder Society many years, until his death. This record, so far as it relates to the genealogical record of the members of said religious society, and their descendants who adhered to their organization, was preserved by him in German manuscript to about the year 1846. In the earlier days, to about 1804, a few records had been kept, but about that time abandoned, when the Rev. Mr. Heebner, copying from those earlier ones, continued his own down to the date mentioned. Without his industry and care it would have been impossible to compile the present work for want of a continuous record. Of a cheerful disposition, and of active and industrious habits, Mr. Heebner always retained the confidence of the entire community in which he lived.

Jeremiah Krauss, son of Christopher Krauss (page 34), married Regina, daughter of Balthasar Krauss (page 49), June 17, 1794. They had children:

Rebecca, born March 22, 1795. Died October 9, 1796.
Carolus, born August 31, 1796. Died November 25, 1820.
Nathan, born March 21, 1798. Died May 25, 1858.
Sophia, born June 7, 1801. Died August 9, 1826.
Maria, born October 13, 1804. Died August 14, 1826.
Regina, wife of J. K., died August 31, 1807, aged 31 years, 10 months, 27 days.
Jeremiah Krauss married, second time, Magdalena Homiller, born June 1, 1775. Had no children.
J. K. died August 17, 1821, aged 62 years, 2 months, 25 days.
Magdalena, his widow, died December 4, 1852. He owned and lived upon the farm now owned by Rev. Jacob Meschter, in Upper Hanover.

John Krauss, son of Balthasar Krauss (page 49), married Rosina, daughter of Melchior Yeakel (page 50), May 11, 1795. Children:
Sarah, born December 9, 1795. Died September 10, 1798.
Maria, born January 7, 1798.
Daughter, born 1800. Died unnamed.
Anthony, born May 23, 1803.
Daniel, born October 16, 1805. Died April 3, 1808.
Daughter, born March, 1811. Died April 7, 1811.
Son, born January 23, 1813. Died January 27, 1813.
Joseph, born November 14, 1814.
Lydia.

John Krauss died February 12, 1819, and his widow died December 8, 1834.

John Wiegner, son of Abraham Wiegner (page 34), married Rosina, daughter of David Kriebel (page 42), September 10, 1795. They had issue:
    Daniel, born September 26, 1797.
    George, born August 25, 1799. Died.
    Joel, born May 14, 1801.
    Abraham, born November 8, 1802.
    Leah, born July 4, 1804.
    John, born November 5, 1806.
    Lydia, born September 9, 1808.
    Ezra, born January 12, 1814.
J. W. died September 6, 1847, aged 82 years, 1 month, 27 days.
Rosina, his widow, died February 11, 1855, aged 82 years, 7 months, 29 days.

Edward Dowers, born February 18, 1796, married Regina, daughter of Abraham Heydrick (page 47). Children:
    Matilda, married Bird Patterson.
    Mary, died single.
    John, died at sea, single.
E. D. died November 28, 1841, and Regina, his wife, died.

Matthias Gehoe married Anna, daughter of George Yeakel (page 48), about 1796. Children:
    Anna, born January 21, 1797.
    Catharine, born March 16, 1799.
    Rosina, born May 7, 1806.
    Sarah, born July 7, 1808.
    Susannah.

Maria.
Jacob.
Daniel.
M. G. died. Anna, his wife, died March 16, 1852.

George Meschter, son of Melchior Meschter (page 56), married Susanna, daughter of Henry Heimbach. Their children were:
Catharine.
George.
Henry, born November 12, 1800.
Susanna.
Daniel.
Magdalena.
Lydia.
David, born 1812.
Regina, born March 18, 1815.
No record of death of George Meschter and wife could be obtained.

Jacob Yeakel, son of Hans or John Yeakel (page 45), married Susanna, daughter of Christopher Souder. Had issue:
Anna.
Mary, born January 12, 1799.
Elizabeth, born 1802.
Magdalena, born October 18, 1804.
Jacob Yeakel died in 1847.

Jacob Gerhard, son of Peter Gerhard (page 40), married Helena, daughter of Balthasar Krauss (page 49), November 12, 1795. They had issue:
John, born April 5, 1797. Died June 24, 1819.
Joseph, born August 27, 1798.

Judith, born December 10, 1799. Died February 15, 1803.
Jesse, born November 11, 1801.
Andrew, born June 16, 1803.
Solomon, born February 15, 1805.
Jacob, born October 29, 1806. Died May 12, 1807.
Hannah, born June 18, 1808.
Susannah, born January 15, 1810.
Lydia, born September 6, 1811.
Samuel, born ———.

J. G. died April 14, 1844, aged 76 years, 5 months, 21 days. He lived in Pennsburg, Upper Hanover, and was Justice of the Peace of said place many years. Helena, his widow, died November 19, 1850, aged 73 years, 19 days.

John Schultz, son of Christopher Schultz (page 51), married Regina, daughter of George Heebner (page 49), May 24, 1796. They had issue:
Sarah, born May 13, 1797.
Maria, born September 5, 1798.
Sophia, born January 28, 1800.
George, born June 14, 1801.
Henry, born March 9, 1804.
William, born March 20, 1806.
John, born July 15, 1808.
Susannah, born February 19, 1810. Died July 8, 1810.
Samuel, born September 1, 1811.
Frederick, born October 23, 1813. Died about 1875. Single.
Christina, born October 23, 1815.
Christopher, born February 9, 1818. Married, to whom and when unknown. Died May 19, 1851.

Anthony, born May 7, 1820.
J. S. died November 3, 1827, aged 55 years, 7 months, 22 days.
Regina, his widow, died September 8, 1862.
This was the Rev. John Schultz. Lived in Hereford Township, Berks County; was a farmer by occupation and a minister of the Schwenkfelder Society. He was highly esteemed for his earnest and impressive piety.

David Wagener, son of David (page 36), married Rosina Beidleman, and had issue as follows:
    Mary, who married Joseph Heister, of Easton.
    Sarah, married Joseph Howell, of Easton.
    Susan, married John Howell, of Easton.
    Catharine.
    Elizabeth, married William Ricker, of Easton.
    Sabina, died January 27, 1868, unmarried.
    Henry, died January 18, 1841.
    Valentine, died September 2, 1836.
    William, died September 14, 1854.
    Jacob.
    David.
D. W. was born in 1771, and died at Easton, Pa., March 9, 1854.

Benjamin Anders, son of Abraham Anders (page 46), married Salome, daughter of Jeremiah Yeakle (page 45), June 2, 1796. They had issue:
    Frederick, born February 5, 1797. Died January 21, 1820.
    Anna, born April 16, 1799.
    Susannah, born April 19, 1805. Died April 6, 1807.

B. A. died May 2, 1843, aged 76 years, 5 months, 2 days. He lived where John Brecht now resides in Worcester, Montgomery County.

Salome, his widow, died April 15, 1847, aged 83 years, less 12 days.

Jacob Cress married Susanna, daughter of Abraham Heydrick (page 47), November 17, 1796. They had issue:
    Daniel, born October 28, 1797. Died March 21, 1846.
    Amelia, born August 20, 1799. Died July 3, 1800.
    Josiah, born January 22, 1800. Died October 31, 1804.
    Mary, born November 29, 1802.
    Edward, born October 6, 1804.
    James, born June 18, 1807. Died March 18, 1808.
    Louis, born January 22, 1809. Died in Stutgard, Europe.
    Augustus, born April 17, 1811. Died March 10, 1838.
    Hamilton, born May 17, 1814.
    Abraham H., born May 10, 1816. Died March 28, 1861.

Susanna, wife of J. C., died February 2, 1847.

Jacob Cress lived at Chestnut Hill, Philadelphia, and died there about 1837 or 1838.

Andrew Krauss, son of Balthasar Krauss (page 49), married Susanna, daughter of Andrew Schultz (page 59), November 30, 1797. They had children:
    Regina, born September 9, 1798.
    Leah, born December 20, 1799.
    Joel, born October 11, 1801.

George, born December 14, 1803.
Samuel, born ———.
Rebecca, born November 20, 1805.
John, born ———.
David, born January 12, 1821.
A. K. died May 11, 1841, aged 69 years, 10 months, 11 days.
Susanna, widow of A. K., died.

David Krauss, son of Christopher Krauss (page 34), married Sarah Huber, in 1797. Their children were:
Maria, born May 24, 1798.
Anna, born December 2, 1801.
Jesse, born March 3, 1803.
Lydia, born February 27, 1806.
Reuben, born June 3, 1807. Died July 13, 1832.
Aaron, born November 27, 1811.
Sarah, born March 17, 1814.
D. K. died November 30, 1814, aged 43 years, less 1 day.
Sarah, wife of D. K., born March 18, 1779. Died June 21, 1817.

Peter Gerhard married, first time, Anna Maria, widow of Abraham Yeakel (page 32), and daughter of Abraham Beyer, Sr. (page 17). No record of children.
Wife died April 10, 1802, aged 77 years and 5 days. He married, second time, Elizabeth, daughter of Christopher Krauss (page 34), December 17, 1802, and died May 14, 1810.
E., his second wife, died April 22, 1828, aged 71 years, 7 months, and 5 days.

Andrew Yeakel, son of Balthasar Yeakel (page 43), married Maria, daughter of Caspar Yeakel (page 57), May 1, 1798. They had children:

Sophia, born July 6, 1799.
Jonas, born December 19, 1800.
Elias, born October 30, 1802.
Sarah, born August 21, 1805.
Susanna, born September 3, 1809. Died October 3, 1809.
Joseph, born December 10, 1811.
A. Y. died April 9, 1837. His descendants now live in Lycoming County, Pa.

Jacob Schultz, son of Christopher Schultz (page 51), married Magdalena, daughter of Peter Gerhard (page 40), April 11, 1799. Their children were:
Maria, born March 6, 1800.
Jonas, born April 24, 1801.
Susanna, born May 29, 1802. Died single.
Esther, born June 27, 1804.
Lydia, born November 26, 1805.
Eleonora, born November, 1807.
Jesse, born October, 1809.
Sophia, born October 30, 1811.
Thomas, born April 24, 1812.
Rachel, born August 28, 1814.
Magdalena, wife of J. S., died March 1, 1839, aged 69 years, 7 months.
J. S. died April 9, 1855, aged 80 years, 9 months, 12 days.

John Yeakel, son of Jeremiah Yeakel (page 45), married Susannah, daughter of George Fisher, October 28, 1799. Child,
Joseph, born July 29, 1800.
Susannah, wife of J. Y., born June 14, 1775. Died September 4, 1801.

J. Y. married, second time, Mary, daughter of George Fisher, April 6, 1802. Children:
  George, born October 2, 1802.
  Henry, born April 8, 1804.
  Susanna, born June 14, 1806.
Mary, second wife of J. Y., died June 30, 1806.
J. Y. married, third time, Susanna, daughter of Samuel Huff, January 27, 1807. Children:
  Sarah, born September 6, 1807. Died.
  Magdalena, born November 28, 1810. Died.
  Catharine, born February 16, 1816. Married —— Bortz.
  Henrietta, born March 16, 1820. Married William Kiebler.
John Yeakel died March 17, 1825, and his wife, born May 9, 1784, died December 6, 1858.

George Heydrick, son of George Heydrick (page 41), married Susanna, daughter of Melchior Yeakel (page 50), November 14, 1799. Issue, one child,
  Anna, born September 21, 1800.
Susanna, wife of G. H., died November 8, 1801, aged 24 years, 4 days.
George Heydrick married, second time, Susanna, daughter of David Kriebel (page 42), May 15, 1804. Their children were:
  Joseph, } twins, born February 18, 1805.
  Abraham,
    Joseph died February 26, 1820.
    Abraham died February 19, 1829.
  Maria, born March 9, 1807.
  Sarah, born September 6, 1808. Died January 22, 1829.
  Susanna, born December 9, 1809.

Elizabeth, born November 18, 1811.
Edith, born September 13, 1813. Died February 15, 1829.
Catharine, born February 5, 1815.
George, born April 14, 1816.
Rebecca, born May 24, 1818.
Regina, born August 31, 1819.
Lydia, born March 21, 1821.
Rosanna, born August 28, 1824. Died April 13, 1853.
Samuel, born September 8, 1826.
Hannah, born November 26, 1829.

Susanna, wife of G. H., died April 14, 1851, aged 68 years, 4 months, 7 days.

G. H. died October 9, 1855, aged 80 years, 6 months, 2 days. He lived and died upon the farm now owned by his son Samuel, in Lower Salford Township, Montgomery County, Pa.

Jacob Snyder, son of Henry Snyder (page 38), married Eve, daughter of Balthasar Schultz (page 48), November 19, 1799. Their children were:

Anna, born October 16, 1800. Died October 26, 1862.
Henry, born January 12, 1802.
Sophia, born July 30, 1804. Died September 26, 1805.
Susanna, born September 17, 1805.
Samuel, born May 27, 1807. Died in June, 1867.
Hannah, born September 2, 1809. Died July 30, 1810.
Esther, born January 2, 1811.
Amos, born ———.
Abigail, born July 30, 1817. Died June 7, 1838.

Eve, wife of J. S., died April 9, 1822, aged 47 years.
J. S. died April 6, 1823, aged 46 years.

Abraham Seipt, son of Caspar Seipt (page 35), married Anna, daughter of George Anders (page 38), November 21, 1799. They had issue:

  George, } twins, born August 6, 1800.
  Susanna,

  Abraham, } twins, born September 25, 1803.
  Joseph,

  Joseph died June 20, 1842.

Anna, wife of A. S., died August 15, 1847, aged 18 years, 5 months.

A. S. died September 19, 1850, aged 83 years, 11 months, 18 days.

Christopher Dresher, son of George Dresher (page 50), married Anna, daughter of Abraham Anders (page 46), November 27, 1799. They had issue:

  Agnes, born November 14, 1804.
  Rebecca, born October 4, 1812.
  George, born June 5, 1816. Died January 6, 1851.
  Eli, born May 15, 1820.

Anna, wife of C. D., died November 23, 1830. She was born April 13, 1780; in her father's record it is 1789, which is an error.

C. D. died January 23, 1839. Dreshertown, Upper Dublin, Montgomery County, was named after him. He owned the farm belonging to the heirs of Jacob Barnitt.

Michael Urffer, son of George Urffer (page 51), married Elizabeth Kohler, May 18, 1800. They had issue:

  Samuel, born November 19, 1803.
  Michael, born November 19, 1805. Died March 9, 1837.

Daniel K., born July 13, 1807.
Maria, born June 1, 1809.
Barbara, born May 18, 1811.
Elizabeth, born April 13, 1814.
Elizabeth, wife of M. U., born December 15, 1769. Died July 6, 1841.
M. U. died May 20, 1854.

George Schultz, son of Balthasar Schultz (page 48), married Barbara, daughter of Balthasar Yeakel (page 43), May 29, 1800. They had issue:
- John, born August 3, 1802.
Susanna, born September 10, 1804.
Sarah, born July 17, 1808.
Barbara, wife of G. S., died July 21, 1823, aged 56 years, 9 months.
G. S. died September 3, 1847, aged 76 years, 2 months, 5 days.

Jacob Bean, born August 6, 1776, married Catharine Beyer, daughter of Jacob Beyer (page 65). Children:
Rachel, born 1801.
Joshua, born November 10, 1807. Died July 15, 1818.
Catharine, born December 23, 1810. Died May 6, 1861.
Jacob, born November 3, 1813. Died September 13, 1840.
Isaac, born July 11, 1817.
Samuel, born January, 1822.
Catharine, wife of J. B., died March 10, 1852.
J. B. died August 5, 1856.

Abraham Yeakel, son of John Yeakel (page 45), married Maria Sauder. Children:

John, born January 14, 1804.
Elizabeth, born January 11, 1806.
Abraham, born February 19, 1808.
Jacob, born March 24, 1810.
Anna, born February 14, 1812.
Mary, born March 15, 1814.
Kate, born August 11, 1816.
Christian, born July 21, 1819.
Henry, born April 23, 1822. Died April 16, 1838.
Lena, born April 8, 1825. Died in infancy.
No record of the deaths of these parents could be obtained.

John Anders, son of George Anders (page 38), married Regina, daughter of Christopher Meschter (page 56), October 23, 1800. Their children were:
Jacob, born June 24, 1801.
Frederick, born May 22, 1803.
Jeremiah, born June 9, 1805.
John, born August 29, 1807.
David, born June 14, 1810.
Catharine, born February 21, 1813.
Mary, born June 30, 1817.
John Anders, Sr., died September 24, 1853, and his wife, Regina, October 31, 1864.

Isaac Yeakel, son of Abraham Yeakle (page 58), married Regina, daughter of Andrew Schultz (page 59), November 4, 1800. They had issue:
Jacob S., born October 16, 1802.
Sarah, born May 19, 1805.
Samuel, born June 10, 1807.
John, born June 10, 1809.
Charlotte, born November 15, 1811. Died June 1, 1854.

Emeline, born August 25, 1814.
Daniel, born March 27, 1816.
Mary, born November 7, 1818.
David W., born December 30, 1821.

I. Y. died October 23, 1847. He lived where his son Daniel now lives, in Springfield, Montgomery County, Pennsylvania.

Regina, his widow, died January 16, 1860.

Christopher Master, son of Christopher (Meschter) Master (page 46), married Mary Kerling, November 18, 1800. Wife born November 14, 1781. They had issue:

    Rachel, born August 21, 1801. Died August 21, 1802.
    Hannah, born November 15, 1802.
    Jacob, born December 27, 1803.
    John, born July 9, 1805.
    James, born April 27, 1807. Died June 30, 1807.
    Eleanor, born May 17, 1808.
    Samuel, born February 15, 1810.
    Aaron, born October 25, 1811.
    Ann, born August 17, 1813.
    Mary, born September 5, 1815.
    Margaret, born June 16, 1817.
    William, born May 17, 1819. Married Mary Garrison.
    Elizabeth, born December 30, 1821.
    Hiram, born November 30, 1824. Died January 26, 1826.

Mary, wife of C. M., died October 10, 1838.
C. M. died November 6, 1859.

Adam Schultz, son of Abraham Schultz (page 52), mar-

ried Regina, daughter of Andrew Kriebel (page 52), May 21, 1801. Their children were:
.Abraham, born April 12, 1803. Died December 5, 1814.
Israel, born June 4, 1805.
Jesse, born April 8, 1808. Died November 7, 1831.
Adam, born September 21, 1810. Died November 12, 1831.
Andrew, born May 19, 1813.
Enoch, born March 31, 1816.
Sarah, born September 1, 1818. Died May 11, 1820.
Regina, born October 9, 1821.
Solomon, born November 19, 1824. Died June 4, 1854.
A. S. died August 30, 1831. He lived in Hereford, Berks County, Pennsylvania.
Regina, his widow, died May 3, 1858.

Abraham Kriebel, son of Andrew Kriebel (page 52), married Christina, daughter of Abraham Kriebel (page 61), June 4, 1801. They had issue:
Sophia, born November 23, 1802.
Isaac, born March 20, 1804.
Maria, born March 17, 1806.
Joseph, born April 27, 1810.
Catharine, born June 9, 1813.
Anna, born February 20, 1818.
Sarah, born February 26, 1821. Died May 17, 1848.
A. K. died April 7, 1844, aged 69 years, 6 months, 10 days. He was a miller, and owned the mill property now in possession of William Kriebel, in Worcester Township.

Christina, his widow, died November 21, 1855, aged 74 years, 10 months, 28 days.

Samuel Dresher, son of George Dresher (page 50), married Anna, daughter of Jeremiah Kriebel (page 62), October 22, 1801. They had issue:
Susanna, born January 1, 1803.
Oliver, born January, 1804.
Levi, born March 3, 1811. Died February 12, 1842.
Daniel, born September 10, 1823.
S. D. died April 1, 1833.
Anna, his widow, died April 3, 1833.

Samuel Kriebel, son of Andrew Kriebel (page 52), married Christina, daughter of Melchior Schultz (page 64), January 3, 1802. Children:
Sarah, born February 24, 1803.
Susanna, born September 13, 1804.
Lydia, born May 10, 1809.
Elizabeth, born December 23, 1812.
William, born October 8, 1815.
Christina, wife of S. K., died April 21, 1819.
Samuel Kriebel, married, second time, Catharine, daughter of Henry Leatherach, July 20, 1824. They had issue:
Sophia, born November 19, 1826.
S. K. died February 1, 1841, aged 64 years, 7 months, 18 days.
Catharine, his widow, died November 16, 1848, aged 53 years, 5 months, 27 days.

John Erb married Elizabeth Reinewald, daughter of Christopher Reinewald (page 43.) Children:
Jacob, born January 4, 1803.

GENEALOGICAL RECORD. 95

George, born December 30, 1804.
Mary, born June 13, 1807.
Abraham, born June 7, 1810. Died April 25, 1813.
Samuel, born July 12, 1813.
Elizabeth, born April 6, 1816.
John, born November 23, 1818.
Anna, born June 25, 1821.
Charles, born August 20, 1824.
Catharine, born July 1, 1827.
J. E. died October 9, 1828, aged 48 years.
Elizabeth, widow of J. E., died November 3, 1864.

Christian Yeakel, son of John Yeakel (page 45), married Mary, daughter of Jacob Souder. They had issue:
  Jacob, born March 17, 1803.
  Anna, born March 30, 1805. Died 1874.
  Samuel S., born September 20, 1807.
  Barbara, born February 10, 1811.
  Christian, born September 11, 1813. After the Mexican war he left for Europe and there was nothing heard from him since.
C. Y. died in 1822, and his wife in 1849.

Abraham Anders, son of Abraham Anders (page 46), married Susanna, daughter of Abraham Dresher (page 60), November 25, 1802. They had issue:
  George, born November 19, 1803.
  Lydia, born July 6, 1805.
  Abraham, born September 2, 1807.
  Anna, born October 24, 1809.
  Samuel, born March 18, 1812.
  Susanna, born October 2, 1815.
  Sarah, born August 8, 1820.

Susanna, wife of A. A., died October 26, 1831, aged 50 years, 3 months.
A. A. died August 2, 1852, aged 78 years, 2 months. He lived in Worcester Township, and owned the farm now in possession of his son Abraham, Sr.

Matthias Gerhard, son of Peter Gerhard (page 40), married Esther, daughter of Caspar Yeakel (page 57), May 24, 1803. They had issue:
    Anna, born May 11, 1805.
    Charles, born September 11, 1806.
    Benjamin, born December 17, 1807.
    Susanna, born November 6, 1809.
    Daniel Y., born June 1, 1816.
    Rebecca, born May 8, 1820.
M. G. died May 27, 1856.
Esther, his widow, died September 12, 1858.

Matthias Schultz, son of Balthasar Schultz (page 48), married Christina, daughter of Melchior Yeakel (page 50), May 24, 1803. They had issue:
    Charles, born April 15, 1804.
    David, born August 30, 1805. Died April 5, 1841.
    Sarah, born May 16, 1807.
    William, born October 27, 1809. Died April 17, 1831.
    Anthony, born December 12, 1811.
    Daniel, born November 21, 1813.
    Regina, born May 16, 1816.
    Christina, born June 5, 1818. Died May 6, 1838.
    Susanna, born September 8, 1821.
Christina, wife of M. S., died July 20, 1829, aged 49 years, 5 months, 13 days.
M. S. died January 30, 1855, aged 77 years, 11 months, and 10 days.

M. S. died January 30, 1855, aged 77 years, 11 months, 10 days.

Abraham Heydrick, son of Abraham Heydrick (page 47), married Susanna, daughter of Jacob Neff, July 11, 1803. Children:
Mary Ann, born June 2, 1805.
Caleb, born December 28, 1806.
George N., born November 1, 1808.
Edward, born November 29, 1809. Died July 4, 1811.
Levi, born October 30, 1811. Died November 11, 1811.
Charles, born February 18, 1813.
Susanna, born April 14, 1822.
Susanna, wife of A. H., born April 15, 1782. Died December 6, 1865.
A. H. died June 16, 1866. He lived at the foot of Chestnut Hill, in Springfield, was a farmer by occupation. He owned the place known as "Heydrick's Hollow," containing hotel, farm, and several other dwellings.

David Yeakel, son of Balthasar Yeakel (page 43), married Susanna, daughter of Gregory Schultz (page 59), October 27, 1803. Children:
Samuel, born July 8, 1804.
Daniel, born August 4, 1808.
Anthony, born July 21, 1810.
Lydia, born September 15, 1812. Died 1826.
David, born November 2, 1814.
Susanna, wife of D. Y., died November 13, 1830, aged 50 years, 6 months, 13 days.
David Yeakel married, second time, Hannah, widow

of Joseph Schultz, and daughter of Rev. Melchior Kriebel (page 55), November, 1836. Had no issue. D. Y. died May 27, 1859, and Hannah, his wife, August 20, 1863.

Christopher Reinewald, son of Christopher Reinewald (page 43), married Barbara, daughter of John Hendricks, in 1803. Wife born November 6, 1784. Their children were:
    Abraham, born 1804.
    Maria, born August 5, 1808.
C. R. died September 26, 1828.
Maria, his widow, died in 1868.

Henry Wiand, born May 31, 1779, married Rosina, daughter of Jeremiah Yeakel (page 45). They had issue:
    George, born April 4, 1804.
    Anna, born February 8, 1806.
    Sophia, born September 25, 1809. Died.
    Christina, born October 9, 1811.
    Susannah, born March 15, 1814.
    Jonas, born August 13, 1816.
    Esther, born December 8, 1818.
H. W. died September 9, 1858.
Rosina, his widow, died August 18, 1860.

John Master, son of Christopher Master (page 46), married Elizabeth De Haven February 21, 1804. Children:
    Rachel, born June 3, 1805.
    Isaac, born July 23, 1807.
    David, born April 20, 1809. Died September 22, 1835.
    Mary, born April 1, 1811. Married John Morgan.

Elizabeth, born May 20, 1813. Married Richard Jaques.
Ann, born February 25, 1816. Married Thomas Steel.
Christopher, born November 4, 1817.
John, born May 17, 1820.
Samuel K., born October 2, 1822.
Jacob, born December 6, 1825.

J. M. died January 16, 1852.
Elizabeth, widow of J. M., died December 5, 1864.
John Master lived in Indiana, where his descendants now reside, and other parts of the West.

Christopher Schultz, son of Andrew Schultz (page 59), married Susannah, daughter of Abraham Yeakle (page 58), May 29, 1804. Children:
Son, born November 2, 1806. Died same day.
Joseph, born April 24, 1808.
David, born October 6, 1809. Died June 14, 1871.
Sarah, born November, 1810.
Regina, born May 26, 1812.
Thomas, born December 25, 1813.
Lydia, born June 1, 1816.
Hannah, born July 17, 1820.
Leah, born November 5, 1823.
Rebecca, born July 10, 1826.

Christopher Schultz was a grandson of the Rev. Christopher Schultz (page 24), and lived in Hereford, Berks County, on the fine farm belonging to the estate of his son Thomas, which he managed very successfully. He was a minister of the Society of the Schwenkfelders, and until his death continued in the ministry. He always drew crowded audiences wherever he preached, whether in his own society or when occupying the pulpit of some neighboring denomination, which was very frequently the case. His fine personal appearance and great fluency of speech always commanded the attention of his audience, accompanied as it was with the most fervent and impressive piety.

The social qualities of his well-stored mind were of the highest order, tempered as it was by a true Christian spirit; he always commanded the respect of those he came in contact with.

Rev. C. S. died March 22, 1843, aged 65 years, and 5 months.

His wife died April 3, 1861, aged 78 years.

Isaac Schultz, son of Abraham Schultz (page 52), married Susanna, daughter of David Schultz (page 64), May 31, 1804. Children:
- Amos, born May 11, 1809.
- Isaac, born June 8, 1811. Died January 2, 1874.
- Abraham, born September 16, 1813.
- Daniel S., born April 10, 1816.
- Christina, born February 15, 1818.
- Joel, born April 2, 1820.
- Philip, born March 11, 1822. Died October 21, 1864.
- Joseph, born March 30, 1824. Died September 1, 1827.

Susanna, wife of I. S., died September 18, 1834.

I. S. died October 15, 1867. He lived upon the property now in possession of Abraham, his son, in Upper Hanover Township, and was a farmer by occupation.

Isaac Kriebel, son of Abraham Kriebel (page 61), married Regina, daughter of Melchior Schultz (page 64), November 1, 1804. One child,

    Isaac S., born April 22, 1806.

I. K. died February 1, 1806.

Leonard Hartranft, Jr., son of Leonard Hartranft (page 61), married Elizabeth, daughter of Henry Engle, of Douglass Township, Montgomery County, and had eight children:

    Henry, born April 3, 1804. Living in Northumberland County.
    Samuel E., born October 6, 1806.
    John, married, and lives in Michigan.
    Susan, married Heimburg. Lived in Michigan.
    Eliza, married to a Mr. Hile. Lived in Michigan.
    Abraham, born November 25, 1820. Married and living in Lycoming County, Pa.
    William, born December 22, 1824. Married, and lived in Clinton County, Pa. Deceased.
    David, married and lived in Michigan. Both deceased.

L. H. died about 1843.

Samuel Schultz, son of Christopher Schultz (page 51), married Rosina, daughter of Jacob Yeakel (page 61), May 9, 1805. Had issue:

    Charles, born March 13, 1806.
    Susanna, born May 11, 1807.
    Jonathan, born September 18, 1808.
    Abraham, born January 5, 1810.
    Jacob, born June 6, 1811.
    David, born November 22, 1812.
    Magdalena, October 7, 1814.
    Lydia, born June 1, 1816. Died November 3, 1828.

Sophia, born March 25, 1818.
Daniel, born April 24, 1820.
Joel, born November 17, 1824.
Rosina, wife of S. S., died January 6, 1840.
S. S. died May 26, 1861. He lived in Milford Township, Bucks County, Pa.

George Krauss, son of Balthasar Krauss (page 49), married, first time, Maria, daughter of Andrew Schultz (page 59), May 21, 1805. Children:
David, born April 24, 1806. Died February 10, 1809.
Jacob, born May 9, 1807.
Maria, first wife, died May 26, 1807.
George Krauss married, second time, Christina, daughter of Andrew Schultz (page 59), November 26, 1807. Children:
Sarah, born November 3, 1808.
Henry, born February 3, 1811.
Susanna, born October 14, 1812. Died April, 1813.
Elizabeth, born June 13, 1814.
Jonathan, born January 8, 1817.
Daniel, born February 27, 1819.
Maria, born December 10, 1821. Died in infancy.
Regina, born July 19, 1824. Died May 5, 1825.
Daughter, born, 1826. Lived only two days.
Charles, born December 12, 1830.
G. K. died June 22, 1844, aged 61 years, 3 months, 18 days.

Andrew Schultz, son of Balthasar Schultz (page 48), married Rosina, daughter of George Snyder (page 63), May 1, 1806. Their children were:
Samuel, born November 24, 1807.

Susanna, born August 29, 1809.
Anna, born June 7, 1811.
Maria, born ———.
Christina, born January 31, 1815.
George, born ———, 1818.
A. S. died May 9, 1818.
Rosina, widow of A. S., died September 28, 1823.

Benjamin Kriebel, son of Jeremiah Kriebel (page 62), married Maria, daughter of Melchior Schultz (page 64), June 5, 1806. Had issue:
Samuel, born 1807.
Abigail, born 1809. Died March 22, 1811.
Maria, wife of B. K., died February 13, 1811.
B. K. died May 24, 1844.

Jeremiah Yeakel, son of Caspar Yeakel (page 57), married Lydia, daughter of Balthasar Krauss (page 49), November 27, 1806. Children:
Daniel, born December 12, 1807. Died March 14, 1813.
Benjamin, born August 9, 1810.
Lydia, wife of J. Y., died January 19, 1812.
Jeremiah Yeakel married, second time, Sarah, daughter of Rev. Melchior Kriebel (page 55). No issue.
Sarah, wife of J. Y., died.
J. Y. died.

Balthasar Urffer, son of George Urffer (page 51), married Regina, daughter of Caspar Yeakel (page 57), November 27, 1806. Child,
Miriam, born November 13, 1808. Married Henry Kemerer.
B. U. went to Trenton for building lumber, and by his horses becoming unruly they run the tongue of

the wagon in his body, from the effects of which he died July 10, 1808.

Regina, his widow, died September 10, 1843.

Andrew Beyer, son of Jacob Beyer (page 65), married Catharine Bean, born September 14, 1783. Date of marriage not given. Children:
    Benjamin, born December 19, 1807.
    Samuel B., born April 18, 1810.
Catharine, wife of A. B., died July 20, 1814.
Andrew Beyer married, second time, Catharine Clemence, born 1794. Date of marriage not given. Children:
    Anna, born October 6, 1816.
    Henry C., born August 20, 1818.
    Jacob C., born April 7, 1822.
    Joseph C., born July 22, 1824.
    William C., born June 18, 1827.
    Margaret, born October 24, 1829. Died June 16, 1852.
    Catharine, born March 5, 1832. Died 1834.
    David C., born February 25, 1834. Died August 14, 1862.
A. B. died August 31, 1846.
Catharine, widow of A. B., died March 30, 1864.

George Yeakel, son of George Yeakel (page 48), married Maria Deisher. No issue.
G. Y. died December 31, 1852.
His wife, born April 5, 1784, died December 13, 1862.

Henry Heebner, son of George Heebner (page 49), married Anna, daughter of Christopher Schultz (page 51), April 21, 1807. Their children were:
    Sarah, born January 30, 1808.

Susannah, born June 25, 1810.
George, born November 24, 1811.
Abraham, born May 14, 1814. Died February 24, 1815.
Hannah, born February 24, 1816.
Maria, born October 31, 1817.
Abigail, born December 29, 1819.
John S., born March 2, 1822.
Anna, born February 28, 1827.

Anna, wife of H. H., died April 2, 1839.

H. H. died March 30, 1847. He was a farmer and lived on the farm now owned by his son, John S. Heebner, in Gwynedd.

Christopher Yeakel, son of Melchior Yeakel (page 50), married Barbara, daughter of Balthasar Schultz (page 48), May 5, 1807. Had no issue.

C. Y. died January 8, 1852.

Barbara, his widow, died May 11, 1860.

Christopher Meschter, son of Christopher Meschter (page 56), married Catharine, daughter of Abraham Anders (page 67), May 14, 1807. Child,
George, born March 28, 1808.

Catharine, wife of C. M., died May 23, 1842.

C. M. died February 14, 1853.

David Schultz, son of Balthasar Schultz (page 48), married Lydia, daughter of Christopher Yeakle (page 66), October 27, 1807. Their children were:
Joshua, born September 11, 1808.
Reuben, born March 12, 1810.
Rebecca, born August 27, 1814. Died November 16, 1872.

Lydia, wife of D. S., died July 5, 1845.

D. S. died April 7, 1851. He resided in Upper Hanover.

Christopher Kriebel, son of George Kriebel (page 54), married Regina, widow of Isaac Kriebel (page 100), and daughter of Rev. Melchior Schultz (page 64), November 12, 1807. Had issue:

    Susanna, born September 21, 1808. Died May 27, 1875.
    Bathseba, born July 8, 1819.
    C. K. died September 12, 1822.
    Regina, widow of C. K., died February 28, 1870.

Jacob Yeakle, son of Abraham Yeakle (page 58), married Gertrude, daughter of George Urffer (page 51), November 1, 1808. Their children were:

    Susan, born September 4, 1809.
    Joseph, born April 11, 1811.
    Leah, born June 4, 1814.
    Charles, born July 7, 1817.
    George, born February 27, 1820.
    William, born November 7, 1821.

Jacob Yeakle was a farmer, and lived in Springfield Township, Montgomery County, Pa., on the farm now owned by his son William, and died there May 29, 1863.

His widow, Gertrude, died February 9, 1868.

David Schubert, son of Melchior Schubert (page 56), married Elizabeth Schiffert, born November 22, 1785. Had issue:

    Anthony, born June 20, 1809.
    Sophia, born June 20, 1811. Died November 24, 1831.
    Anna, born February 4, 1814.

Louis, born April 15, 1816.
Rebecca, born March 2, 1818.
Oliver, born February 18, 1820.
Elizabeth, born September 18, 1822.
Charles, born September 24, 1824.
Sarah, born April 27, 1827.
Rachel, born December 4, 1829.

Elizabeth, wife of D. S., died December 25, 1831.

David Schubert married, second time, Susanna, daughter of John Yeakel (page 86). Child,
Daughter.

D. S. died July 1, 1861.

Susanna, widow of D. S., died November 22, 1873.

Michael Van Fossen, born December 12, 1785, married Christianna, daughter of Jacob Beyer (page 65). Date of marriage not given. Had issue:
Joseph, born June 6, 1810.
Charlotte, born December 22, 1815.
Jacob, born September 3, 1818.
Eli, born August 31, 1828.

Michael Van Fossen died January 30, 1865.

John Overholtzer married Abigail, daughter of Abraham Yeakle (page 77), 1809. Children:
Noah. Died single.
Matilda. Died single.
Reuben, born November 24, 1816.
Abraham, born October 12, 1818.
Isaac, born May 8, 1820.
Joseph, born May 24, 1822.

Death record of these parents could not be found.

Isaac (Meschter) Master, son of Christopher Meschter (page 46), married Mary Clemence, May 11, 1809. Children:

John, born March 7, 1810.
Elizabeth, born September 11, 1811. Still born.
George, born December 23, 1813. Died October 1, 1874.
Sarah Ann, born January 23, 1816. Married Benjamin Shupe.
Abraham, born April 11, 1818. Died July 7, 1853.
Mary, born May 7, 1820. Married Edward Ellis.
Isaac, born January 25, 1822. Died July 30, 1834.
Hannah, born December 18, 1824. Married Benjamin Erb.
Catharine, born August 3, 1826.
Samuel, born June 19, 1828.
Nancy, born March 29, 1830.
Eliza, born July 2, 1832. Married John Stringer.
Henry, born March 27, 1834.
Lewis, born January 8, 1836. Died August 15, 1836.
Lucinda, born January 29, 1837.
I. M. died June 21, 1853.
Mary, widow of I. M., died May 26, 1870.
His descendants reside in Canada West, where Isaac Meschter moved to many years ago.

Andrew Schultz, son of David Schultz (page 64), married Sophia, daughter of Andrew Kriebel (page 52), June 1, 1809. They had issue:
Susanna, born June 28, 1810.
Anna, born January 14, 1812.
Lydia, born January 23, 1814.
Elizabeth, born March 21, 1816.
Andrew K., born May 3, 1818.
A. S. died November 17, 1817.
Sophia, widow of A. S., died March 24, 1857.

David Urffer, son of George Urffer (page 51), married Mary, daughter of Abraham Yeakle (page 58), November 26, 1809. Their children were:
   Daniel Y., born July 18, 1820.
   George, } died when young.
   Sarah,
   Hannah. Married John Reed.
   Christina.
   Magdalene. Married Frank Cope.
   Susan. Married William F. Reed, Esq.
   D. U. died April 6, 1847.
   His wife died April 20, 1840.

Solomon Kriebel, son of Rev. Melchior Kriebel (page 55), married Maria, daughter of Balthasar Meschter (page 57), November 28, 1809. They had issue:
   Susanna, born January 28, 1811. Died July 17, 1877.
   Elias, born February 1, 1814. Died March 14, 1815.
   Levi, born February 20, 1816.
   Sarah, born July 24, 1818. Died June 19, 1838.
   Maria, born July 29, 1821.
   Elizabeth, born May 30, 1823.
   S. K. died August 17, 1853. He was a carpenter, and lived in Gwynedd.
   Maria, widow of S. K., died April 28, 1868.

John Peters, son of Michael Peters, married Mary, daughter of Abraham Heydrick (page 47), about 1810. Children:
   Delinda.
   Susanna.
   John.

Franklin.
Elizabeth.
Charlotte.
Caroline.
J. P. died May 31, 1832.
Mary, his widow, died August 26, 1866.

Solomon Yeakel, son of Melchior Yeakel (page 50), married Regina, daughter of Melchior Schubert (page 56). Had issue:
    Jammin, born September 9, 1811. Died March 9, 1812.
    Leah, born April 14, 1813.
S. Y. died April 6, 1814.
Regina, his widow, married John Schlicher, and had one daughter:
    Thamar, born November 28, 1817. Married Dr. Wm. Addison Shelly, and left issue.
Regina, wife of J. S., died June 5, 1867.
John Schlicher was born in 1791, and died, aged about 26 years, in 1817.

Christopher Yeakel, son of Jacob Yeakel (page 61), married Elizabeth, daughter of Caspar Yeakel (page 57), May 10, 1810. Their children were:
    Abigail, born October 9, 1811.
    Samuel, born January 27, 1813.
    Reuben, born August 3, 1816. Died.
    Joel, born November 18, 1817.
    Deborah, born March 24, 1821.
    Joseph, born December 10, 1823.
Elizabeth, wife of C. Y., died February 27, 1864, and he died March 25, 1874. He lived in Upper Hanover, on the farm now owned by his son Joseph.

David Kriebel, son of Andrew Kriebel (page 52), married Rosina, daughter of David Schultz (page 64), May 24, 1810. Children:
  Anna, born July 11, 1812.
  Mary, born December 26, 1813.
  Philip, born December 6, 1815.
Rosina, wife of D. K., died December 27, 1817.
David Kriebel married, second time, Elizabeth, daughter of Frederick Alderfer, January 14, 1819. Wife born January 11, 1802. Children:
  Henry, born July 8, 1819.
  Susanna, born March 17, 1821.
  Magdalene, born October 21, 1822.
  Septimus, born August 3, 1825.
  Barbara, born September 3, 1827.
  Hannah, born January 5, 1829.
  Elizabeth, born January 18, 1832.
D. K. died July 1, 1842.
Elizabeth, widow of D. K., died August 12, 1878.

Caspar Schultz, son of Christopher Schultz (page 51), married Christina, daughter of Jacob Yeakel (page 61), June 7, 1810. Children:
  Sarah, born March 4, 1811.
  Maria, born July 9, 1812.
  Susanna, born April 20, 1814. Died December 27, 1818.
  Jacob, born August 10, 1815.
  Magdalena, born March 9, 1819.
  Lydia, born May 27, 1821. Died August 18, 1821.
  Elias, born March 3, 1825. Died April 6, 1837.
  Son, born September 21, 1826. Died September 27, 1828.
  Jonas, born March 31, 1829.

C. S. died March 15, 1858.
Christina, widow of C. S., died April 9, 1862.

Joseph Snyder, son of Henry Snyder (page 68), married Sophia, daughter of Abraham Kriebel (page 71), April 25, 1811. Children:
- Jesse, born February 15, 1812.
- Margaret, born April 14, 1814.
- Hannah, born July 25, 1816.
- Elizabeth, born August 31, 1818. Died August 1, 1876.
- George, born July 16, 1821.

Sophia, wife of J. S., died September 4, 1824.
J. S. died December 1, 1858.

Michael Nuss married Barbara, daughter of George Urffer (page 51). Children:
- Nathan, } twins, born March 2, 1812.
- Leah,
- Aaron, born June 20, 1815.
- Sarah, born August 5, 1817.
- Susan, born June 19, 1819.
- Charles, born September 9, 1821.
- Joseph, born July 13, 1824.
- John Mahlon, born February 11, 1827.

M. N. lived where Greenville is now located, and died there July 25, 1870.
Barbara, his wife, died July 6, 1869.

Henry Althouse, son of Yost Althouse, married Juliana, daughter of David Schultz (page 54), about the year 1811. They had issue:
- Daniel, born April 13, 1812.
- Samuel, born 1815. Died young.

Lydia, born 1818.
Henry, born 1820.
Hannah, born 1822.
Catharine, born 1829. Married Anthony Seibert. The time of the deaths of H. A. and wife could not be ascertained.

Jeremiah Meschter, son of Christopher Meschter (page 56), married Christina, daughter of Jacob Kriebel (page 71), May 9, 1811. Their children were:
Lydia, born April 6, 1813.
Sophia.
Samuel.
Jacob, born October 3, 1818.
Christina, born August 11, 1821.
Jeremiah, born November 27, 1823.
Christina, wife of J. M., died January 28, 1831.
J. M. died October 5, 1849. He lived in Upper Hanover Township, Montgomery County, Pa.

William Schultz, son of David Schultz (page 64), married Salome, daughter of Andrew Kriebel (page 52), November 14, 1811. They had children:
Christina, born December 6, 1812.
Samuel, born September 13, 1814.
Maria, born October 6, 1816. Died February 27, 1833.
W. S. died December 25, 1817.
Salome, widow of W. S., died November 4, 1869.

Benjamin Cassel, born December 19, 1789, married Sarah, daughter of Abraham Heebner (page 73), November 28, 1811. Their children were:
Abraham, born December 7, 1812.
Elizabeth, born April 4, 1814.

Hannah, born November 22. 1816.
Jacob, born February 5, 1820. Died March 27, 1848.
Joseph, born March 8, 1822.
Benjamin, born February 26, 1825.
Sarah, born January 4, 1828.
Catharine, born January 12, 1831.
Enos, born April 2, 1833.
Susanna, born March 4, 1837.
Sarah, wife of B. C., died June 30, 1841.
B. C. died May 30, 1861.

Andrew Yeakel, son of Jacob Yeakel (page 61), married Susanna, daughter of Caspar Yeakel (page 57), April 23, 1812. Children:
Jacob, born March 3, 1813.
Maria, born January 31, 1815. Died December 18, 1837.
Jonas, born February 18, 1818. Died November 10, 1836.
George, born August 16, 1820. Died June 3, 1848.
Susanna, born September 7, 1822. Died May 19, 1838.
Andrew, born April 26, 1824. Died September 8, 1848.
Joel, born August, 1831.
A. Y. died April 6, 1837.
Susanna, widow of A. Y., died July 21, 1863.

Joseph Beyer, son of Jacob Beyer (page 65), married Hannah Bean. Children:
Jacob, born January 17, 1813.
William, born July 29, 1814.
Joseph, born April 17, 1817.

J. B. died May 10, 1818.
Hannah, widow of J. B., died January 20, 1850.

George Schultz, son of Christopher Schultz (page 51), married Hannah, daughter of Melchior Schubert (page 56), May, 1812. They had issue:
  Michael, born July 13, 1814.
  Anthony, born October 21, 1815.
  Rebecca, born June 19, 1817.
  Solomon, born August 3, 1819.
  Nathan, born January 24, 1821.
  Mary, born May 2, 1826.
  William, born December 26, 1827.
G. S. died October 29, 1851. He lived in Worcester, and owned the farm now in possession of his son Solomon.
Hannah, widow of G. S., died August 18, 1869.

Joseph Schultz, son of Abraham Schultz (page 52), married Eve, daughter of Gregory Schultz (page 59), May 19, 1812. No issue.
Eve, wife of J. S., died August 16, 1816.
Joseph Schultz married, second time, Hannah, daughter of Rev. Melchior Kriebel (page 55). No issue.
J. S. died March 3, 1833.

Gabriel Schultz, son of David Schultz (page 54), married Catharine Schwab. Children:
  Sarah, born September, 1814.
  David, born December 15, 1815.
  Henry, born April, 1817.
  Joseph.
  Daniel.
  Elizabeth.

G. S. died many years ago, and is buried somewhere near Boyertown, Berks County.

Christopher Schubert, son of Melchior Schubert (page 56), married Maria, daughter of Melchior Yeakel (page 50). Had issue:
    Theresa, born August 22, 1814. Died April 24, 1837.
    Christina, born October 1, 1816. Married Glaser, and died April 6, 1848.
    Lydia, born September 27, 1818.
    Timothy, born August 14, 1820.
    Reuben, } twins, born June 21, 1822.
    Simon,
Maria, wife of C. S., died April 8, 1823.
Christopher Schubert married, second time, Sabina, daughter of Isaac Yeakle (page 71).
Sabina, wife of C. S., died January 10, 1855.
C. S. died.

Benjamin Kriebel, son of Abraham Kriebel (page 66), married Catharine, daughter of Melchior Yeakel (page 50), 1813. Had issue:
    Agnes, born December 5, 1814.
    Gideon, born September 7, 1818. Died January 29, 1819.
    Judith, born January 22, 1820.
    Maria, born May 17, 1823.
    Isaac, born October 19, 1825.
B. K. died October 20, 1863. He lived in Upper Hanover.
Catharine, his widow, died September 30, 1868.

Samuel Kline, born December 20, 1788, married Mar-

garet, daughter of Jacob Beyer (page 65), in February, 1813. Children:
  Rachel, born July 13, 1815.
  Samuel, born May 29, 1820.
S. K. died October 10, 1867.
Margaret, widow of S. K., died November 6, 1867.

John Kriebel, son of Rev. Melchior Kriebel (page 55), married Agnes, daughter of Christopher Yeakle (page 66), November 9, 1813. Their children were:
  Charles, born September 12, 1814.
  Samuel, born May 23, 1816.
  Mary, born January 31, 1819.
  Susanna, born June 12, 1821.
  Sarah, born August 4, 1828.
J. K. died December 5, 1863.
Agnes, widow of J. K., died July 20, 1873.
John Kriebel, after he married, lived on a farm on Chestnut Hill, Philadelphia. His residence, or farmhouse, is now occupied as a hotel immediately adjoining the depot of the C. H. & G. RR. He sold his farm just previous to the building of the C. H. RR., and moved to Worcester and died there.

Daniel Schultz, son of Gregory Schultz (page 59), married Sarah, daughter of Jacob Yeakel (page 61), November 25, 1813. Had issue:
  Twins, born June 28, 1815. Died August 5 and 6, 1815.
  Lydia, born November 2, 1816. Died August, 1836.
  Susanna, born December 23, 1819.
  John, born September 30, 1824. Died February 13, 1826.

D. S. died September 5, 1862. He lived in Upper Hanover.

Sarah, widow of D. S., died December 23, 1862.

Hannah Heebner, daughter of Abraham Heebner (page 73), married Garrett Metz, son of Jacob Metz, December 13, 1813. Their children were:

Joseph, born April 28, 1815.

Catharine, born August 1, 1817. Died August 20, 1819.

Jacob, } twins, born March 10, 1821.
Eve,

Eve died March 16, 1866.

Abraham, born September 1, 1823. Died August 25, 1825.

Sarah, born July 21, 1826. Died October 5, 1843.

Mary, born February 27, 1829.

John, born February 29, 1832. Died July 28, 1864.

Susanna, born January 21, 1835.

Abraham Yeakel, son of Caspar Yeakel (page 57), married Sarah Miller April 17, 1814. Wife born May 10, 1793. They had issue:

Edward, born January 18, 1816.

Joseph, born June 18, 1818.

Anna, born August 20, 1820.

Hiram.

Maria, born November 15, 1823.

Levi, born March 24, 1825.

Nimrod, born April 14, 1827.

Solomon, born November 22, 1828.

Sarah, born September 1, 1830.

A. Y. died October 27, 1865.

Sarah, widow of A. Y., died October 3, 1875.
Abraham Yeakel was a millwright, and lived in Upper Hanover, Montgomery County, Pa.

Melchior Schultz, son of Abraham Schultz (page 52), married Mary, daughter of David Schultz (page 64), April 28, 1814. Children:
David, born July 7, 1819.
Lydia, born October 17, 1821. Died February 26, 1833.
Mary, born July 14, 1824.
M. S. died November 5, 1875.
Mary, widow of M. S., died January 29, 1877.

Abraham Snyder, son of Henry Snyder (page 68), married Susanna, daughter of Balthasar Schultz (page 48), May 5, 1814. Their children were:
Regina, born February 10, 1815.
Daniel, born January 1, 1817.
Sarah, born May 1, 1820.
Anna, born January 6, 1825.
A. S. died May 23, 1858.
Susanna, widow of A. S., died October, 15, 1862.

Henry W. Schultz, son of Rev. Melchior Schultz (page 64), married Anna, daughter of Christopher Yeakle (page 66), November 8, 1814. They had issue:
Harriet Y., born June 21, 1817.
Selina Y., born 1819.
Ella Y., born April 25, 1824. Died May 5, 1866.
Amanda Y., born May 5, 1826. Died August 6, 1845.
H. W. S. died December 30, 1846. He resided in

Whitemarsh, upon the farm now owned by Elias H. Phipps.

Anna, widow of H. W. S., died February 20, 1869.

David Kriebel, son of Rev. Melchior Kriebel (page 55), married Sarah, daughter of Rev. Melchior Schultz (page 64), April 11, 1815. Their children were:
 Barbara, born September 1, 1816.
 Jacob, born December 22, 1817.
 Jesse, born January 11, 1820. Died July 26, 1843.
 Adam, born June 9, 1823.
 Dinah, born October 6, 1825. Died July 9, 1848.
 Sarah, born September 30, 1828.
 Hannah, born June 20, 1834.
Sarah, wife of D. K., died April 28, 1837.

D. K. died April 23, 1848. He was a farmer, and lived near Centre Point, in Worcester Township. He was a minister of the Society of Schwenkfelders for some length of time, and an eloquent and earnest preacher.

Carl Yeakel, son of Jacob Yeakel (page 61), married Susanna, daughter of David Yeakel (page 69), May 1, 1815. Children:
 Sarah, born June 4, 1817.
 Jesse, born February 15, 1820.
 Jacob, born January 8, 1824.
 Reuben, born August 3, 1827.
 Lydia, born April 13, 1831.
Carl Yeakel died October 6, 1874, and wife September 9, 1877.

Humphrey White, M.D., son of James White, married

Susanna, daughter of Abraham Yeakle (page 77), in 1816. Their children were:
  Sarah, born June 29, 1817.
  Elizabeth, born November 2, 1818.
  Franklin, born December 2, 1820. Died.
  Melinda, born November 27, 1823.
  Abraham, born July 16, 1826. Died August 1, 1874.
  Sylvester, born November 2, 1828. Died.
Dr. H. W. died March 16, 1829. He was a physician, and followed his profession in Gwynedd, Montgomery County, Pa.

Daniel Yeakel, son of Melchior Yeakel (page 50), married Susanna, daughter of Matthias Geho (page 80), January 26, 1816. Children:
  George, born June 9, 1816.
  Sarah, born October 31, 1817. Died December 27, 1819.
  Elizabeth, born November 19, 1819.
  Agnes, born January 23, 1821.
  John, born November 21, 1823.
  Daniel, born January 15, 1826.
  Susanna, born September 9, 1831.
  Hannah, born May 23, 1833.
  Lydia, born October 10, 1835.
  Emeline, born December, 1843.
D. Y. died August 11, 1859.
Susanna, his widow, died April 5, 1875.

Margaret Heebner, daughter of Christopher Heebner (page 74), married, first husband, George Reiff, October 29, 1816. Children:
  Elizabeth, born July 16, 1817. Married Henry Longaker, and died in 1878.

Christopher, born October 5, 1819.

G. R., her husband, died in the year 1820. She married, second time, William O. Roberts, in 1822. Children:
David, born December 25, 1823.
William, born April 21, 1825.
Hannah, born September 12, 1829.
Daniel W., born January 27, 1834. Died May 10, 1855.
Josephus, born November 26, 1836.

W. O. Roberts was born April 20, 1792, and died April 3, 1858. His widow died January 5, 1867.

Job Kriebel, son of Rev. Melchior Kriebel (page 55), married Esther, daughter of George Anders (page 76), April 20, 1817. Had issue:
Catharine, born June 4, 1818.
Joseph, born March 10, 1820. Died October 21, 1851.
George A., born October 17, 1824.

J. K. died November 24, 1825.
Esther, widow of J. K., died January 20, 1849.

Christopher K. Schultz, son of David Schultz (page 64), married Sarah, daughter of Christopher Yeakle (page 66), May 13, 1817. Children:
Matilda Y., born March 14, 1827.
Hiram, born February 17, 1831. Died January 15, 1834.

C. K. S. died December 11, 1856.
Sarah, widow of C. K. S., died December 1, 1862.

Schultzville, Berks County, was named after C. K. S. He was a storekeeper and farmer.

Jacob Kriebel, son of Abraham Kriebel (page 66), married Anna, daughter of Caspar Yeakel (page 57), November 6, 1817. Had children:
 Reuben, born September 11, 1820.
 Hannah, born April 6, 1823.
 Leah, born October 8, 1825.
 Daniel, born August 5, 1828. Died May 2, 1831.
 David, born December 19, 1831.
 Solomon, born January 31, 1836.
J. K. died May 1, 1869.
Anna, widow of J. K., died March 17, 1875.
Jacob Kriebel was a miller by trade, and owned the mill property on the Hosensack now in possession of Joel Yeakel.

Jacob Wagener, son of Daniel Wagener (page 68), married Sabina Michler, daughter of Nathaniel Michler, Esq., May 5, 1818. Children:
 Emma. Married the Hon. William A. Porter, of Philadelphia, son of the late Governor Porter.
 Elizabeth. Married William P. Newlin, of Philadelphia, merchant.
Jacob Wagener, after obtaining an excellent English education, pursued the business of a merchant, chiefly in partnership with his brother David, until they had each acquired a competence, and then retired from business and devoted himself to literature and science. He became exceedingly well read in English literature. He was at one time an efficient trustee of Lafayette College. He devoted much of his time to mineralogy and geology, and at the period of his death his min-

eral cabinet was believed to be the best in Pennsylvania out of the city of Philadelphia, many of its specimens having been collected at large cost from foreign countries.

J. W. died December 14, 1859.

Samuel Kriebel, son of Jeremiah Kriebel (page 62), married Elizabeth, daughter of Peter Boorse, in 1818. They had issue:
  Joseph B., born October 23, 1819.
  Jeremiah.
  Samuel.
  Aaron.

Sarah Heebner, daughter of Christopher Heebner (page 74), married Andrew Bossert January 5, 1819. Children:
  Christopher, born November 13, 1819.
  Charles, born March 31, 1823.
  James, born August 23, 1825.
  Andrew J., born January 1, 1830.
  Sarah Ann, born December 17, 1833.
  Amanda, born January 30, 1836.
  Isaiah, born April 5, 1837.
A. B. was born August 6, 1792.

John Robinson, son of John Robinson, married Mary, daughter of George Dresher (page 50), about 1819, and had issue:
  Charles. Married.
  Lydia.   Married John Avery.
  Sarah.   Married Dr. Benjamin Lawson.
  Daniel. Married Emeline Stackhouse.
  Edwin.   Died in infancy.

Moved to Cincinnati many years ago, where his descendants now reside.

Israel Kriebel, son of Andrew Kriebel (page 52), married Sarah, daughter of Rev. John Schultz (page 82), May 6, 1819. Children:
    Christina, born October 12, 1820. Died October 10, 1864.
    John, born February 4, 1822.
    Samuel, born November 11, 1823. Died June 16, 1825.
    Susanna, born January 8, 1825.
    Elizabeth, born August 10, 1826.
    Henry, born March 25, 1828.
    Elias, born October 13, 1829.
    Regina, born October 7, 1831.
    Joseph, born June 28, 1833. Died December 29, 1859.
    Andrew, born August 8, 1835.
    Anna, born March 5, 1838. Died April 27, 1845.
    Sarah, born June 27, 1841. Died April 27, 1845.
    Mary, born July 14, 1846.
Sarah, wife of I. K., died March 1, 1859.
I. K. died June 14, 1860. He was a miller and lived in Hereford, Berks County, Pa.

Mary Yeakel, daughter of Jacob Yeakel (page 81), married George Lyster, January 7, 1819. Had issue as follows:
    Jacob, born November 19, 1819.
    Lucy Ann, born August 15, 1821. Died September 5, 1821.
    Abraham, born August 15, 1822. Died September 1875.

Elizabeth, born December 21, 1824.
Samuel, born March 30, 1827.
Susanna, born October 19, 1829.
John, born January 15, 1832.
Augustus, born May 16, 1834.
George, born November 27, 1837. Died August 7, 1876.
Mary, born December 1, 1839.
Catharine, born April 6, 1841.
Sarah, born March 15, 1843.
Elemina, born July, 1845. Died August, 1846.
George Lyster died November 7, 1878, at the age of 81 years.

Anthony Kriebel, son of Abraham Kriebel (page 66), married Christina, daughter of David Schultz (page 64), May 11, 1819. Children:
Sarah, born July 5, 1822.
Mary, born July 4, 1825.
Susanna, born September 9, 1830.
Christina, wife of A. K., died June 3, 1869.

Abraham Kriebel, son of Jacob Kriebel (page 71), married Lydia, daughter of Andrew Kriebel (page 76), May 27, 1819. No issue.
A. K. died March 2, 1828.
Lydia, widow of A. K., died December 6, 1844.

Melchior Kriebel, son of Rev. Melchior Kriebel (page 55), married Rosina, daughter of Rev. Melchior Schultz (page 64), ———, 1820. Children:
Ephraim, born February 16, 1821.
Salome, born January 16, 1823.
Anna, born March 17, 1825. Died July 12, 1825.

Maria, born December 16, 1826.
Rosina, born December 22, 1829. Died May 10, 1848.
Susanna, born April 17, 1836.
M. K. died February 13, 1868.
Rosina, widow of M. K., died April 7, 1872.

Jonathan Kriebel, son of Abraham Kriebel (page 66), married Anna, daughter of George Heydrick (page 87), April 22, 1820. Children:
George, born January 24, 1821. Died November 6, 1821.
Abraham, born July 10, 1823.
Charles, born March 7, 1828. Died February 21, 1838.
Anna, wife of J. K., died April 9, 1836.
J. K. died April 10, 1873.

Jeremiah Schultz, son of David Schultz (page 64), married Mary, daughter of Rev. John Schultz (page 82), June 1, 1820. Children:
Henry, born June 16, 1821.
Edward, born June 20, 1824.
John, born September 6, 1828.
Solomon S.
Mary, wife of J. S., died February 2, 1873.
J. S. died February 3, 1874. He lived where his son Henry now lives, in Hereford, Berks County, Pa.

Daniel Rittenhouse, born November 17, 1798, married Rachel, daughter of Jacob Beyer (page 65), September 10, 1820. Children:
Catharine, born November 9, 1821.
Aaron, born November 19, 1823. Died February 18, 1870.

Silas, born August 15, 1826.
D. R. died December 21, 1876.

Joseph Yeakel, son of John Yeakel (page 86), married Lydia, daughter of Abraham Kriebel (page 66), September 20, 1820. No issue.
Lydia, wife of J. Y., died November 3, 1834.
Joseph Yeakel married, second time, Anna Maria, daughter of Christian Zellner, May 22, 1836. Children :
  Joseph, born January 31, 1837.
  William, born August 28, 1839.

Samuel Newman, son of Christopher Newman (page 69), married Regina, daughter of Andrew Krauss (page 84), October 15, 1820. Children :
  Leah, born September 27, 1821.
  Esther, born October 15, 1824.
  George, born August 4, 1826. Died December 24, 1830.
  Sarah, born December 21, 1828.
  Enos, born February 12, 1832.
S. N. died March 30, 1862.

Andrew Gerhard, son of Jacob Gerhard (page 81), married Catharine, daughter of Jacob Kriebel (page 71), November 12, 1820. Had issue:
  Judith, born March 18, 1828.
  Jacob, born January 10, 1831. Died October 23, 1831.
  David, born February 2, 1833. Died April 5, 1833.
  Henry, born September 25, 1834.
  Jonas, born January 23, 1838.
Catharine, wife of A. G., died February 3, 1860.

A. G. died December 25, 1876. He was a blacksmith and farmer, and lived in Milford, Bucks County, Pa.

Jacob Meschter, son of Balthasar Meschter (page 57), married Catharine, daughter of John Hendricks, November 14, 1820. Their children were:
  Charles, born September 2, 1821.
  Jesse, born September 17, 1823.
  Antrim, born January 7, 1825.
  Elizabeth, born June 28, 1827.
  Sarah, born October 29, 1831.
  James, born February 2, 1834. Died September 2, 1838.
  Mary, born January 7, 1836. Died December 5, 1851.
  Isaac, born April 19, 1838.
  Barbara, born August 6, 1840.
J. M. died December 18, 1851.

George Schuler, son of Samuel Schuler, married Sophia, daughter of Abraham Kriebel (page 66), December 26, 1820. Had issue:
  Sarah, born April 15, 1821.
  Raham, born March 20, 1823.
  Thomas, } twins, born December 24, 1825.
  Amandus, }
  Jethro, born December 26, 1828.
  Mahlon, born August 1, 1830.
  Elijah, born August 25, 1833. Died August 27, 1846.
  Willoughby, born March 27, 1837. Died August 23, 1846.
G. S. died June 28, 1842. He was a carpenter in Upper Milford, Lehigh County, Pa.
Sophia, widow of G. S., died July 20, 1878.

Caroline M. Heydrick, daughter of Dr. Christopher Heydrick (page 74), married Thomas J. Brown, November, 1821, leaving issue:

    Alexander F., born February 18, 1823.
    Harriet H., born July 15, 1824.
    James, born March 26, 1826.
    Charles H., born December 22, 1827. Married Mary A. Black, December 17, 1874.
    Albert G., born September 6, 1830.
    Christopher H., born March 22, 1836.
    Mary E., born November 18, 1837. Married Emlin P. Thorn, and died December 8, 1871.
    Benjamin F., born May 11, 1842. Died 1843.

C. M. B., wife of Thomas J. Brown, died March 2, 1874. Thomas Jacobs Brown was born in Westmoreland County, Pa., in May, 1801; removed with his parents to Mercer County, Pa., in 1808, where he subsequently laid out the now borough of Sandy Lake, formerly called Brownsville, erected a saw mill, flouring mill, oil mill, woollen factory, and turning mill, all propelled by water power, and was engaged many years in general merchandising; was appointed Justice of the Peace in 1840, and elected to the same office in 1845; appointed Associate Judge of the several Courts of Mercer County in 1855, to fill a vacancy, and elected to the same office in 1856 for the term of five years; again appointed Justice of the Peace in 1875, to fill a vacancy, and again elected for a full term in 1876.

David Seibert, son of Jacob Seibert (page 63), married Susanna, daughter of Matthias Gerhard (page 59), in 1821. Children:

    Anthony, born August 30, 1822.
    Joshua, born January 15, 1824.

Esther, born May 29, 1825. Married William Winkler.
Jonas, born May 8, 1827.
Maria, born June 20, 1829. Married Joel Walter.
Joel, } twins, born April 3, 1831. Died August
Levi,   3, 1831.
Nathan, born September 19, 1832.
Susanna, born February 10, 1835. Married Levinus Schell.
Elizabeth, born April 26, 1839. Married Josiah Long.
Susanna, wife of D. S., died August 6, 1863.
D. S. died May 12, 1875. He was a weaver by trade, and lived in Upper Milford, Lehigh County, Pa.

Joseph Metz, born August 18, 1800, married Mary, daughter of Jacob Beyer (page 65), September 11, 1821. Children:
    John B., born October 22, 1822.
    Jacob B., born September 8, 1826.
    Elizabeth, born June 3, 1829.
    Joseph, born June 7, 1833. Died June 10, 1833.
    Mary, born August 17, 1838.
J. M. died January 10, 1860.

David D. Wagener, son of Daniel Wagener (page 68), married Mary Knauss, September 20, 1821, and had issue:
    Daniel, born August 8, 1822. Died July 8, 1878. A lawyer by profession and unmarried.
    John O.
    Elizabeth K. Married Thomas H. Leary, Esq.
    Susan B. Married Dr. J. Brackenridge Clemens.
    Sarah E. Married L. Caufman Hepburn, Esq.

David D. Wagener was a merchant, but in early life turned his attention to politics, and became a leader in the party to which he belonged. He served as a member from Northampton in the State Legislature during the administration of Governor Wolf. He occupied a seat in Congress for four successive terms, from 1832 to 1840. On retiring from political life he was elected President of the Easton Bank, an office which he filled with acceptance to the community until the period of his death, which took place on the first day of October, 1860.

His wife died February 13, 1833.

Jacob Beyer, son of Jacob Beyer (page 65), married Magdalena Boorse in 1822. Children:

Samuel, born February 13, 1823.
John, born April 8, 1824.
Jesse, born September 13, 1825.
Adam, born August 24, 1827.
Elizabeth, born October 31, 1828.
Daniel, born June 27, 1830.
Albert, born January 8, 1832. Died January 5, 1851.
Jacob, born June 21, 1834.
Benjamin, born March 4, 1836. Died April 23, 1849.
James, born October 29, 1838.
Franklin, born June 28, 1840. Died April 16, 1852.
Charles, born April 30, 1842. Died January 19, 1848.
Sarah, born April 13, 1844.

Magdalena, wife of J. B., died March 30, 1848.

Jacob Beyer married, second time, Elizabeth Oberholtzer in 1855. No issue.

Joseph Anders, son of Andrew Anders (page 69), married Hannah, daughter of Andrew Kriebel (page 76), May 23, 1822. They had issue:
  Andrew, born August 29, 1823.
  Joseph, born 1826.
J. A. died March 11, 1831, aged 38 years, 2 months, less 10 days.
Hannah, widow of J. A., died March 1, 1870.

Samuel Kriebel, son of Rev. Melchior Kriebel (page 55), married Sarah, daughter of Samuel Kriebel (page 94), October 31, 1822. Children:
  Jonas, born March 22, 1824.
  Susanna, born June 28, 1826.
  Lydia, born March 8, 1829.
  Samuel, born September 16, 1833.
  Catharine, born December 24, 1836. Died August 28, 1860.
  William, born February 3, 1840. Died August 4, 1860.
S. K. died August 13, 1853.

John Beyer, son of Jacob Beyer (page 65), married Lydia Frick. They had issue:
  Henry F., born 1824.
  Elias, born August 22, 1826.
  Aaron, born September 10, 1828. Died January 31, 1844.
  Ann, born January 18, 1831. Died July 25, 1846.
J. B. died from a fall at a mill, July 24, 1832.
Lydia, widow of J. B., died September 11, 1856.

Jacob Dresher, son of Abraham Dresher (page 60), married Regina, daughter of Christopher Kriebel (page 67), 1823. Children:
  Reuben, born April 26, 1824.

Susanna, born November 27, 1825.
Jacob, born March 9, 1828.
Abraham, born November 21, 1830.
J. D. died March 29, 1833.

Abraham Heebner, son of Christopher Heebner (page 74), married Elizabeth Saylor, January 1, 1823. No issue.
A. H. died May 16, 1843.
His widow died February 16, 1876, aged 74 years, 9 months, and 1 day.

Samuel Yeakle, son of Christopher Yeakle (page 66), married Lydia, daughter of Abraham Anders (page 95), November, 1823. Children:
    William A., born October 20, 1824.
    Charles A., born October 25, 1826.
    Abraham A., born April 4, 1830.
Lydia, wife of S. Y., died December 26, 1846.
Samuel Yeakle married, second time, Susanna, daughter of Samuel Dresher (page 94), November 19, 1850. He commenced farming in 1824 on the farm now occupied by his son Charles A., in Whitemarsh, Montgomery County, Pa., and continued until about 1853, when he removed to the borough of Norristown and retired from business.

Christian Detweiler, born April 30, 1802, married Catharine Heebner, daughter of Abraham Heebner (page 73), January 15, 1824. Children:
    Abraham, born May 12, 1824.
    Samuel, born February 18, 1827.
    Margaret, born January 16, 1829.
    Mary, born November 8, 1831.
    Enos, born August 4, 1834.

Catharine, born November 5, 1837.

Christian, born August 29, 1839. Died August 12, 1840.

Isaiah, born September 23, 1841.

Christian, born November 16, 1842.

Lydia, born October 7, 1845.

C. D. died December 3, 1861.

Rachel Master, daughter of John Master (page 98), married Thomas Glidewell, March 6, 1824. Children:

Alison, born December 28, 1824. Died January 22, 1835.

Elizabeth, born May 31, 1825.

Joann, born May 20, 1827.

Mary, born June 16, 1829.

John, born May 10, 1830.

Selah, born November, 1832.

Robert, born February 8, 1835.

Sarah Ann, born November 1, 1837.

Lavina, born September 8, 1839.

Rachel Martha, born October 29, 1841. Died April 29, 1856.

Thomas, born December 18, 1843.

Christopher, born July 9, 1848. Died September 8, 1874.

Thomas Glidewell was born November 25, 1803, and died October 29, 1868.

Benjamin Kriebel, son of Christopher Kriebel (page 67), married Elizabeth, daughter of Henry Snyder (page 68), May 1, 1823. They had issue:

Euphemia, born 1823.

Regina, born October 25, 1824.

Isabella, born November 11, 1826. Died February 26, 1828.

Abigail, born August 26, 1828.
Edith, born November 24, 1830.
Joel S., born March 4, 1833.
Job, born May 1, 1835.
Benjamin, born July 27, 1838.

Anthony S. Heebner, son of Balthasar Heebner (page 77), married Lydia, daughter of David Krauss (page 85), May 18, 1824. Their children were:
Levi, born May 30, 1825.
Saraam, born June 18, 1830. Died December 15, 1832.
Maria, born June 7, 1833.
Anthony K., born November 7, 1835.
Lydia, wife of A. S. H., died November 9, 1840.
Anthony S. Heebner married, second time, Anna, daughter of Matthias Gerhard (page 96), January 25, 1842. No issue.
Anna, wife of A. S. H., died February 25, 1865.
A. S. H. died June 14, 1866. He lived upon and owned the farm now in possession of his son, A. K. Heebner, in Worcester.

Jacob Yeakel, son of David Yeakel (page 69), married Maria, daughter of John Krauss (page 79). One child,
Joshua, born December 26, 1825. Died July 15, 1850.
Jacob Y. died June 16, 1837, and his wife died afterwards.

David Heebner, son of Christopher Heebner (page 74), married Mary Hahn March, 1824. No issue.
Wife was born in 1795, and died March 13, 1825.
He married, second time, Sarah Rush, June 27, 1833.
Wife born October 10, 1808. Children:

John, born June 28, 1835. Died February 22, 1862.
Charles, born December 25, 1838.
David, Jr., born February 16, 1842.
Stephen, born June 24, 1844.
D. H. died May 14, 1864.

George Kriebel, son of Andrew Kriebel (page 76), married Sophia, daughter of Abraham Kriebel (page 93), May 20, 1824. Had issue:
Mary, born November 11, 1825. Died May 2, 1835.
Anna, born December 15, 1827.
Andrew, born November 22, 1829.
Aaron, born October 30, 1831. Died April 30, 1835.
Abraham, born March 11, 1834.
Susanna, born March 20, 1836.
Charles, born December 2, 1837.
Christina, born August 24, 1839.
George, } twins, born September 27, 1841.
Joseph, }
George died October 21, 1841.
Joseph died October 26, 1841.
Sarah, born December 7, 1842.
Hannah, born June 11, 1845. Died May 9, 1853.
Isaac, born May 7, 1847. Died September 4, 1850.
G. K. died September 15, 1869. He was a farmer, and resided in Towamencin Township, where his son Abraham now lives.

George Scipt, son of Abraham Scipt (page 89), married Anna, daughter of Balthasar Heebner (page 77), September, 1824. Children:
Anthony H., born October 2, 1825.

Susanna, born November 20, 1826.
Mary, born March 29, 1828.
Abraham II., born September 4, 1829.
Anna, born April 14, 1832.
Lydia, born March 5, 1835. Died March 25, 1838.
George II., born April 3, 1837.
Daughter, born August 10, 1840. Died same day.
William, born February 6, 1843.
Anna, wife of G. S., died March 29, 1848.

William Barns married Susanna, daughter of Abraham Kriebel (page 66), January 1, 1825. Children:
Lavina, born July 29, 1825.
William, born July 12, 1829.
Daniel, born October 16, 1830.
Mary, born February 19, 1833.
Andrew, born May 27, 1835.
Susanna, born January 28, 1838.
Sarah, born April 1, 1839.
Amandus, born February 28, 1842.
Benjamin, born April 13, 1844. Died January 13, 1846.
Isaac, born October 21, 1846.
William Barns lives at Menomonee Falls, Waukesha County, Wisconsin.

Anthony Krauss, son of John Krauss (page 79), married Sarah, daughter of Isaac Yeakel (page 91), May 17, 1825. Children:
Lavina, born April 25, 1832.
Isaac Y., born February 10, 1836.
Elmira Regina, born November 23, 1838.
Harrison, born July 20, 1840.
Hannah, born May 23, 1842.
Emma, born April 19, 1845.

Sarah, born February 20, 1846. Died October, 1846.

Matilda, born May 15, 1847. Died March 4, 1854.

James, born February 11, 1850.

A. K. died January 24, 1852.

Sarah, widow of A. K., died April 24, 1874.

Anthony Krauss lived in Kraussdale, about two miles northeast from Pennsburg, where he carried on the machine business quite extensively.

Isaac Heydrick, son of Balthasar (page 70), married Elizabeth Wasser July 31, 1825, and had issue:
  David, born November 11, 1826.
  William W., born November 16, 1828.
  Mary, born January 10, 1831.
  Charles, born September 20, 1832.
  James Henry, born November 29, 1835. Died November 26, 1837.
  Samuel, born April 22, 1838. Died December 20, 1843.
  George, born January 22, 1841. Died January 22, 1847.
  Anna, born July 14, 1844. Died February 12, 1876.
  E., wife of I. H., was born December 4, 1802, and died October 12, 1854.
  I. H. died November 24, 1846. He lived in Bridesburg, Philadelphia.

Jonas Reinewald, son of Melchior Reinewald (page 48), married Susanna, daughter of George Schultz (page 90), October 13, 1825. One child,
  Sarah, born September 29, 1826.

J. R. died November 9, 1829.

George Anders, son of Abraham Anders (page 95), married Susanna, daughter of Samuel Kriebel (page 94), October 27, 1825. They had issue:
  Sarah, born June 3, 1828. Died September 3, 1828.
  Elizabeth, born May 15, 1830.
  Abraham K., born October 5, 1833.
  Rosanna, born October 16, 1836. Died same day.
  Samuel K., born November 3, 1838.
  William K., born June 12, 1841.
  Daniel K., born September 19, 1846.
Susanna, wife of G. A., died May 21, 1857.
G. A. died January 23, 1876.

Jacob Anders, son of John Anders (page 91), married Lydia, daughter of Christopher Kriebel (page 67), November 3, 1825. No issue.
Lydia, wife of J. A., died November 16, 1876.

Henry Y. Schultz, son of Andrew Schultz (page 59), married Elizabeth Strunk, November 6, 1825. Children:
  Joel, born July 26, 1826.
  Susan, born April 10, 1828.
  Joseph, born April 16, 1830.
  Anna, born September 1, 1832.
  Aaron, born September 6, 1834.
  William, born October 21, 1836.
  Elizabeth, born September 7, 1838.
  Sarah, born October 13, 1840. Married William Deisher.
  Lydia, born April 2, 1843.
  Peter, born June 18, 1846.
  John, born October 27, 1848.
H. Y. S. fell from a horse, of which he died October 23, 1858.

Charles H. Heydrick, son of Dr. Christopher Heydrick (page 74), married, first, Mary Ann, daughter of James Adams, March 2, 1826, who died September 28, 1838.

He married, second time, Ann, daughter of Jesse Adams. Children:

James A., born January 28, 1827.
Harriet E., born August 1, 1828.
Christopher, born May 19, 1830.
Jesse A., born September 19, 1832.
Peter C., born September 12, 1834.
Charles William, born October 17, 1836.
Mary Ann, born June 25, 1843.
Joseph H., born July 22, 1845.
Caroline E., born September 3, 1847. Died March 18, 1862.
Thomas B., born October 13, 1851.

Charles Henry Heydrick was born at Chestnut Hill, Philadelphia, March 5, 1799. Educated at the University of Pennsylvania, removed to Venango County, Pa., in 1826, where he has ever since resided. Was elected County Auditor in 1842, appointed Deputy Surveyor for Venango County by the Surveyor-General January 22, 1845, reappointed May 29, 1845, and held the office under the latter appointment until it became elective, under the title of County Surveyor, in 1850, when he was elected for the term of three years; re-elected in 1853 and again in 1856. The Indian village of Custalogastown was located on his farm, and the remains of wigwams were visible when he first visited the place in 1819.

Joseph R. Heebner, son of Abraham Heebner (page 73),

married Susanna, daughter of Henry Letherach, March 21, 1826. Children:
　Henry L., born December 8, 1826.
　Abraham L., born September 5, 1828.
　David L., born August 25, 1830. Died August 28, 1830.
　Catharine, born December 24, 1831.
　Ann, born February 9, 1834.
　Benjamin L., born August 17, 1835.
　Joseph L., born April 7, 1837.
　William L., born January 1, 1840.
　Enoch M., born June 20, 1843.

Frederick Anders, son of John Anders (page 91), married Catharine, daughter of Balthasar Heebner (page 77), April 18, 1826. Had issue:
　John H., born December 1, 1827.
　Susanna, born August 22, 1829. Died August 13, 1856.
　William, born February 13, 1831.
　Jacob H., born March 19, 1833.
　David, born February 28, 1835.
　Nathaniel H., born October 4, 1837.
　Joseph, born March 29, 1842.

George Anders, son of George Anders (page 76), married Susanna, daughter of Andrew Kriebel (page 76), May 11, 1826. No issue.

Samuel Heydrick, son of Balthasar (page 70), married Leanna, daughter of Michael Kline. Had no issue. S. H. lived in Flourtown, Pa., and died February 1, 1850, aged 51 years, 9 months, and 21 days.

Jesse Krauss, son of David Krauss (page 85), married
Mary Sell September 17, 1826. Wife born October
15, 1807. Their children were:
    Mary, born September 26, 1827.
    Catharine, born February 3, 1829.
    David, born October 30, 1830. Died February 23, 1833.
    Nathaniel, born August 5, 1832.
    Isaac, born October 14, 1834.
    Mahlon, born June, 1836.
    Anna, born September 8, 1839.
    Elizabeth, born May 31, 1841.
    Angeline, born November 5, 1843.
    Ambrose, born October 10, 1845.
    Emma, born December 4, 1849. Died November 4, 1851.
    Adelaide, born March 7, 1851.
    Wilson, born March 29, 1855.
  J. K. died January 23, 1863.
  Mary, widow of J. K., died March 22, 187–.

Joseph Cassel, son of John Cassel, born April 28, 1805, married Rebecca, daughter of Abraham Heebner (page 73), November 9, 1826. Children:
    Mary, born September 7, 1827.
    Amos, born June 23, 1830. Died March 2, 1858.
    Sarah, born January 31, 1832.
    Henry, born May 30, 1834.
    Edith, born October 28, 1836.
    Susanna, born April 4, 1839.
    Mahlon, born April 10, 1840.
    Hannah, born July 29, 1845.
    Christian, born November 19, 1846.
    Leah, born April 21, 1850.

Jacob Kriebel, son of Jacob Kriebel (page 71), married Anna, daughter of Jacob Deisher, December 24, 1826. Wife born October 25, 1808. Children:
- Enos, born September 8, 1827.
- George, born April 26, 1829.
- Joel, born September 29, 1830.
- Maria, born July 10, 1832. Died January 1, 1854.
- Sarah, born December 19, 1835. Died June 12, 1869.
- Lydia, born January 17, 1838. Died April 20, 1841.
- Anna, born June 23, 1840.

J. K. died February 6, 1840, and his wife April 4, 1861.

Magdalena Yeakel, daughter of Jacob Yeakel (page 81), married Michael Erdman October 18, 1826. Had issue:
- Mahlon, born July 1, 1827. Died married.
- William A., born December 16, 1829. Died in 1848.
- John A., born July 20, 1832. Died September 30, 1877.
- Susanna, born March 21, 1834.
- Amanda, born September 28, 1836. Died aged 3 months.
- Rebecca, born December 10, 1837.
- Richard, born September 26, 1840.
- David R. P., born February 11, 1843.
- George M., born February 16, 1846.

M. E. died March 23, 1846, aged 44 years, 10 months, and 14 days. She lives in Nicetown, Philadelphia.

Anna Yeakel, daughter of Jacob Yeakel (page 81), married Philip Lyster and had one daughter,

Elizabeth. Married to Abraham Souder.
Anna Lyster died about twenty years ago.

Elizabeth Yeakel, daughter of Jacob Yeakel (page 81), married Abraham Wambold. They had five children. They lived in New Jersey, where Elizabeth, the wife, died about ten years ago.

John Heebner, son of Christopher Heebner (page 74), married Susannah Barndollar January 7, 1827. Had issue:
  Sarah B., born October 8, 1827.
  Ann Eliza, born March 6, 1829.
  Christopher B., born July 31, 1831.
  John, born March 10, 1833. Died July 5, 1838.
  Hannah, born December 19, 1837.
J. H. died June 8, 1850.
Susannah, his wife, was born November 30, 1801, and died May 12, 1860.

Frederick W. Schultz, son of Rev. Melchior Schultz (page 64), married Mary K., daughter of Abraham Kriebel (page 93), May 31, 1827. Children:
  Dinah K., born February 23, 1828. Died January 21, 1846.
  Adonia K., born March 25, 1830.
  Naomi K., born October 21, 1832.
  Mary K., born December 17, 1834.
  Lydia K., born January 4, 1839. Died January 28, 1846.
  Joseph K., born April 9, 1841.
  Sarah K., born April 12, 1845.
  F. W. S. died April 12, 1867. His son, Joseph K.

Schultz, now owns and occupies his place in Worcester Township.

Mary K., widow of F. W. S., died July 20, 1875.

Isaac Kriebel, son of Abraham Kriebel (page 93), married Anna, daughter of Rev. Abraham Haldeman, September 1, 1827. Children:

    Abraham H.
    Henry H.
    Moses H.
    Samuel H.
    Lavina.
    Sarah.
    Joseph H.
    Isaac H.
    Noah H.
    Elizabeth.
    1 Ann. Died in infancy.
    2 Ann.
    William H.
    Mary.

I. K. died April 20, 1876.

Anna, widow of I. K., died February 5, 1877, aged 70 years, 2 months, 8 days.

Isaac Kriebel moved to Ohio, where his descendants now live.

Israel Schultz, son of Adam Schultz (page 92), married Anna, daughter of Benjamin Anders (page 83), November 22, 1827. Children:

    Samuel, born August 27, 1828. Died October 7, 1828.
    Salome, born February 19, 1830.
    Benjamin, born August 29, 1831.

Regina, born October 13, 1833. Died January 2, 1853.
Elizabeth, born February 4, 1835.
James A., born April 25, 1836.
Jesse, born October 13, 1838. Died May 7, 1838.
Maria, born November 29, 1839.
I. S. died July 16, 1844. He lived in Worcester.
Anna, widow of I. S., died March 17, 1867.

Abraham Yeakel, son of Abraham Yeakel (page 90), married Susanna Moyer, born January 15, 1808. Children:
Noah, born September 7, 1829.
Jacob, born March 6, 1831. Died young.
John, born November 1, 1834.
Anna, born October, 1837. Died January 3, 1876.
Abraham, born November 29, 1844. Died January 30, 1872.
Margaret, born February 11, 1851. Died September 2, 1876.
A. Y. died April 17, 1866.
Susanna, widow of A. Y., died November 20, 1877.

John Metz, born June 26, 1803, married Elizabeth, daughter of Jacob Beyer (page 65), January 6, 1828. Had issue:
Catharine, born August 29, 1829.
Samuel, born March 23, 1832. Died February 26, 1847.
Eli, born December 9, 1839. Died July 18, 1856.
Elizabeth, born April 20, 1844.

Daniel Schiffert, born March 16, 1808, married Rachel, daughter of Abraham Kriebel (page 66), April 15, 1828. Had issue:

Sarah Ann, born April 5, 1829.
Tilera, born January 16, 1830.
Leanna, born November 11, 1831.
Susanna, born December 25, 1833.
Charles, born September 24, 1836.
Daniel Wayne, born October 25, 1838. Died November 28, 1865.
Son, born February 2, 1841. Died March 7, 1841.
Elwina, born April 7, 1842. Died May 12, 1843.
Mentes, Juliana, } twins, born July 18, 1844.
  Mentes died August 24, 1846.
  Juliana died September 2, 1846.
Eddie, Erwin, } twins, born March 23, 1847.
  Erwin died January 21, 1875.
This family lives in the State of Indiana.

John Master, son of Christopher Master (page 92), born in Chester County, Pa., married Susanna, daughter of Jacob Harris, April 15, 1828. Children:
  Mary, born January 16, 1829. Married Roderick R. Spencer.
  Jacob H., born March 31, 1831.
  John Q., born December 26, 1832.
  Jane, born January 16, 1835.
  Thomas W., born June 26, 1838. Married Susanna Hayward. No issue.
  Wm. Christopher, born June 10, 1841.
  Samuel Benson, born June 30, 1843.
  Levi Kerling, born August 25, 1847.
John Master resides in the State of Indiana.

GENEALOGICAL RECORD. 149

Abraham Heebner, son of Abraham Heebner (page 72), married Susanna, daughter of Henry Heebner (page 104), May 22, 1828. Had issue:
  Elias, born July 4, 1832.
  Christina, born January 9, 1834. Died November 20, 1834.
  Henry H., born February 1836.
  Anna Maria, born August 11, 1838. Died November 3, 1855.
  Sarah, born July 24, 1841.
  Deborah, born May 5, 1845. Died April 12, 1846.
  Anna, born April 28, 1847.
A. H. died October 4, 1877. He lived in Worcester Township, Montgomery County, Pa., on a farm which his son Henry H. now occupies.

Joshua K. Urffer, son of Michael Urffer (page 89), married Elizabeth, daughter of Abraham Hendricks, May 29, 1828. Wife born June 19, 1801. Children:
  Sarah, H., born July 19, 1830.
  Israel H., born September 17, 1832.
  Joel H., born January 21, 1837.
J. K. U. died May 17, 1861.

Jacob Erb, son of John Erb (page 94), married Susanna, daughter of Abraham Seipt (page 89), in 1829. Children:
  Lavina, born November 21, 1829. Died 1830.
  Mahlon, born July 30, 1832.
  Samuel, born July 17, 1835.
  Aaron, born May 14, 1839.

John Springer, son of John Springer, born March 22, 1794, married Maria, daughter of Christopher Reinewald (page 98), in 1829. One child,

Abraham R., born December 20, 1829.
J. S. died in 1866.

Christopher Wiegner, son of Abraham Wiegner (page 76), married Susanna, daughter of Andrew Schultz (page 108). Their children:
  Sophia, born September 3, 1830.
  Elizabeth, born May 31, 1833.
  Anna, born May 21, 1835.
  Abraham, born May 25, 1837.
  Samuel, born January 29, 1840.
  Sarah, born February 11, 1843.
  Susanna, born March 11, 1846. Died September 5, 1850.
C. W. died March 12, 1853. He lived in Hereford, Berks County, Pa.
Susanna, widow of C. S., died April 26, 1876.

Henry Meschter, son of George Meschter (page 81), married Judith, daughter of John Grikery, January 3, 1829. Children:
  Henrietta, born September 3, 1829.
  Joseph, born July 4, 1831.
  Ann Elizabeth, born June 12, 1833.
  Judith Susanna, born April 11, 1835.
  Sarah Ann, born November 15, 1837.
  Manoah, born August 13, 1841.
Judith, wife of H. M., was born July 4, 1799. Died March, 1877.

Samuel Engle Hartranft, son of Leonard Hartranft (page 101), married Lydia, daughter of George Bucher, of New Hanover Township, Montgomery County, Pa., in 1829. Had one child,

John Frederick, born December 16, 1830.
S. E. H. resides in Norristown, Pa.

Joseph Kriebel, son of Abraham Kriebel (page 71), married Elizabeth, daughter of Andrew Anders (page 69), May 7, 1829. Children:
Abraham, } twins, born November 25, 1830.
Andrew,
Elizabeth, wife of J. K., died.
J. K. died.

Oliver Dresher, son of Samuel Dresher (page 94), married Anna, daughter of Abraham Anders (page 95), June 5, 1829. Had issue:
Samuel, born March 7, 1830.
Theresa, born January 28, 1832. Died March 29, 1853.

Isaac Master, son of John Master (page 98), married Martha Drake December 24, 1829. Children:
Mary Elizabeth, born October 10, 1830.
James K., born May 12, 1834.
John W., born June 3, 1837.
Rachel Ann, born October 28, 1839.
William H. H., born May 6, 1841.
Martha Oliva, born March 22, 1854.

Anna Yeakel, daughter of Christian Yeakel (page 95), married John S. Moyer October 10, 1829, and had issue as follows:
Henry Y., born September 12, 1830.
Mary, born December 9, 1831.
Salome, born January 6, 1836. Died May 25, 1859.
Anna, wife of J. S. Moyer, died October 15, 1874.

Jacob Master, son of Christopher (page 92), married Juliann Kearns January 5, 1830. Children:
- Mary, born December 17, 1830. Died July 1, 1832.
- Henry, born February 9, 1832.
- Christopher, born December 21, 1833. Died March 29, 1861.
- Aaron, born November 9, 1836.
- Jacob K., born November 4, 1838.
- Ellenor, born March 8, 1841. Died January 6, 1853.
- John W., born June 26, 1843.
- Juliette, born March 1, 1846.
- Webster, born August 6, 1848. Died September 12, 1851.
- Hannah, born September 15, 1851.
- Leander, born September 5, 1856.

Jacob S. Yeakel, son of Isaac Yeakel (page 91), married Lydia, daughter of Philip Brey. Wife born January 18, 1807. Children:
- Carolina, born February 28, 1831.
- Amanda, born November 17, 1833.
- Elamina, born November 10, 1835.
- Anna Regina, born May 27, 1842.
- Franklin B., born July 1, 1849.

Lydia, wife of J. S. Y., died April 28, 1862.

J. S. Y. died May 30, 1863. He lived and died on the farm now in possession of Joseph Nash, in Springfield, Montgomery County, Pa.

Samuel Urffer, son of Michael Urffer (page 89), married Mary, daughter of Michael Weber, in 1830. Wife born June 30, 1809. Children:

Mary, born January 17, 1831. Died June 4, 1850.
Daniel, born December 5, 1833. Died March 14, 1857.
Elizabeth, born January 31, 1837. Married Joseph Beyl.
Adam, born December 29, 1839. Died December 12, 1857.
Samuel, born March 3, 1844.
Charles, born September 6, 1852.
Mary, wife of S. U., died March 14, 1857.
S. U. died July 10, 1862.

George Schultz, son of Rev. John Schultz (page 82), married Regina, daughter of David Schultz (page 64), May 11, 1830. They had issue:
Levi, born June 14, 1832. Died May 3, 1853.
Anna, born March 24, 1836.
Christian, born April 6, 1838.

Joseph Yeakel, son of Christopher Yeakel (page 110), married Susan Stahl, who was born May 5, 1830, daughter of Daniel Stahl. Had only one child, Henry, who died aged 19 years, 9 months.

John Yeakel, son of Abraham Yeakel (page 90), married Margaret, daughter of Michael Moyer, in 1830. Wife born November 4, 1808. Children:
Henry, born May 14, 1831. Died in Andersonville prison.
Elizabeth, born June 14, 1833. Died in 1835.
Catharine, born June 8, 1835.
Abraham, born December 20, 1841. Died October 27, 1875.

Mary, born October 21, 1844. Married Thomas Carson. No issue:

Sarah,
Elizabeth, } twins, born January 10, 1849.

Elizabeth died in July 1849.

George Meschter, son of Christopher Meschter (page 105), married Sophia, daughter of Andrew Kriebel (page 76), May 13, 1830. Children:

Catharine, born May 7, 1831.
Abraham, born August 31, 1833.
Maria, born April 6, 1836. Died September 29, 1836.
Jacob, born July 4, 1837.
George, born May 2, 1840.
Lydia, born June 5, 1843.
John, born June 15, 1847.
Aaron, born April 17, 1852. Died May 6, 1852.

Sophia, wife of G. M., died April 24, 1852.

This is the Rev. George Meschter, a minister of the Society of Schwenkfelders, and lives in Lower Salford, near the village of Mainland.

Jacob Krauss, son of George Krauss (page 102), married Lydia, daughter of Samuel Kriebel (page 94), September 26, 1830. They had issue:

Amos, born March 21, 1833.
Amanda, born June 19, 1834.
Selina, born June 1, 1837.
Samuel, born August 23, 1839.
Jacob, born February 1, 1842. Died.
Catharine, born March 21, 1844.
Mary, born October 23, 1846.

Jacob Krauss lives in Upper Milford Township, Lehigh County, Pa.

John Master, son of Isaac Master (page 107), married Nancy Stauffer October 30, 1830. Wife born August 4, 1811. Children:
  Sallie Ann, born February 6, 1833.
  Isaac, born March 19, 1835.
  Mary, born March 12, 1837.
  Hannah, born June 4, 1839.
  Levi, born February 8, 1841.
  Harriet, born March 14, 1843.
Nancy, wife of J. M., died May 13, 1843.
John Master married, second time, Catharine Reichard, April 30, 1844. Wife born May 15, 1811.

Jacob Yeakel, son of Christian Yeakel (page 95), married Catharine, daughter of Jacob Kratz, and their children are:
  Samuel K., born March 25, 1832.
  Mary, born September 18, 1839.
  John K., born March 28, 1843. Married Arimenta Van Gilder.
  Catharine, born July 27, 1847.
Jacob Yeakel died May 5, 1864.

John Reed, born March 3, 1804, son of Philip Reed, married Hannah, daughter of David Urffer (page 109), December 11, 1830. Had issue:
  Floranda M., born May 3, 1832.
  Servatius W., born December 19, 1834.
  Wellington J., born March 28, 1836.
Hannah, wife of J. R., died May 8, 1866.

Solomon Gerhard, son of Jacob Gerhard (page 81), married Catharine Ragers February 10, 1831. Wife born June 5, 1811. Their children were:

Benjamin F., born December 16, 1831. Died July 6, 1851.
Joseph, born June 21, 1833. Died July 6, 1833.
Thomas R., born November 19, 1837.
Jacob R., born March 26, 1841.
Samuel, born August 7, 1843.
Resides in Camden, N. J.

Jonathan Schultz, son of Samuel Schultz (page 101), married Sarah, daughter of George Krauss (page 102), April 3, 1831. Had children:
Sarah, born January 3, 1840. Married Michael Housekeeper.
Jonathan, born February 3, 1842.
David, born April, 1843. Died 8 days old.
J. S. lives in Dudley, Berks County, and some of his descendants in Venango County, Pa., and others in Ohio.

Ann Heebner, daughter of Christopher Heebner (page 74), married Peter Griffith April 5, 1832. He was born December 12, 1805. Children:
Amanda, born July 3, 1833.
Myra B., born July 7, 1834.
Worthington, born July 3, 1836.
Elizabeth, born September 11, 1838.
Elbridge, born February 24, 1841.
Susanna, born July 20, 1843.
Mansfield, born November 7, 1845.

Joel Wolf, born May 25, 1810, son of Jacob Wolf, married Elizabeth, daughter of George Krauss (page 102). Their children were:
David K. Died August, 1832.
Emeline K., born March 30, 1837.

Henry W. K., born April 1, 1839.
Christina M. K., born September 23, 1840. Died May 10, 1864.
Susanna K., born November 9, 1841. Died June 3, 1863.
George K., born 1843. Died August 7, 1844.
Caroline K., born February 17, 1845.
Mary Elizabeth K., born September 15, 1846. Died January 12, 1868.
Leanna K., born March 12, 1848.
Edwin K., born July 5, 1849.
Sarah J. K., born December 26, 1850.
Oswin K., born April 8, 1852. Died in 1852.
Joel K., born October 30, 1853.
Jonathan K., born March 4, 1855.
Daniel K., born March 21, 1857.
Horace K., born January 16, 1860.
Edwin. K., born May 14, 1861.

Benjamin Beyer, son of Andrew Beyer (page 104), married Hannah Cassel. Children:
Susanna, born June 5, 1832. Died June 19, 1852.
Catharine, born September 15, 1834.
Enos, born April 12, 1836.
Elizabeth, born September 5, 1839. Died January 17, 1840.
Nathaniel, born February 8, 1841.
Benjamin, born December 8, 1846. Died April 18, 1848.
Lewis, born December 12, 1849.
Amanda, born September 16, 1853.
Samuel, born March 22, 1858. Died August 18, 1858.
Reuben, born March 4, 1860.

Jeremiah Anders, son of John Anders (page 91), married Catharine, daughter of Abraham Kriebel (page 93), April 26, 1832. Children:
  Anna, born May 5, 1833. Died May 3, 1835.
  Lydia, born March 26, 1836.
  Abraham, born May 24, 1838. Died May 7, 1848.
  Sophia, born August 29, 1840.
  John, born May 15, 1843.
  Sarah, born March 1, 1846. Died April 19, 1848.
  Aaron, born December 18, 1848. Died October 15, 1867.
  Jeremiah K., born September 11, 1852.

Samuel Yeakel, son of David Yeakel (page 97), married Sophia, daughter of Rev. John Schultz (page 82), April 19, 1831. No issue.
S. Y. died March 3, 1871.

Henry H. Schultz, son of Rev. John Schultz (page 82), married Susanna, daughter of Andrew Schultz (page 102), April 21, 1831. They had issue:
  Joel, born May 12, 1832.
  Sophia, born November 24, 1833. Died October 10, 1862.
  Enos, born February 23, 1838.
  Christina, born March 27, 1840. Died October 18, 1862.
  Caroline, born February 6, 1842.
  William, born January 3, 1845.
  Samuel, born January 2, 1847.
  Ezra, born December 18, 1849.

Isaac S. Kriebel, son of Isaac Kriebel (page 100), married Christina, daughter of William Schultz (page 113), May 5, 1831. Children:

William, born June, 8, 1832.
Son, born October 10, 1833. Died October 12, 1833.
Carolina, born September 28, 1834. Died October 24, 1851.
Phœbe, born January 20, 1837.
Noah, born December 4, 1838. Died August 16, 1839.
Sarah, born September 24, 1840.
Jesse, born October 11, 1842.
Daniel, born December 2, 1845.
Enos, born February 1, 1847. Died February 12, 1847.
Amanda, born May 20, 1850.
Selina, born May 30, 1853.
Son, born November 15, 1856. Stillborn.

I. S. K. is a farmer and lives in Worcester Township.

Daniel Seibert, son of Jacob Seibert (page 63), married Charlotte, daughter of Isaac Yeakle (page 71), May 31, 1831. No issue.

Charlotte, wife of D. S., died May 4, 1832.

Daniel Seibert married, second time, Elizabeth, daughter of John Wagner, April 29, 1838. Children:
William, born October 2, 1839. Died July 31, 1855.
Daniel, born December 15, 1841.
Jonathan, born February 21, 1844.
Anna, born February 11, 1846.
Susanna, born December 27, 1847.
Willoughby, born May 31, 1851.

Job Snyder, son of Henry Snyder (page 68), married Susanna, daughter of Abraham Wiegner (page 76), in 1831. They had issue:

Henry, born December 6, 1831.
Edith, born November 11, 1833. Died.
Sophia, born September 2, 1836.
Joseph, born July 14, 1839.
Elizabeth, born November 22, 1841. Died August 9, 1843.
Susanna, born June 24, 1844.
Maria, born October 13, 1846. Died April 22, 1852.
Charles, born May 8, 1849.
J. S. died November 14, 1871.

Joseph Kriebel, son of Jeremiah Kriebel (page 62), married Elizabeth, daughter of George Heydrick (page 87), in 1831. Their children were:
Samuel, born February 5, 1832. Died July 26, 1844.
Abraham, born August 22, 1833.
Charles, born February 17, 1835. Died.
George, born October 23, 1836. Died February 16, 1840.
John, born May 31, 1839. Died February, 1840.
Elizabeth, wife of J. K., died April 18, 1840.
Joseph Kriebel married, second time, Lydia, daughter of George Heydrick (page 87), in 1842. Children:
Joseph, born December, 24, 1842.
Daniel, born April 3, 1854.
J. K. died November 10, 1853.
Lydia, widow of J. K., married, second time, Joseph Smith. Had one child,
Josiah.
L. S. died in 1860.

Isaac B. Cassel, born October 25, 1809, married Mary, daughter of Abraham Heebner (page 73), October 20, 1831. Their children were:
  Abraham II., born January 30, 1833.
  Joseph, born October 24, 1835.
  Jesse, born January 7, 1838. Died January 26, 1871.
  Rebecca, born March 29, 1840.
  Catharine, born March 5, 1843.
  Samuel, born November 30, 1846.

John Nase, son of Dewalt Nase, born January 23, 1807, married Barbara, daughter of Christian Yeakel (page 95), January 15, 1832. Their issue:
  Samuel, born January 18, 1833.
  James, born November 14, 1834. Died in April, 1862.
  Ann, born August 8, 1836. Died October 11, 1874.
  Mary, born February 19, 1839.
  Leanna, born September 12, 1841. Died in December, 1862.
  Aaron, born August 29, 1844.
  Elizabeth, born February 21, 1849.
J. N. died some years ago.

Jacob Yeakel, son of Abraham Yeakel (page 90), married Catharine, daughter of William Meyer, January 22, 1832. Wife born October 2, 1811. Their children:
  Mary Ann, born January 21, 1833.
  Sarah, born September 5, 1834. Died July 14, 1872.
  Amanda, born October 18, 1836. Died October 4, 1864.

Susannah, born April 25, 1839.
William, born October 24, 1841.
Catharine, born February 10, 1844.
Sophia, born January 25, 1846. Died September 3, 1865.
Jacob, born February 25, 1848.
Elizabeth, born September 23, 1850. Died November 27, 1869.
Oliver, born January 13, 1853. Died January 14, 1853.
Anna, born October 9, 1858. Died October 9, 1859.
J. Y. died June 29, 1863.

Abraham Kriebel, son of Andrew Kriebel (page 76), married Anna, daughter of John Bergey, April, 1832. They had issue:
Mary, born October 27, 1835.
Lydia, born November 6, 1837.
Catharine, born October 5, 1839. Died.
John B., born December 18, 1841.
Andrew, born April 11, 1844.
Hannah, } twins, born September 3, 1846.
Susanna, }
Sophia B., born August 12, 1849.
Aaron B., born December 29, 1851.
Abraham B., born November 13, 1859. Died April 9, 1868.

A. K. lives in Worcester Township, and is a farmer by occupation.

Samuel Kriebel, son of Benjamin Kriebel (page 103), married Abigail, daughter of Christopher Kriebel (page 67), April, 1832. Their children:

Jacob, born April 29, 1833. Died.
Jonathan. Died April 22, 1837.
Sophia, born December 23, 1835. Died April 29, 1837.
Oliver, born August 2, 1839. Died February 7, 1841.
Isaac, born February 9, 1841.

Charles Schultz, son of Samuel Schultz (page 101), married Hannah, daughter of Jacob Gerhard (page 81), April 23, 1832. Children:
Lydia, born April 29, 1838.
Samuel, born September 16, 1836.
Jacob, born December 8, 1837. Died September 26, 1838.
Helena, born November 5, 1839.
Susanna, born May 29, 1841. Died September 6, 1841.

David S. Heebner, son of Rev. Balthasar Heebner (page 77), married Anna, daughter of —— Derstein, May 3, 1832. They had issue:
Joseph, born June 11, 1833. Died April 3, 1838.
James, born August 6, 1836. Died April 8, 1838.
Mary Ann, born April 2, 1839.
Isaac, born January 18, 1841.
Addison, born June 18, 1843. Died August 23, 1843.
Josiah, born July 5, 1844.
Jacob, born August 10, 1846.
William, born September 27, 1848.
David, born August 22, 1851. Died June 15, 1852.
Anna, wife of D. S. H., died June 18, 1853.
David S. Heebner married, second time, Regina, daughter of Rev. Christopher Schultz (page 99), in 1852. Child,

Abram S., born May 22, 1857. Died October 6, 1862.

D. S. H. resides at Lansdale, and is the senior member of the firm of D. S. Heebner & Sons, machinists, of that place.

Samuel Schultz, son of Andrew Schultz (page 102), married Abigail, daughter of Christopher Yeakel (page 110), November 15, 1832. Children:
  Reuben, born January 3, 1835.
  George, born December 9, 1839.
  Lydia, born February 25, 1843.
  Joseph Y., born February 15, 1850.
Samuel Schultz died. His wife died May 13, 1879.

George Kriebel, son of Abraham Kriebel (page 71), married Deborah, daughter of Abraham Heebner (page 72), October 18, 1832. No issue.

G. K. died February 27, 1877.

Charles E. Boyer, born in Philadelphia, Pa., January 25, 1829, married Anna H., daughter of George Seipt (page 137), October 27, 1853. Children:
  George S., born August 5, 1854. Married Mary Ann Reigel.
  Samuel S., born March 30, 1856.
  Susanna S., born February 25, 1859.
  Charles S., born March 11, 1861. Died July 31, 1864.
  Isaiah S., born July 27, 1862. Died August 4, 1864.
  Erwin S., born January 7, 1865.
  Mary Ann, born November 22, 1867.
  Ida Jane, born January 23, 1870.
  Franklin, born January 17, 1872.

Ella Irene, born December 24, 1874.

C. E. Boyer moved, about 1866, from Montgomery County, Pa., to Kankakee County, Ill., where he now resides.

Isaac Snyder, son of Henry Snyder (page 68), married Christina Henning November 6, 1832. Wife born October 12, 1811. Children:
    Elizabeth, born January 25, 1834.
    Henry, born July 2, 1835. Died February 23, 1849.
    Dinah, born April 18, 1838.
    Isaac, born September 26, 1840.
Isaac Snyder, Sr., died July 6, 1840.

Abraham Wiegner, son of Abraham Wiegner (page 76), married Magdalena, daughter of Jacob Cassel, November 6, 1832. Issue:
    Mary, born July 26, 1833.
    Joseph, born October 7, 1837.
    Elizabeth, born February 23, 1842.
    Susanna, born June 7, 1846. Died August 22, 1847.
    Abraham, born July 22, 1850.
    Magdalene, born May 7, 1853.

Joshua Heebner,* son of Christopher Heebner (page 74), married Eliza Williams December 13, 1832, and had issue:
    Child, born October 6, 1833. Died.
    Susanna, born January 5, 1835. Died February 20, 1835.
    William, born February 18, 1836. Married Catharine Rumford.

---

* By reference to his father's record it will be seen that the name of Joshua is omitted.

Myra, born January 19, 1838. Died December 23, 1848.

Thaddeus S., born November 22, 1839. Married Ellen D. Jones.

Catharine, born June 1, 1841. Married Thomas U. Francis.

Uriah, born April 25, 1843. Married Catharine Custer.

Eliza Ann, born December 15, 1844.

Joshua, Jr., born August 1, 1846.

Margaret, born January 16, 1849. Married John Weikle.

John, born May 1, 1850. Died January 6, 1857.

Myra, born March 21, 1852.

Christopher, born July 17, 1853.

Richard, born April 2, 1856. Died July 29, 1856.

Eliza, wife of Joshua Heebner, was born March 10, 1813; and died October 16, 1869.

John Yeakel, son of Isaac Yeakel (page 91), married Amy, daughter of Israel Mitchner, December 18, 1832. Wife born March 11, 1808. Children:

Isaac, born November 26, 1833. Died June, 1834.

William M., born December 25, 1834.

Marietta, born December 31, 1836. Died October 9, 1856.

Josephus, born April 19, 1839.

J. Y. died April 26, 1846.

Joseph Kriebel, son of Abraham Kriebel (page 93), married Catharine, daughter of John Anders (page 91), April 11, 1833. Children:

John, born February 8, 1834. Died April 28, 1835.

Abraham, born September 28, 1835.
Maria, born February 21, 1840. Died November 16, 1851.
Regina, born November 21, 1842.

J. K. is a farmer, and lives in Worcester.

Joel Wiegner, son of John Wiegner (page 80), married Sarah, daughter of Henry Heebner (page 104), in 1833. Children:
Anna, born September 3, 1834.
Lydia, born July 26, 1837. Died May 25, 1865.
Abigail, born November 1, 1842. Died March 16, 1868.

J. W. died March 13, 1857.

Joseph Wiegner, son of Abraham Wiegner (page 76), married Agnes, daughter of Christopher Dresher (page 89), in 1833. Children:
Abraham, born January 9, 1837. Died.
Eli D., born March 23, 1843.
Joseph, born July 5, 1846.
Rebecca Ann.

Agnes, wife of J. W., died November 19, 1868.
J. W. died August 22, 1873. He lived in Dreshertown, Upper Dublin Township, and owned the farm now in possession of his son, Eli D. Wiegner.

Daniel Wiegner, son of John Wiegner (page 80), married Margaret, daughter of Joseph Snyder (page 112), April 8, 1833. One child,
Maria, born February 27, 1844. Died July 16, 1850.

D. W. died December 11, 1866.

Amos Schultz, son of Isaac Schultz (page 100), married Elizabeth, daughter of Samuel Kriebel (page 94), April 16, 1833. Had issue:
Sarah, born August 25, 1836.
Susanna, born September 4, 1838.
Joseph K., born November 20, 1840.
Amanda K., born April 5, 1843. Died November 14, 1862.
Lucina K., born November 10, 1845.
Edwin K., born August 1, 1848.
Owen K., born March 23, 1851.
Elizabeth K., born May 4, 1853.

Amos Schultz resides in Washington Township, Berks County, and is a farmer by occupation.

Augustus Yeakle, son of Isaac Yeakle (page 71), married Ellenora, daughter of Jacob Schultz (page 86), May 14, 1833. They had issue:
Matilda, born December 12, 1834.
Thomas, born May 2, 1836.
Lydia, born August 19, 1838.
Isaac S., born May 13, 1841.
Jacob S., born April 15, 1846.

A. Y. died May 2, 1876. He lived in Upper Hanover.

Ellenora, widow of A. Y., died January 13, 1878.

Susanna Krauss, daughter of Andrew Krauss (page 84), married Charles W. Wiand, born March 3, 1809, son of David Wiand, May 16, 1833. Children:
Maria, born March 27, 1834.
David A., born October 6, 1842. Died July 26, 1846.
Sarah, born December 30, 1844.

Charles S., born February 28, 1848.

Susanna, born August 7, 1850.

Laura Elizabeth, born February 17, 1857. Died June 23, 1859.

Susanna, wife of C. W. W., died July 20, 1877. By some error her name is omitted in her father's record.

John Anders, son of John Anders (page 91), married Lydia, daughter of Andrew Schultz (page 108), October, 1833. Their children were:

Edith, born October 18, 1834. Died May 10, 1835.

Elizabeth, born June 17, 1835.

Judia, born May 19, 1837. Died September 26, 1853.

Catharina, born July 23, 1839.

Sophia, born October 12, 1841.

Magdalena, born September 3, 1845.

Mary Ann, born August 8, 1847.

Matilda, born December 25, 1850.

J. A. died May 2, 1855.

Lydia, widow of J. A., died May 1, 1874.

Christopher Heebner, son of Christopher Heebner (page 74), married Ann Mitchell November 7, 1833. Wife born October 20, 1813. Children:

Elizabeth, born July 21, 1834.

George, born May 14, 1836.

Martha, born April 11, 1838.

Edward, born November 19, 1839.

James B., born December 10, 1841.

Henry, born March 1, 1844. Died August 5, 1844.

C. H. is engaged in the milling business, and lives in Norristown, Pa.

Samuel Krauss, son of Andrew Krauss (page 84), married Barbara, daughter of Michael Urffer (page 89), February 8, 1834. Their children were:
  Anna, born November 2, 1835.
  Andrew, born March 10, 1838. Died May 10, 1868.
  Mendon, born November 14, 1840.
Barbara, wife of S. K., died February 7, 1841.
Samuel Krauss married, second time, Catharine Ann, daughter of Abraham Gerhard, September 17, 1842. Wife born November 29, 1821. Children:
  Matilda, born September 6, 1843.
  Hannah, born November 8, 1844.
  Charles, born September 4, 1846.
  Dianna, born August 8, 1848. Died March 24, 1860.
  Samuel, born April 8, 1850.
  Abraham, born October 2, 1854. Died August 6, 1855.

Charles Huber married Susanna, daughter of George Heydrick (page 87). Had one child,
  Catharine Ann, born May 1, 1835.
Susanna, wife of C. H., died November 28, 1836.
C. H. died some time afterward.

Benjamin Yeakel, son of Jeremiah Yeakel (page 103), married Elizabeth Brenner May 12, 1834. Had issue:
  Solomon B., born January 3, 1836.
  Lydia E., born January 17, 1839.
  Susanna M., born July 5, 1841.
  Daniel B., born May 19, 1844. Died June 3, 1844.
  Joseph B., born March 7, 1845.
  Simon H., born October 24, 1848.

B. Y. died January 12, 1871, in Allentown, Pa.
Elizabeth, widow of B. Y., died January 20, 1875.

Charles Gerhard, son of Matthias Gerhard (page 96), married Sarah, daughter of Rev. Christopher Schultz (page 99), May 20, 1834. Had issue:
  Helena, born February 8, 1836.
  Hannah, born March 2, 1838.
  Sarah, born July 9, 1840.
  Isaac, born November 6, 1842.
  Susanna, born October 1, 1848. Died February 4, 1875.
  Thomas, born February 8, 1852.

Jacob Kile, son of Isaac Kile, married Anna, daughter of Abraham Yeakel (page 90), August, 1834. Children:
  Mary, born July 12, 1835.
  John, born April 9, 1838.
  Sophia, born June 10, 1842.
  Anna, wife of J. K., died.

George N. Heydrick, son of Abraham Heydrick (page 97), married Ann, daughter of John Huston, December 9, 1834. She was born March 6, 1815. Their children were:
  Emily D., born November 29, 1835.
  Harriet A., born June 20, 1838.
  William H. H., born July 5, 1840.
  Loretta Susanna, born August 10, 1843.
  Anna Clara, born April 20, 1845. Died April 2, 1846.
  John Abraham, born September 27, 1848. Died October, 1856.

Joseph Yeakle, son of Jacob Yeakle (page 106), married, first, Elizabeth, daughter of John Huston. Wife born April 1, 1813. They had issue:

    Huston, born December 13, 1835. Died November 12, 1840.
    James, born December 8, 1837. Died April 7, 1843.
    Emily, born October 15, 1839.
    Elenora, born April 29, 1842. Died May 15, 1843.
    Daniel W., born November 24, 1844.
    Jacob, born January 25, 1847.
    Elvie, born September 5, 1850.
    John H., born August 12, 1853. Died March 7, 1854.
    Thomas C., born January 19, 1855.

Elizabeth, first wife of J. Y., died June 18, 1852, and his second wife, Mary Huston, born February 19, 1817, died February 14, 1877.

George Yeakle, son of John Yeakle (page 86), married Mary, daughter of George Caldovy, 1835. One child:

    Sarah Ann, born March 1, 1840.

Abraham Schultz, son of Samuel Schultz (page 101), married Lydia, daughter of John Krauss (page 79), 1835. No issue:

Lydia, wife of A. S., died in the spring of 1862.

Abraham Schultz married, second time, Mary Livingstone, March 12, 1863.

Joshua Schultz, son of David Schultz (page 105), married Anna, daughter of Andrew Schultz (page 102), February 24, 1835. Had issue:

    Susanna, born March 10, 1842.

Mary, born June 16, 1845.
Manoah, born November 23, 1847.
Josiah, born April 8, 1850. Died May 15, 1851.
Samuel S., born April 16, 1852.
Anna, wife of Rev. J. S., died September 24, 1871.
Joshua Schultz is a minister of the Society of Schwenkfelders, and lives in Hereford, Bucks County, Pa.

Anthony Anders, son of George Anders (page 76), married Hannah, daughter of Joseph Snyder (page 112), 1835. Their children were:
George, born March 23, 1836. Died July 9, 1840.
Judia, born June 23, 1840.
George, born January 24, 1843.
Joseph, born April 27, 1846.
Anthony, born October 15, 1849. Died August 24, 1850.

David Anders, son of John Anders (page 91), married Maria, daughter of Andrew Schultz (page 102), February, 1835. Children:
Susanna, born February 14, 1836. Died March 10, 1836.
Rachel, born March, 1837.
Anna, born November 29, 1839. Died June 26, 1872.
John, born February 28, 1842.
George, born May 14, 1845. Died October 31, 1848.
Edith, born May 14, 1845.
Mary, born September 9, 1850.
Christina, born November 3, 1854.
Maria, wife of D. A., died October 20, 1872.

Aaron Krauss, son of David Krauss (page 85), married
Lydia, daughter of Balthasar Heebner (page 77), May
7, 1835. Their children were:
  Joel, born March 23, 1836.
  Sarah, born December 6, 1837. Died January 10,
    1861.
  David, born March 10, 1841. Married Emma
    Kneedler.
  Susanna, born May 2, 1843.
  Isaac, born August 3, 1845. Died April 4, 1848.
  Amanda, born November 23, 1847.
  William, born February 12, 1850.
  Anna, born July 8, 1852.
A. K. is a farmer, and resides in Worcester, Montgomery County, Pa.

Caleb Heydrick, son of Abraham Heydrick (page 97),
married Sarah Faust May 16, 1835. Children:
  Matilda A., born August 29, 1836.
  Mary C., born February 23, 1848. Died May 13,
    1854.
Sarah, wife of C. H., died March 19, 1854.

Samuel S. Yeakel, son of Christian Yeakel (page 95),
married Anna, daughter of Abraham Moyer, December 13, 1835. She was born September 10, 1810.
Had issue:
  Henry, born September 17, 1836.
  Elizabeth, born August 29, 1838. Died 1864.
  Mary, born December 2, 1840.
  Anna, born March 23, 1843.
  Abraham, born April 3, 1846.
  Sarah, born March 22, 1848.
  Hannah, born August 12, 1851.

S. S. Y. resides in the village of Perkasie, in Bucks County, Pa.

Henry Krauss, son of George Krauss (page 102), married Christina, daughter of Rev. John Schultz (page 82), November 8, 1835. They had issue:
    Solomon, born February 17, 1837.
    Abraham, born January 2, 1838.
    George, born September 22, 1839.
    Sophia, born January 15, 1841.
    Regina, born November 14, 1842.
    Christina, born December 30, 1844.
    Henry S., born October, 12, 1846.
    John Mahlon, born September 29, 1848.
    Rebecca, born August 21, 1851.
    Susanna, born February 9, 1853.
    Leanna, born December 24, 1854. Died March 18, 1858.
    Priscilla, born May 21, 1857.
    Attilla, born March 8, 1859. Died September 24, 1860.

George S. Krauss, son of Andrew Krauss (page 84), married Elizabeth Bechtel October 13, 1836. Wife born December 8, 1816. Their children were:
    Edwin B., born March 1, 1838.
    Allen B., born March 1, 1840. Died February 18, 1859.
    Susan B., born January 16, 1846.

Jacob B. Beyer, son of Joseph Beyer (page 114), married Elizabeth Cassel October 20, 1836. Had issue:
    Hannah, born September 10, 1837.
    Isaac, born January 25, 1840.

Sarah, born November 27, 1845. Died March 23, 1862.

Elizabeth, wife of J. B., born April 4, 1814.

Jesse Snyder, son of Joseph Snyder (page 112), married Maria, daughter of Henry Heebner (page 104), November 17, 1836. Had issue:

    Hannah, born October 20, 1837. Died November 19, 1839.

    Margaret, born November 8, 1838. Died November 2, 1839.

    Lydia, born October 16, 1840.

    John, born January 3, 1843.

    Elias, born August 24, 1845.

    Susanna, born November 22, 1847. Died December 29, 1874.

    Aaron, born October 29, 1850.

    Elizabeth, born March 11, 1853.

    Mary, born January 4, 1856.

    Jesse, born February 2, 1859.

    Sarah, born March 4, 1862. Died September 10, 1863.

Jesse Snyder lives in Towamencin, and is a farmer by occupation.

Eli Krupp, born in Montgomery County, Pa., married Sarah, daughter of Dr. Humphrey White (page 120), and had issue as follows:

    Sarah Ann, born August 17, 1837. Married Henry Krips, now deceased. Her children are Annie and Henry.

    Milton, born August 1, 1840. Married. No issue.

    Susannah, born July 18, 1842. Married J. M. Kirby.

    Elizabeth, born January 17, 1845. Married Wm.

II. Neely. Left two children, Joseph L. and Jamie. She died March 20, 1878.

Mary, born October 22, 1847. Married J. L. Keebler.

Charles, born August 30, 1850. Died October 9, 1850.

Caroline, born March 26, 1853. Married John J. White.

Franklin, born April 15, 1856.

Eli Krupp resides in Philadelphia, has been quite successful in business, and was at one time a member of the Common Council of the city.

Jacob Schultz, son of Samuel Schultz (page 101), married Rebecca Eberhard December 22, 1836. No issue.

Amos Corson, son of Benjamin Corson, married Mary Ann, daughter of Abraham Heydrick (page 97), February 9, 1837. One child,

Sarah J., born January 19, 1838.

Amos Corson was a farmer by occupation, and lived in Springfield on the property owned by his father-in-law until a few years previous to his death, when he purchased the farm adjoining the Union Church in Whitemarsh, and died there April 9, 1876.

Samuel Yeakel, son of Isaac Yeakel (page 91), married Maria, daughter of George Rex. Children:

Isaac, born June 26, 1838. Died January, 1857.

George R., born July 25, 1840. Died March 3, 1846.

Emily, born November 18, 1842. Died April 3, 1850.

Amanda, born February 3, 1845. Died March 8, 1846.

S. Y. died July 23, 1866, and his widow afterwards married Charles Heydrick, son of Abraham.

Peter Stroh, born August 26, 1802, son of Peter Stroh, married Sophia, daughter of Melchior Schubert (page 56), in 1837. One child,
Charles, born November 25, 1838.
Sophia, wife of P. S., died May 28, 1875.

George Heebner, son of Henry Heebner (page 104), married Anna, daughter of Andrew Schultz (page 102), April 4, 1837. No issue.
Anna, wife of G. H., died April 22, 1838.
George Heebner married, second time, Mary Krupp, July 16, 1843. Their children were:
Noah. Died December 20, 1846.
George, born August 11, 1846. Died October 22, 1846.
G. H. died October 27, 1846.

Myra Heebner, daughter of Christopher Heebner (page 74), married P. P. Bodley April 6, 1837. Children:
Mary, born January 18, 1838. Died December 30, 1839.
Ann, born April 21, 1847. Died November 16, 1852.
Charles, born September 28, 1853.
P. P. Bodley was born June 20, 1810, and died February 14, 1875.

Susanna Heebner, daughter of Christopher (page 74), married Abraham Masson April 9, 1837.
A. M. died November 3, 1869.

John Wiegner, son of John Wiegner (page 80), married
Maria, daughter of John Anders (page 91), April 11,
1837. Children:
  Jacob, born November 15, 1838.
  Abraham, born December 16, 1839. Died December 16, 1871.
  George, born April 3, 1845.
  Catharine, born November 27, 1847. Died June 6, 1848.
  Catharine, born February 27, 1849.
  John, Daniel, } twins, born November 24, 1851.
  John died March 17, 1856.
  Daniel died January 4, 1852.
  J. W. died February 27, 1865.
  Maria, widow of John Wiegner, died October 24, 1869.

Samuel B. Beyer, son of Andrew Beyer (page 104), married Harriet Gouldy April 16, 1837. Wife born October 19, 1814. Their children were:
  Charles W., born January 20, 1838.
  Josephus, born March 16, 1843.
  James M., born January 4, 1848.
  Eugenia E., born July 7, 1850.

Samuel Schultz, son of William Schultz (page 113), married Susanna, daughter of Abraham Anders (page 95), April 20, 1837. Had issue:
  William A., born February 15, 1838.
  Sarah, born April 9, 1840. Died July 19, 1844.
  Susanna, born December 1, 1843.
  Amanda, born July 25, 1846.
  Samuel A., born February 2, 1849.

S. S. lives in Worcester, near Centre Point, and is a farmer by occupation.

Thomas L. Bates, born April 24, 1809, married Leah, daughter of Jacob Yeakle (page 106), April 20, 1837. Had issue:
    Gertrude, born May 13, 1838.
    Jacob Y., born May 17, 1842.
    Leah Eliza, born September 13, 1844.
    Ella A., born September 26, 1847.
    Horace Y., born January 25, 1851. Died February 17, 1855.
    Laura, born March 4, 1857.
    Mary Ida, born March 9, 1860.
T. L. Bates resides on Chestnut Hill, Philadelphia, near the depot.

Joseph Schultz, son of Rev. Christopher Schultz (page 99), married Susanna, daughter of Matthias Gerhard (page 96), June 5, 1837. Their children were:
    Regina G., born September 20, 1840.
    Susanna G., born February 19, 1843. Died April 4, 1845.
    Rebecca G., born June 29, 1845.
    Cornelius G., born December 16, 1847.
    Harriet G., born September 1, 1849.
Susanna, wife of J. S., died November 14, 1855.
J. S. died May 17, 1874.

William Beyer, son of Joseph Beyer (page 114), married Elizabeth Cassel November 5, 1837. Wife born May 19, 1812. Children:
    Mary, born September 10, 1838. Died February 26, 1843.
    Susanna, born July 8, 1841.

Catharine, born February 4, 1843.
Elizabeth, born May 17, 1849.
Rebecca, born April 20, 1856. Died June 5, 1865.
Elizabeth, wife of W. B., died January 5, 1859.

Charles Schultz, son of Matthias Schultz (page 96), married Maria, daughter of John George Reichenbach, October 1, 1837. Wife born January 3, 1802. Children:
    Lydia, born May 25, 1838. Died May 25, 1845.
    Christina, born May 8, 1840.
    Edwin, born October 30, 1843. Died March 9, 1845.
    C. S. died March 14, 1870.

Jacob Yeakel, son of Rev. Andrew Yeakel (page 114), married Catharine, daughter of Daniel Wiand, December 23, 1837. Wife born October 4, 1820. Their children were:
    Jonas, born May 20, 1839. Died 7 years old.
    Sarah, born July 5, 1841.
    Daniel, born February 28, 1843.
    Isaac W., born February 20, 1848.
    Irwin C., born March 4, 1852.
    Julian, born March 2, 1855.
J. Y. lived in Schuylkill County, Pa., and died there August 13, 1874.

Joel Krauss, son of Andrew Krauss (page 84), married Emeline, daughter of Isaac Yeakel (page 91). Their children were:
    Florence Aletha, born May 3, 1839. Died June 5, 1842.
    George. Died young.
J. K. died September 27, 1852.
Emeline, his widow, married Jacob Boas, of Harrisburg, and died November 29, 1872.

Samuel Hagy married Mary, daughter of Isaac Yeakel (page 91), January 23, 1838. Children:
- Kate F., born August 23, 1843.
- John F., born August 28, 1846.
- Emma C., born April 22, 1850.
- Bushrod W., born March 20, 1852.
- Mary Flora, born November 10, 1854.

S. H. resides in Roxborough, Philadelphia, Pa.

George R. Detwiler married Anna, daughter of Andrew Beyer (page 104), January 28, 1838. Children:
- Andrew B., born January 11, 1839.
- Daniel B., born March 5, 1841. Died July 2, 1876.
- Joseph B., born May 7, 1843.
- Benjamin B., born April 7, 1845. Died December, 1851.
- John B., born May 9, 1848.
- Catharine B., born September 27, 1850.
- George B., born December 27, 1852.
- Anna B., born March 20, 1855.
- Jacob B., born July 3, 1858.

George Snyder, son of Christian Snyder (page 72), married Sarah, daughter of Christian Sauder, February 11, 1838. Their children were:
- David, born March 19, 1839. Died September, 1839.
- Mary, born September 16, 1840. Married Caleb Fox.
- Noah, born March 14, 1843.
- Abraham, born December 4, 1845.
- Amanda, born January 27, 1849. Died March 15, 1876.
- Elizabeth, born September 4, 1851.

Joseph Krauss, a native of Germany, married Susanna, widow of Jonas Reinewald (page 139), and daughter of George Schultz (page 90), March 27, 1838. Children :
  Jonas, born September 7, 1839.
  Christina, born February 3, 1841.
  Susanna, born April 19, 1844.
J. K. died.
Susanna, his widow, died August 11, 1876.

Jesse Sheppard, born September 30, 1814, son of Thomas Sheppard, married Harriet, daughter of Henry W. Schultz (page 119), April 5, 1838. Had issue:
  Sarah A., born December 24, 1838.
  Anna Eliza, born August 23, 1842.
  Henry Schultz, born March 16, 1846.
  Charles Edwin, born May 15, 1848.
  John S., born May 15, 1854.
J. S. resides in Hickorytown, Plymouth Township, Montgomery County, Pa.

Samuel Anders, son of Abraham Anders (page 95), married Lydia, daughter of Jeremiah Meschter (page 113), November 20, 1838. One child,
  Charles, born January 10, 1840. Died July 13, 1842.
Lydia, wife of S. A., died July 21, 1842.
Samuel Anders married, second time, Christina, daughter of Jeremiah Meschter (page 113), October 17, 1844. Children :
  Sarah, born October 3, 1845.
  Hiram, born December 6, 1847.
  Aaron, born March 21, 1849. Died August 28, 1850.

Mary Ann, born January 26, 1851. Died April 27, 1854.
Susanna, born March 23, 1853.
James, born July 18, 1854.
Daniel, born November 1, 1856.
Ellen, born April 5, 1858.
Samuel, born August 4, 1860. Died November 4, 1867.
Samuel Anders is a farmer, and resides in Lower Providence, Montgomery County, Pa.

Samuel Yeakel, son of Christopher Yeakel (page 110), married Hannah, daughter of Daniel Bertolet, February 13, 1838. One child,
Isaac B., born July 7, 1840.
S. Y. died April 15, 1842.

Anthony Yeakel, son of David Yeakel (page 97), married Elizabeth, daughter of Daniel Yeakel (page 121), April 9, 1839. Their children were:
Sarah, born March 1, 1840.
Mary, born June 10, 1841. Died March 25, 1844.
Anna, born April 4, 1843.
Edward, born May 22, 1844. Died March 28, 1857.
Helena, born May 16, 1846.
William, born November 27, 1847. Died July 27, 1854.
Ambrose, born March 25, 1849.
Nathan, born August 20, 1851. Died March 21, 1857.
Levi, born July 21, 1853. Died May 18, 1877.
Jonas, born July 10, 1855. Died October 25, 1875.
Franklin, born October 22, 1856.
A. Y. died December 31, 1856.

Abraham Anders, son of Abraham Anders (page 95), married Rebecca, daughter of George Schultz (page 115), May 14, 1839. Children:
   William S., born August 30, 1840.
   Joseph S., born March 23, 1842.
   Susanna S., born March 24, 1844.
   Charles S., born August 15, 1847.
   Abraham S., born February 12, 1850. Died November 23, 1862.
   Mary S., born March 5, 1853.
   Amos S., born February 14, 1855.
Abraham Anders lives in Worcester, upon the farm formerly occupied by his father and grandfather.

Samuel Gerhard, son of Jacob Gerhard (page 81), married Susanna, daughter of Daniel Schultz (page 117), May 28, 1839. Had issue:
   Abraham, born June 10, 1840.
   Isaac, born May 8, 1841.
   Sarah, born September 17, 1844.
   Susanna, wife of S. G., died.

Lewis Schubert, son of David Schubert (page 107), married Esther Kline June 8, 1839. Wife born February 11, 1811. Children:
   Sarah, born March 9, 1841.
   William, born November 25, 1842.
   Daniel, born November 3, 1847.
   Henry, born October 30, 1849.
   Franklin, born July 31, 1852.
L. S., some years ago, moved from Lehigh County, Pa., to Tiffin, Ohio, where he now resides.

Anthony Schultz, son of George Schultz (page 115), mar-

ried Maria, daughter of Joseph Bitting, November 12, 1839. Wife born October 24, 1818. Children:
James, born February 25, 1843. Died 1877.
Isaac, born January 25, 1845.
Sarah, born January 16, 1848.
Anthony B., born April 25, 1852.
Emeline, born September 27, 1854.
Hannah, born January 16, 1857.
Mary, born September 23, 1861.
Mary, wife of A. S., died January 8, 1870.

Joseph B. Beyer, son of Joseph Beyer (page 114), married Lydia Rittenhouse November 17, 1839. Children:
Amy, born July 22, 1841. Died May 13, 1851.
Abraham, born August 15, 1843. Died May 13, 1851.
Levi, born September 4, 1845.
Lydia, wife of J. B. B., died May 23, 1847.
Joseph B. Beyer married, second time, Mary Rittenhouse June 15, 1848. Issue:
Amos, born March 11, 1849.
Joseph R., born November 4, 1850. Died February 2, 1875.
John R., born December 21, 1852.
Elizabeth R., born January 15, 1854.
Anna R., born May 31, 1855.
William R., born January 14, 1857.
Mary R., born July 27, 1858. Died May 27, 1859.
Samuel R., born May 12, 1860.
Sarah R., born February 5, 1862. Died December 5, 1865.
Deborah R., born March 28, 1863.

Ida R., born October 20, 1865.
J. B. B. died January 4, 1867.

David Schultz, son of Samuel Schultz (page 101), married Christina, daughter of Isaac Schultz (page 100), February, 1839. No issue.
David S. was a minister of the Society of Schwenkfelders only a short time, and connected himself with the Evangelical Association, and died in the year 1850.
His wife died August 3, 1857.

Reuben Schultz, son of David Schultz (page 105), married Hannah, daughter of Henry Heebner (page 104), November 19, 1839. Children:
Lydia, born September 24, 1840. Died November 18, 1841.
Daniel, born November 24, 1841.
Sarah, born November 21, 1843.
Jeremiah, born October 9, 1846.
Edwin, born November 24, 1848.
Mary, born December 7, 1852.
R. S. resides in Upper Hanover Township, on the Hosensack Creek.

Nathan Nuss, son of Michael Nuss (page 112), married Leah, daughter of Solomon Yeakel (page 110), December 10, 1839. No issue.
Leah, wife of N. N., died March 16, 1876.

Adam Fisher, son of Jacob Fisher, came in 1836 to Pennsylvania and married Maria, daughter of George Heydrick (page 87), December 22, 1839. Children:
Susanna.
Mary.
Adam.

John Schultz, son of Rev. John Schultz (page 82), married Rebecca, daughter of Christopher Yeakle (page 66), February, 1840. No issue.
J. S. resides on Chestnut Hill, Philadelphia, late the residence of Christopher Yeakle.

Rosina Kriebel, daughter of Abraham Kriebel (page 71), married George Smith, a native of Germany, in 1840, and about 1847 they left Gwynedd Township, Montgomery County, Pa., for Germany, and settled in Lahr, where she died July 6, 1862, at the age of 72 years and 3 months. She left no issue.

Jacob H. Hartman, born July 25, 1812, son of George Hartman, married Sarah S., daughter of Gabriel Schultz (page 115), April 10, 1840. Had issue:
Catharine S., born November 12, 1842.
Matilda S., born October 19, 1844.
Henry S., born April 10, 1848.
Franklin S., born January 19, 1858. Died in June, 1858.
Sarah S., wife of J. H. H., died September 19, 1875.

Bernard B. Freyer married Catharine, daughter of Job Kriebel (page 122), September 13, 1840. Children:
Hester, born August 31, 1841.
Jacob, born April 26, 1844.
Judia, born October 2, 1846.
Susanna, born November 13, 1850.

Henry Kriebel, son of David Kriebel (page 111), married Sarah Rahn December 6, 1840. Wife born April 20, 1822. Children:
David, born July 26, 1841.
Isaac, born August 16, 1845.

Septimus, born June 17, 1849.
Henry, born May 9, 1853. Died May 30, 1853.
Amanda, born March 11, 1855.
George, born June 10, 1857.
Sarah, born March 20, 1859.
Reinard, born November 17, 1861.
Philip, born August 8, 1864.

George C. Master, son of Isaac Master (page 107), married Emeline Adsett December 29, 1840. Wife born January 13, 1825. Had issue:
Lewis E., born November 3, 1842.
Edward Ellis, born November 2, 1845.
Jared K., born February 19, 1848.
Melissa, born May 3, 1856.

David Meschter, son of George Meschter (page 81), married Catharina, daughter of Christian Hunsberger, in 1841. Wife born March 10, 1815. Children:
John, born 1841.
Mary, born May 6, 1842.
Henry, born August 18, 1843.
Eben, born October 27, 1845. Married George Rittenhouse.
William.
George Washington.
David, born December 10, 1849.
Milton, born September 21, 1855.
Catharine Ann, born October 25, 1858.
James.

Jacob Clemens married Sophia, daughter of Jacob Schultz (page 86), in 1841. Their children were:
William, Adeline, } twins, born January, 24, 1845.

Jacob, born October 8, 1846.
Sophia, wife of J. C., died November 3, 1854.

Joseph Bechtel, born September 7, 1818, son of John Bechtel, married Maria, daughter of Andrew Krauss (page 84), January 11, 1841. Children:
Matilda, born July 7, 1842.
Rebecca, born August 13, 1844.
David, born November 13, 1845.
Edwin, born January 17, 1850.
Sarah, born February 4, 1852.
William, born March 22, 1853. Died.
Harris, born May 10, 1855.

John Krauss, son of Andrew Krauss (page 84), married Rachel, daughter of Adam Schultz (page 92), February 3, 1841. Had issue:
William, born March 24, 1842. Died April 18, 1862.
Adam, born 1844.
Rachel, wife of J. K., died September 15, 1852.
John Krauss married, second time, Lizzie Wiedner April 18, 1871. No issue.

Charles Krieble, son of John Krieble (page 117), married Sarah, daughter of Abraham Anders (page 95), February 18, 1841. Children:
. Hiram A., born May 26, 1842.
Mary Ann, born February 6, 1845.
C. K. is a farmer and resides in Whitpain Township, Montgomery County, Pa.

George Yeakel, son of Daniel Yeakel (page 121), married Lydia, daughter of Rev. Christopher Schultz (page 99), April 4, 1841. One child,
Maria, born March 30, 1842.

G. Y. died February 24, 1842. His widow afterwards married Miller, who died and left issue.

Daniel Schultz, son of Samuel Schultz (page 101), married Anna, daughter of Jacob Gerhard (page 81), April 17, 1841. No issue.

Michael Schultz, son of George Schultz (page 115), married Rachel, daughter of Abraham Snyder (page 119), April 20, 1841. Children:
    Mary Ann, born February 5, 1842.
    Hiram, born October 3, 1843.
    Abraham, born October 27, 1845.
    Hannah, born September 21, 1847. Died March 21, 1850.
    Franklin, born November 9, 1850. Died March 6, 1855.
    Addison, born February 5, 1853.
    Daniel, born September 6, 1856.

Gabriel Griesmer, born December 27, 1813, son of Isaac Griesmer, married Regina, daughter of George Meschter (page 81), September 2, 1841. Children:
    Elizabeth, born November 26, 1842.
    Susanna, born June 23, 1843.
    Sarah Ann, born May 8, 1845.
    Matthew, born January 31, 1847. Died July 12, 1848.
    Owen, born May 12, 1848.
    Mary Ann, born June 23, 1850.
    Percival, born June 8, 1853.
    Joseph, born March 17, 1857.

Joseph Schultz, son of Gabriel Schultz (page 115), married Elizabeth, daughter of Samuel Burdan, September 12, 1841. Children:

Henry, born January 27, 1842. Died February 19, 1856.
William, born January 7, 1844.
Milton, born November 18, 1846. Died August 8, 1852.
Sarah, born October 21, 1849.
Mary Ann, born August 12, 1852.
Catharine, born September 21, 1854.
Edwin, born December 31, 1860.
Elam, born April 11, 1863.

Henry S. Schultz, son of Gabriel Schultz (page 115), married Catharine, daughter of John Smith, October 3, 1841. Wife born in November, 1816. No issue.

Aaron Master, son of Christopher Master (page 92), married Cynthia Clark October 20, 1841. Children:
David W., born November 9, 1842. Died January 24, 1864.
Mary Kerling, born April 11, 1845.
Quincy Adams, born January 30, 1847.
Winfield Scott, born April 24, 1849.
James Madison, born April 2, 1852.
Lewis Clark, born July 6, 1855.
Cynthia, wife of A. M., died December 31, 1858.
Aaron Master married, second time, Mary Ann Erb October 4, 1866. One child,
Allen Willie, born August 14, 1867.

William Kriebel, son of Samuel Kriebel (page 94), married Mary, daughter of Michael Zilling, October 24, 1841. Children:
Samuel Z., born April 24, 1842.
Amos Z., born August 16, 1843.

Michael Z., born January 10, 1845.
Susanna, born August 18, 1846.
Francis Z., born January 21, 1849.
William Z., born September 19, 1851.
Elizabeth, born March 23, 1852.
Mary, born August 15, 1855.
Chester Z., born October 16, 1856.
Edwin, born March 31, 1859.
Elmer Ellsworth, born February 23, 1863.
Emma, born May 10, 1865.
William Kriebel is a miller by trade, and resides in Worcester.

Levi Kriebel, son of Solomon Kriebel (page 109), married Eliza, daughter of George Krupp, November, 1841. Wife born October, 1820. Had children:
Elijah, born November, 1843.
Franklin, born August, 1848. Died July, 1850.

Daniel S. Schultz, son of Isaac Schultz (page 100), married Mary, daughter of John Krieble (page 117), November 11, 1841. Children:
Caroline, born January 1, 1843. Died February 11, 1851.
Addison, born March 24, 1844.
Joshua, } twins, born August 6, 1847.
Caleb, }
Joshua died August 23, 1847.
Caleb died August 26, 1847.
Sarah Agnes.
Susanna.
Joanna.
Mary. Died July 23, 1876.
Ellen.

Alice, born February 24, 1862. Died November 21, 1878.

D. S. S. resides at Schultzville, Berks County, Pa., where as Magistrate, Surveyor, and Conveyancer, he performed his several duties to the satisfaction of the community. He is now engaged in the coal and lumber business at Barto Station, Colebrookedale RR.

Samuel Krichel, son of Abraham Krichel (page 66), married Catharine Snyder November 14, 1841. Wife born November 8, 1806. No issue.
S. K. died August 22, 1858.

Enoch Schultz, son of Adam Schultz (page 92), married Leah, daughter of Samuel Neuman (page 128), November 14, 1841. Children:
Sarah, born January 8, 1843.
Lydia, born April 19, 1844.
Levi, born December 15, 1845.
Edwin N., born July 26, 1847.
Regina, born August 6, 1849.
Susanna, born September 4, 1850.
Esther, born March 27, 1854. Died April 28, 1876.
Daniel, born November 9, 1855.
Mary, born June 6, 1859.
Emma, born February 13, 1863.
E. S. resides in Hereford Township, Berks County, Pa., where his father lived.

Henry C. Beyer, son of Andrew Beyer (page 104), married Sophia Hartel November 23, 1841. Wife born November 2, 1816. Children:
Elmira, born August 23, 1843. Died August 9, 1862.

Edward H., born April 23, 1846. Died January 3, 1867.

Jacob Schultz, son of Caspar Schultz (page 111), married Anna, daughter of David Kriebel (page 111), March 29, 1842. Children:
Lavina.
Anna.
James.
Philip.
Jacob, born August 13, 1851.
Jonas.

Henry Schultz,* born January 26, 1818, son of Henry Y. Schultz (page 140), married Sarah, daughter of Dr. Abraham Schelly, April 24, 1842. Children:
Ambrose, born December 18, 1843.
Benneville, born June 29, 1852. Died August 30, 1854.
Angeline, born December 28, 1854.

Edward Yeakel, son of Abraham Yeakel (page 118), married Matilda Drake April 30, 1842. Children:
Amos A., born February 26, 1843.
Emma R., born January 24, 1846.
Samuel M., born August 8, 1849. Died October 17, 1856.
Sarah F., born January 27, 1856.
Resides in West Greenville, Mercer County, Pa.

Isaac Rose married Eleanor, daughter of Christopher Master (page 92), May 18, 1842. Had issue:
Margaret, born January 19, 1843.
Tamson, born December 29, 1844.
Drucilla, born October 14, 1846.

---

* The name of Henry Schultz is omitted in his father's record.

Phœbe, born May 3, 1848.
Eleanor, wife of I. R., died July 7, 1863.
I. R. resides in Franklin County, Indiana.

Andrew K. Schultz, son of Andrew Schultz (page 108), married Magdalena, daughter of John High, September 11, 1842. Children:
- Henry H., born July 17, 1844.
- Mary Ann, born October 13, 1846.
- Andrew H., born August 7, 1848.
- Amanda, born September 14, 1850.
- Edwin H., born April 8, 1852.
- Magdalena, born September 31, 1853.
- John H., born May 10, 1855.
- Diana, born April 1, 1857. Died, aged 5 months.
- Samuel H., born September 9, 1858. Died, aged 12 days.
- Emma, born December 24, 1861.

Daniel Wiand, born January 1, 1816, son of Daniel Wiand, married Judith, daughter of Benjamin Kriebel (page 116), October 30, 1842. Children:
- Elizabeth, born October 3, 1843.
- William, born October 28, 1845.
- Maria, born November 19, 1853.

Judith, wife of D. W., died March 5, 1861.

Jonathan Krauss, son of George Krauss (page 102), married Magdalene, daughter of Caspar Schultz (page 111), November 1, 1842. Children:
- Enos S., born July 3, 1844.
- Edward S., born October 17, 1845.
- Sarah, born November 27, 1846.
- Benjamin S., born March 29, 1848.
- Oswin S., born January 25, 1850.

Joel S., born June 3, 1852. Died.
Jonathan S., born March 23, 1855.
Maria S., born September 25, 1856.
Allen S., born November 26, 1859. Died.
Daniel S., born June 8, 1863.
J. K. is a farmer, and resides near Kraussdale, in Upper Hanover.

Thomas Schultz, son of Jacob Schultz (page 86), married Elizabeth, daughter of Abraham Klemmer, November 27, 1842. Wife born November 18, 1819. One child,
    Washington, born October, 1848. Died.
Elizabeth, wife of T. S., died—time not given.
Thomas Schultz married, second time, widow Elizabeth Johnson October 15, 1850. No issue.

Daniel K. Urffer, son of Michael Urffer (page 89), married Rebecca, daughter of Andrew Krauss (page 84). Had issue:
    Henry K.
    David. Died.
    George K., born November 9, 1844. Died May 28, 1849.
    Susanna, born February 1, 1849. Died same day.
    Lydia. Probably the oldest child.
This record is not regular and probably very deficient.
Rebecca, the wife, died June 6, 1852.
D. K. U. died June 27, 1852, and is buried at Allentown, Pa.

Joel Yeakel, son of Christopher Yeakel (page 110), married Sarah, daughter of Anthony Kriebel (page 126), October 29, 1842. Children:
    Daniel, born November 2, 1844.

Mary Ann, born April 22, 1847.
Elizabeth, born June 3, 1849.
Sarah, born November 12, 1853.
Milton, born December 12, 1855.
Emilia, born November 29, 1857.
William, born March 31, 1860.
Abraham, born July 9, 1862. Died.
Ellen, born August 30, 1865.

Solomon S. Moyer, born March 3, 1820, married Lydia, daughter of Christopher Schubert (page 116), January 1, 1843. Children:
Mary, born April 12, 1844. Died August 4, 1875.
William, born July 10, 1846. Died November 10, 1875.
Susan, born September 19, 1848.
Sarah, born March 25, 1852.
Caroline, born January 29, 1854.
Thomas, born April 19, 1857.
Amelia, born September 9, 1860.
Lydia, wife of S. S. M., died May 24, 1876.

David Schultz, son of Melchior Schultz (page 119), married Mary, daughter of Caspar Schultz (page 111), January 27, 1843. Children:
Abraham S., born August 13, 1845.
Isaac S., born June 12, 1847.

Jacob Raudenbush, son of Henry Raudenbush, married Sophia, daughter of Samuel Schultz (page 101), February 5, 1843. Children:
Edwin S., born September 20, 1845.
Amanda S., born August 22, 1852.
Sarah S., born September 7, 1855.

Lavina S., born September 12, 1858.
J. R. born December 15, 1810.

Ezra Wiegner, son of John Wiegner (page 80), married Maria, daughter of Samuel Gehman, February 26, 1843. Children:
John, born July 18, 1844.
Samuel, born May 11, 1846. Died July 19, 1848.
Amanda, born June 5, 1847. Died August 1, 1847.
Mary, born February 13, 1849.
Maria, wife of E. W., died February 19, 1849.
Ezra Wiegner married, second time, Rebecca, daughter of George Diehl, February 29, 1852. Children:
Sarah Catharine, born February 2, 1854.
Lucy Ann, born January 3, 1857.

Charles Yeakle, son of Jacob Yeakle (page 106), married Sarah, daughter of Michael Nuss (page 112), March 16, 1843. One child,
Levi, born December 13, 1844. Died February 1, 1861.

Joseph B. Kriebel, son of Samuel Kriebel (page 124), married Margaret, daughter of Abraham Schwenk, May 14, 1843. Had issue:
Amanda, born February 26, 1844.
Samuel, born January 6, 1851.
Elizabeth, born November 6, 1853.

George Snyder, son of Joseph Snyder (page 112), married Abigail, daughter of Henry Heebner (page 104), September 7, 1843. Had issue:
Joseph, born May 7, 1844.
Sarah, born October 31, 1845. Died June 4, 1848.
Anna, born March 16, 1848.

Reuben, born November 3, 1850. Died January 3, 1853.
Amanda, born March 17, 1853.
George, born November 11, 1855. Died March 20, 1859.
Lizzie, born October 27, 1858.
Hannah, born March 20, 1861.

Jeremiah Kriebel, son of Samuel Kriebel (page 124), married Susanna Mininger October 8, 1843. Children:
William, born September 20, 1849. Died November 8, 1849.
Jeremiah, born September 20, 1849.
J. K. died in 1851.

Abraham S. Moyer, son of Jacob Moyer, born November 15, 1822, married Sarah Y., daughter of Carl Yeakel (page 120), October 9, 1843. Children:
Isaac Y., born July 8, 1846.
Jacob Y., born April 4, 1848.
Charles Y., born November 9, 1850.
Susanna Y., born May 26, 1853.
Emeline Y., born August 10, 1856.
William Y., June 9, 1858.
Abraham Y., born October 12, 1860. Died December 3, 1863.
Elizabeth Y., born February 5, 1864.

Jacob Kriebel, son of Rev. David Kriebel (page 120), married Susanna, daughter of Jacob Dresher (page 133), October 19, 1843. Children:
David D., born November 30, 1844.
Reuben D., born December 18, 1846.
Lydia, born September 20, 1848.
Four children died in infancy between 1852 and 1860.

Joseph Detweiler, born January 15, 1820, son of Daniel
Detweiler, married Rachel, daughter of Jacob Schultz
(page 86), November 5, 1843. Children:
    Jacob, born January 23, 1846. Married Annie
      Cassel.
    Kate, born September 25, 1848.
    Mary, born October 19, 1850. Married Jesse Clem-
      mence.

Daniel Y. Gerhard, son of Matthias Gerhard (page 96),
married Susanna, daughter of John Krieble (page 117),
November 7, 1843. Children:
    Ambrose, born June 4, 1845.
    Josephus, born July 16, 1853.
    Josiah, born February 19, 1856.
    Selina, born September 17, 1858.

Jacob Heebner, son of Abraham Heebner (page 72),
married Bathseba, daughter of Christopher Kriebel
(page 106), November 12, 1843. No issue.
Bathseba, wife of J. H., died June 18, 1845.
Jacob Heebner married, second time, Catharine, daugh-
ter of George Heydrick (page 87), February 11, 1847.
No issue.
Catharine, wife of J. H., died May 29, 1862.
J. H. died November 18, 1862.

Jesse Yeakel, son of Carl Yeakel (page 120), married
Maria, daughter of Melchior Schultz (page 119), November 23, 1843. Had issue:
    Matilda, born February 15, 1851. Died August
      25, 1856.
    Emma, born May 26, 1852. Died June 17, 1856.
    Sarah Jane, born March 25, 1854.
    Ellen, born July 16, 1856.

> Charles, born August 14, 1858.
> Uriah, born November 18, 1860.
> Henry, born September 12, 1863. Died April 17, 1864.
> William, born October 12, 1867. Died December 9, 1875.
>
> This is the Rev. Jesse Yeakel, a clergyman of the Evangelical Church, and resides in the city of Philadelphia.

Jacob Meschter, son of Jeremiah Meschter (page 113), married Agnes, daughter of Daniel Yeakel (page 121), November 28, 1843. Children:
> Charles, born September 20, 1844.
> Susanna, born September 14, 1846.
> Daniel, born October 14, 1848.
> Levi, born June 10, 1850.
> William, born June 19, 1852.

Agnes, wife of J. M., died December 25, 1872.

Jacob Meschter married, second time, Hannah S., daughter of Charles Gerhard (page 171), February 22, 1876.

This is the Rev. Jacob Meschter, a minister of the Society of Schwenkfelders, and resides at Palm, in Upper Hanover Township, Montgomery County, Pa.

Samuel H. Schultz, son of Rev. John Schultz (page 82), married Elizabeth, daughter of Andrew Schultz (page 108), February 4, 1844. Children:
> Sarah, born May 31, 1845.
> Lydia, born June 14, 1847. Died September 18, 1849.
> Benneville, born March 18, 1849.
> Isaac, born June 18, 1851.

Alfred, born August 1, 1853.
Susanna, born October 12, 1855.
Elizabeth, born March 25, 1860.
Elizabeth, wife of S. H. S., died May 20, 1877.

Joseph Krauss, son of John Krauss (page 79), married —— Kulp March 17, 1844. Children:
- John, born September 17, 1845. Died March 28, 1853.
- Erwin, born September 24, 1847. Died December 1, 1850.
- Sarah Ann, born July 5, 1849.
- Edwin, born September 17, 1851. Died November 23, 1857.
- Emma Louisa, born May 21, 1855.
- Elmira Jane, born October 27, 1858.
- Nevin, born July 4, 1861.
- Clement, born July 7, 1865. Died May 1, 1877.

J. K. died in 1871, and his wife, who was born February 2, 1824, died February 13, 1875.

Uriah Rose married Elizabeth, daughter of Christopher Master (page 92), March 23, 1844. Children:
- Mary S., born January 17, 1845.
- Tamson, born November 9, 1847.
- Emons R., born October 7, 1850. Died August 29, 1853.
- Christopher, born December 29, 1852. Died May 2, 1860.
- Elnora, born December 23, 1855.
- Elizabeth, born January 26, 1858.
- William W., born April 20, 1861.
- Josephine, born July 1, 1863.

Abraham Schultz, son of Isaac Schultz (page 100), mar-

ried Rebecca, daughter of Matthias Gerhard (page 96), May 14, 1844. Children:
Miriam, born September 17, 1845. Died October 21, 1845.
Matilda, born January 3, 1847. Died May 7, 1871.
Hiram, born June 25, 1848.
Levi, born March 4, 1851.
Susanna, born October 10, 1855.
Regina, born July 28, 1858.
Rebecca, wife of A. S., died June 6, 1875.

Samuel Beyer, son of Jacob Beyer (page 132), married Hannah Brunner in 1844. Had issue:
Mary Ann, born January 1, 1846.
Martha Jane, born June 1, 1847.
Emily, born January 18, 1849.
Elizabeth, born September 15, 1850. Died November 13, 1851.
Franklin, born March 23, 1852.
Cyrus, born April 7, 1855.
Lydia, born January 29, 1857.
Amanda, born December 10, 1862.
Eva, born April 7, 1866.

Abraham Wiegner, son of John Wiegner (page 80), married Barbara, daughter of Rev. David Kriebel (page 120), October 24, 1844. Had issue:
Son, born September 4, 1845. Died September 21, 1845.
Lydia, born November 15, 1847.
Sarah, born January 29, 1850.
Rosanna, born March 23, 1852. Died March 15, 1874.
Ann, born January 17, 1855. Died November 22, 1857.

Samuel Y. Krieble, son of John Krieble (page 117), married Mary, daughter of George Schultz (page 115), November 26, 1844. No issue.

Amos Snyder, born May 14, 1824, married Catharine, daughter of Isaac Master (page 107), December 31, 1844. Children:
　Isaac, born December 4, 1845.
　Hannah, born May 10, 1847. Died September 2, 1848.
　Mary, born June 6, 1848.
　George, born July 11, 1850.
　Eliza, born March 6, 1852.
　Henry W., born October 12, 1853.
　John Wesley, born May 11, 1856.
　Clemens, born December 29, 1858.
　Rachel, born May 5, 1861.
　Lydia Ann, born November 17, 1863.
　Elsie, born May 23, 1866.
　Rebecca, born November 28, 1868.

Anthony Schultz, son of Rev. John Schultz (page 82), married Mary, daughter of David Kriebel (page 111), January 28, 1845. One child,
　Regina, born July 11, 1846.
　A. S. died August 23, 1848.

Hannah Schultz, daughter of Rev. Christopher Schultz (page 99), married William Bechtel, born December 2, 1819, son of John Bechtel, February 2, 1845. Issue:
　Elam, born August 22, 1845.
　James, born July 6, 1847.
　Daughter, born August 6, 1851. Stillborn.
　John, born November 7, 1854.
　Hannah, wife of W. B., died December 10, 1861.

Solomon Schultz, son of George Schultz (page 115), married Sophia, daughter of Samuel Kriebel (page 94), April 8, 1845. Children:
  Amanda, born March 26, 1847.
  Catharine Ann, born June 25, 1849.
  Chester, born August 3, 1851.
  Wilson Henry, born December 21, 1853.
  Elizabeth A., born February 22, 1857.
  Ellen Jane, born July 15, 1860.
  Sophia K., } twins, born March 21, 1863.
  Salina K.,
  Samuel K., born May 14, 1865. Died April 29, 1871.

Paul Keiser married Elizabeth, daughter of Jacob Meschter (page 129), October 28, 1845. No issue.

Andrew Schultz, son of Adam Schultz (page 92), married Sarah, daughter of Andrew Mohr, November 16, 1845. Wife born March 17, 1827. Had issue:
  Emma, born 1846.
  Mary Ann, born June 9, 1849.
  Harrison, born April 13, 1864.

Abraham Kriebel, son of Jonathan Kriebel (page 127), married Regina, daughter of Matthias Schultz (page 96), November 27, 1845. Children:
  Susanna, born January 30, 1847. Died October 10, 1876.
  Jonas, born August 19, 1848.
  Charles, born March 23, 1850.
  Sarah, born July 28, 1852.
  Samuel, born August 12, 1854. Died October 27, 1860.

John, born September 7, 1856.
Daughter, born May 3, 1859. Died.
William, born April 28, 1861. Died August 23, 1862.

George A. Kriebel, son of Job Kriebel (page 122), married Susanna, daughter of Israel Kriebel (page 125), January 26, 1846. Children.
John, born May 31, 1847.
Enos, born June 21, 1849.
Sarah, born March 17, 1852. Died September 15, 1853.
Edwin, born July 22, 1854.
Emma, born February 25, 1856.
G. A. K. was a soldier in the Union Army, and was killed in the attack on Fredericksburg, Va.

Daniel Snyder, son of Abraham Snyder (page 119), married Christina, widow of Isaac Snyder (page 165), February 12, 1846. Children:
Susanna, born December 1, 1846.
Hannah, born May 3, 1849.
John, born August 9, 1857.
Christina, wife of D. S., died November 13, 1858.

Joel Schultz, son of Isaac Schultz (page 100), married Leah, daughter of Rev. Christopher Schultz (page 99), February 17, 1846. One child,
Oliver, born November 29, 1850.
J. S. died December 12, 1864.
Leah, wife of J. S., died March 3, 1875.

Anthony Schultz, son of Matthias Schultz (page 96), married Sophia, daughter of Jeremiah Meschter (page 113), April 13, 1846. Children:

Daughter, born February 26, 1847. Died May 19, 1847.
Edwin, born April 14, 1850.
Nathan, born November 27, 1852.
Elizabeth, born April 7, 1857.

Henry F. Beyer, son of John Beyer (page 133), married Hannah, daughter of George Schlotterer, March 6, 1845. Wife born March 25, 1826. Had issue:
George, born January 18, 1847. Died March 4, 1848.
Ann, born October 11, 1848.
Cornelius, born December 1, 1851.
Kate, born April 27, 1854.
H. F. B. resides at Belplain, Iowa.

George Schultz, son of Andrew Schultz (page 102), married Anna, daughter of Abraham Yeakel (page 118), June 7, 1846. Had issue:
Lucianna, born April 30, 1847.
Levi, born September 9, 1849.
Rosina, born January 22, 1852.
Amandus, born December 6, 1854.
Carolina, born July 24, 1856.
G. S. died September 18, 1857.

Aaron Kriebel, son of Samuel Kriebel (page 124), married Catharine, daughter of Jacob Wisler, August 2, 1846. No issue.

John S. Heebner, son of Henry Heebner (page 104), married Susanna, daughter of Samuel Kriebel (page 133), September 22, 1846. Children:
Amanda, born November 9, 1847.
Sarah, born October 14, 1849.

Catharine, born January 31, 1852. Died July 20, 1853.
Samuel, born November 1, 1854.
Susanna, born August 16, 1857.
Ellen, born February 22, 1860.
William, born August 21, 1862.

Joseph C. Beyer, son of Andrew Beyer (page 104), married Mary Ann Y. Kugler November 3, 1846. Wife born February 26, 1826. Children:
Augustus, born August 7, 1847. Died October 24, 1847.
Oliver K., born May 6, 1850.
Charles C., born October 19, 1857.

Isaac Kriebel, son of Benjamin Kriebel (page 116), married Sarah, daughter of Daniel Wiand, February 7, 1847. Children:
William, born October 8, 1850.
Benjamin F., born February 13, 1854.
Daniel, born November 14, 1865.

Richard F. Smith, son of Jacob Smith, married Elizabeth, daughter of Gabriel Schultz (page 115), February 9, 1847. Children:
Andora E., born April 1, 1847. Died May 21, 1874.
Jacob A., born April 6, 1849.
Abraham R., born October 2, 1851. Died August 2, 1852.
Hetty Amanda, born June 23, 1853.
Irwin Samuel, born April 1, 1861.

Jacob Barnit, son of John Barnit, married Rebecca,

daughter of Christopher Dresher (page 89), December 8, 1842, and had issue as follows:
Clarenda, born January 3, 1844.
Albert, born January 15, 1848.
Anna Elizabeth, born October 28, 1853.
J. B. was a farmer, and lived in Dreshertown, Upper Dublin, Montgomery County, Pa. He died January 22, 1879, aged 69 years, and his wife died November 30, 1871.

Timothy Schubert, son of Christopher Schubert (page 116), married Catharine Esterly. Wife born September 2, 1823. Had issue:
Reuben, born September 7, 1848.
Maria, born August 12, 1850.
Abraham, born June 5, 1853.
William, born January 3, 1856.
Charles, born October 21, 1857.
Emma, born September 16, 1859.
T. S. died November 24, 1876.

Daniel S. Yeakel, son of David Yeakel (page 97), married Rebecca, daughter of George Heydrick (page 87), February 11, 1847. No issue.
Rebecca, wife of D. S. Y., died October 31, 1861.
Daniel S. Yeakel married, second time, Regina, daughter of Henry Krauss (page 175), May 8, 1869. No issue.

Samuel B. Kriebel, son of Samuel Kriebel (page 124), married Lavina, daughter of John Wagoner, April 25, 1847. Wife born May 3, 1827. Children:
Elizabeth, born June 17, 1848. Married William Hunsberger.
Mary Ann, born August 16, 1849.

Rosalinda, } twins, born April 6, 1852.
Angeline,

William Moyer, son of Peter Moyer, married Susanna, daughter of David Kriebel (page 111), July 11, 1847. Children:
  David, born January 8, 1848.
  Septimus, born June 10, 1849. Died August 31, 1850.
  Daniel, born March 16, 1851.
  Enos, born November 21, 1852.
  William K., born February 25, 1855.
  Peter, born June 9, 1859.

Amos Snyder, son of Jacob Snyder (page 88), married Mary Ann Demuth September 21, 1847. Children:
  Edgar Callender, born September 6, 1859.
  George Agnew, born March 3, 1866.
  Mary Kline, born November 24, 1871. Died June 15, 1872.
  A. S. died September 28, 1874.

Abraham Anders, son of George Anders (page 76), married Salome, daughter of Melchior Kriebel (page 126), October 21, 1847. No issue.

Jonas Kriebel, son of Samuel Kriebel (page 133), married Mary, daughter of George Seipt (page 137), November 23, 1847. Children:
  Urias S., born March 17, 1849. Died July 14, 1860.
  Daniel S., born May 18, 1853.
  Samuel S., born January 4, 1855.
  Susanna S., born April 29, 1856.
  Addison S., born October 18, 1857.
  Sarah Ann S., born October 19, 1859. Died July 15, 1860.

William S., born August 31, 1861.
James S., born April 9, 1864.
George Edwin S., born August 1, 1867.
Emma Jane S., born September 13, 1869. Died September 30, 1869.

Jonas Kriebel moved some years ago to the State of Indiana, in Kankakee County, where he purchased a tract of land and engaged in farming, where he still resides.

Harriet H. Brown, daughter of Thomas J. Brown (page 130), married Dr. L. G. Rosenbury November 24, 1847. Issue:

    Emily A., born November 27, 1848. Died November 20, 1860.
    Thomas B., born September 9, 1850. Died November 18, 1860.
    John R., born March 25, 1852.
    Mary E., born June 12, 1853. Died November 22, 1860.
    Caroline M., born May 14, 1855. Died September 14, 1857.
    M. J., born April 11, 1857.
    Hattie J., born August 6, 1859.
    Albert B., born January 12, 1862. Died August 2, 1865.
    Hattie E., born July 26, 1865. Died January 18, 1867.
    Agnes B., born January 1, 1868. Died March 19, 1868.

Daniel Yeakel, son of Isaac Yeakel (page 91), married, first wife, Amanda, daughter of Adam Heilig.
Amanda, wife of D. Y., died 1849.

Daniel Yeakel married, second time, Amanda, daughter of John Bush, June 2, 1868. Children:
  Emma B., born December 8, 1869.
  D. Dawson, born March, 1871.

Daniel S. Schultz, son of Gabriel Schultz (page 115), married Sarah, daughter of Jacob Yerger. Children:
  Milton, born March 18, 1849. Died December 26, 1857.
  Malinda, born November 10, 1851.
  Amanda, born November 8, 1858.
  John, born April 3, 1867.

Joseph Yeakel, son of Abraham Yeakel (page 118), married Josephine, daughter of Joseph Neis, 1848. Wife born July 4, 1828. Children:
  Amanda, born January 11, 1849.
  Amelia, born March 5, 1850.
  Wellington N., born September 12, 1851.
  Uriah G., born August 4, 1863.
  Wesley L., born April 11, 1868.

Frederick Bookheimer, born April 5, 1816, son of Frederick Bookheimer, married Regina, daughter of Benjamin Kriebel (page 135), January 30, 1848. Their children:
  Mary, born 1848.
  Amanda, born September 10, 1851.
  Addison, born April 15, 1853.
  Elizabeth, born March 1, 1855.
  Lydia, born December 24, 1856.
  Samuel, born November 24, 1858.
  John, born March 1, 1861.
  Hannah, born July 11, 1864.

Daniel Krauss, son of George Krauss (page 102), married Esther, daughter of Samuel Neuman (page 128), March 19, 1848. No issue.

Eli Dresher, son of Christopher Dresher (page 89), married Elizabeth M., daughter of Cornelius Conrad, March 30, 1848. Children:
George B., born May 3, 1849.
William H., born February 17, 1851.
Emma L., born February 11, 1853.
E. D. died December 10, 1855. He was a farmer, and resided in Dreshertown, Upper Dublin Township, Montgomery County, Pa.

Jacob C. Beyer, son of Andrew Beyer (page 104), married Margaret Ann McCarter August 15, 1848. Children:
Manning, born June 23, 1849. Died August 31, 1863.
James Marshall, born November 4, 1851.
Margaret A., wife of J. C. B., died December 15, 1856.
Jacob C. Beyer married, second time, Susan Landis January 15, 1860. Children:
William H., born August 9, 1863.
Nettie K., born January 3, 1876.

William C. Beyer, son of Andrew Beyer (page 104), married Catharine Kugler September 30, 1848. Wife born February 4, 1830. Children:
Isabella, born August 31, 1852.
Mary E., born March 27, 1855.
Worthington, born July 31, 1858.

Reuben Kriebel, son of Jacob Kriebel (page 123), married Maria, daughter of Melchior Kriebel (page 126), November 30, 1848. Children:

  Hosea, born September 12, 1849.

  Aaron, born July 16, 1852. Died February 26, 1860.

  Daniel, born December 4, 1856.

  Hannah Maria, born September 30, 1859. Died September 23, 1860.

Maria, wife of R. K., died October 30, 1859.

Reuben Kriebel married, second time, Hannah, daughter of George Heydrick (page 87), May 14, 1861. Had issue:

  Sophia, born October 31, 1865.

  Susanna, born December 10, 1869.

Jacob Yeakel, son of Carl Yeakel (page 120), married Hester, daughter of Michael Brunner, January 4, 1849. Wife born July 26, 1823. Children:

  Mary, born November 26, 1852.

  Obadiah, born July 30, 1856.

Elias Beyer, son of John Beyer (page 133), married Juliana Moser February 8, 1849. Wife born April 6, 1830. Children:

  Lydia, born August 3, 1850.

  Isabella, born September 14, 1853.

  Josiah, born June 8, 1855.

  Sarah, born September 19, 1859.

  Mary Emma, born May 11, 1862.

  Henry M., born October 22, 1863.

  Elias Vernon, born October 4, 1869.

Jacob Shupe, born June 19, 1822, married Sallie Ann, daughter of John Master (page 155), February 7, 1849. Children:

John W., born November 18, 1849.
Wellington, born February 20, 1851.

Jacob Rodenberger, born July 7, 1805, son of Peter Rodenberger, married Maria, daughter of Michael Urffer (page 89), March 25, 1849. No issue.
J. R. died April 27, 1861.

William Anders Yeakle, son of Samuel Yeakle (page 134), married Caroline, daughter of John Hocker, of Whitemarsh, January 25, 1849. Had issue:
  Annie H., born August 2, 1851.
  Samuel, born August 16, 1853.
Caroline, wife of W. A. Y., was born August 30, 1825, and died May 16, 1857, aged 31 years, 8 months, and 17 days.

Jonas Seibert, son of David Seibert (page 130), married Sarah, daughter of Jonas Reinewald (page 139), March 27, 1849. Children:
  Noah, born December 15, 1849.
  Susanna, born December 25, 1852.
  Lydia, born April 20, 1856.
  Henry, born January 24, 1858.
  Samuel, born August 6, 1860.
  William, born September 20, 1862. Died May 13, 1875.
  Sarah, born October 28, 1865.
  Mary, born October 28, 1868.
  Jonas, born March 21, 1873. Died January 10, 1877.

Levi Miller, born February 25, 1825, married Lydia, widow of George Yeakle (page 190), and daughter of Rev. Christopher Schultz (page 99), June 10, 1849. Their children are:

Rebecca, born February 22, 1850.
Ambrose, born May 26, 1856.
L. M. died February 23, 1859.
Lydia, his wife, married, third time, Delong, and resides in Reading, Pa.

Jacob Dresher, son of Jacob Dresher (page 133), married Catharine, daughter of Samuel Weil, October, 1849. Children:
  Susanna, born September 20, 1850.
  Mary, born December 14, 1851.
  Samuel, born October 10, 1856.
  Jacob, born April 8, 1867.
  Reuben, born April 20, 1869. Died May 4, 1869.
Catharine, wife of J. D., born April 13, 1830.

John Yeakel, son of Daniel Yeakel (page 121), married Lydia, daughter of Samuel Kriebel (page 133), October 9, 1849. Children:
  Samuel, born October 27, 1850.
  Jefferson, born September 1, 1852.
  Susanna, born March 14, 1855.
  Edwin, born September 2, 1857.
  Sarah Jane, born May 5, 1860. Died October 5, 1860.
  Emma, born May 30, 1862.
  William, born January 27, 1865.
  Ella, born January 7, 1869.
  John, born February 28, 1872.
John Yeakel lives in Ogle County, Indiana, and is a farmer by occupation.

Andrew Anders, son of Joseph Anders (page 132), married Anna, daughter of Henry Heebner (page 104), October 10, 1849. Children:

William, born October 29, 1850.
Hannah, born July 17, 1852.
Anna, wife of A. A., died September 18, 1852.
Andrew Anders married, second time, Naomi, daughter of Frederick Schultz (page 145), April 15, 1856. Children:
  Edwin, born July 18, 1857.
  Samuel, born April 16, 1862. Died July 14, 1862.
  Mary Ann, born September 27, 1863. Died August 17, 1864.
  Isaiah, born February 10, 1866.

Samuel Master, son of Isaac Master (page 107), married Barbara Hoffman October 16, 1849. Wife born October 15, 1827. Had issue:
  Elizabeth, born September, 17, 1850.
  Angeline, born September 27, 1855.
  David, born September 29, 1856.
S. M. died February 5, 1860.

David Z. Evans, son of Isaac Evans, married Susanna, daughter of Abraham Heydrick (page 97), October 29, 1849. Children:
  Charles H., born March 17, 1851.
  David Z., Jr., born March 4, 1852.
  Edward A., born March 15, 1855. Died July 15, 1855.
  Mary M., born November 15, 1858. Died July 29, 1859.
  Burd P., born September 7, 1860.
  Isaac H., born April 16, 1862.
  Helena N., born July 21, 1864. Died July 4, 1865.
  William H., born October 12, 1865. Died March 30, 1866.

Andrew Evans, born November 3, 1825, married Sarah, daughter of Jacob Meschter (page 129), November 11, 1849. Children:
  Jacob M., born June 10, 1851.
  Charles J., born October 4, 1853.
  John N., born April 15, 1856.
  Mark V., } twins, born July 25, 1860.
  Andrew J.,
  William S., born June 25, 1863.
  Benjamin F., born August 15, 1865.
  Howard S., born August 4, 1868.

John H. Anders, son of Frederick Anders (page 142), married Elizabeth, daughter of —— Rosenberger, November 13, 1849. Children:
  Henry, born October 20, 1850.
  Catharine, born July 25, 1852.
  Josiah, born September 24, 1854.
  Nathaniel, born February 27, 1864.
  J. H. A. died January 14, 1879. He lived in Towamencin Township, Montgomery County, Pa.

William Yeakle, son of Jacob Yeakle (page 106), married Mary, daughter of Jacob Wentz, December 27, 1849. Wife born September 24, 1826. Children:
  Atwood, born October 18, 1850.
  Gertrude, born June 13, 1852.
  Ambrose, born October 14, 1854.
  John, born August 21, 1857.

John Beyer, son of Jacob Beyer (page 132), married Sarah Schwenk 1850. Children:
  Theodore, born April 14, 1852. Died June 22, 1852.
  Margaret Schwenk, born October 20, 1853.

Sarah Jane, born December 31, 1854.
Sophia H., born June 9, 1856.
Elizabeth, born October 16, 1860.

Roderick R. Spencer married Mary, daughter of John
Master (page 148), April 4, 1850. Children:
　John Edwin, born June 24, 1851.
　Willie, born January 12, 1859. Died same day.
　Susan Alma, born October 13, 1863. Died February 22, 1864.
　Hattie Jane, born December 2, 1866. Died January 16, 1874.
　Charlie V., born August 28, 1869.

Levi Heebner, son of Anthony S. Heebner (page 135),
married Sarah, daughter of Samuel Newman (page
97), March 5, 1850. Child,
　Priscilla, born April 6, 1852.
Sarah, wife of L. H., died December, 1860.
Levi Heebner married, second time, Lizzie R., daughter of Samuel Hoffman, March 5, 1865. One child,
　Lucina Mary, born April 1, 1872.

Henry Schultz, son of Jeremiah Schultz (page 127), married Barbara, daughter of David Kriebel (page 111),
May 23, 1850. Children:
　Franklin, born March 12, 1853.
　Solomon, born April 26, 1855.
　Jeremiah, born October 6, 1857.
　Wesley, born August 21, 1859.
　Horace, born February 7, 1861.
　Ambrose, born March 24, 1863.
　Mary, born August 16, 1865.
　Elizabeth, born February 1, 1868.

Amanda, born July 17, 1869.
Annie, born November 6, 1874.

Jacob Master, son of John Master (page 98), married Frances Whorton June 17, 1850. Had issue:
Sylvester, born May 6, 1851. Died August 4, 1851.
Elizabeth Alice, born July 27, 1852.
Mary Frances, born August 11, 1856. Died October 21, 1856.
Frances, wife of J. M., died September 25, 1856.
Jacob Master married, second time, Elcey Lee Curry April 4, 1857. Children:
John C., born May 7, 1858.
Christopher A., born June 2, 1861.
Milton D., born August 2, 1864.
Curnel, born March 7, 1867.

Harriet E., daughter of Charles H. and Mary Ann (Adams) Heydrick (page 141), married James E. Shaw July 25, 1850.
Harriet E., wife of J. E. S., died October 5, 1864.

Adam Kriebel, son of Rev. David Kriebel (page 120), married Mary, daughter of Joseph Cassel (page 143), December 14, 1850. Children:
Susanna, born November 16, 1853.
James, born November 11, 1857. Died December 9, 1857.

Abraham Scipt, son of Abraham Scipt (page 89), married Maria, daughter of Henry Bardman, 1851. Wife born September 6, 1825. Children:
Franklin, born November 15, 1851.
George, born October 7, 1853.

Abraham, born February 8, 1855.
Susanna, born May 28, 1857.
William, born September 24, 1858. Died April 15, 1859.
Maria, wife of A. S., died May 14, 1874.

Nathan Cole, born January 7, 1824, son of Jacob Cole, married Abigail, daughter of Benjamin Kriebel (page 135). Children:
Elizabeth Ann, born January 1, 1851. Died September 18, 1867.
Henry Ellwood, born July 16, 1855.
Mary Catharine, born March 19, 1859.
Benjamin Jacob, born January 21, 1864.
Emma Jane, born May 29, 1870.
Abigail, wife of N. C., died October 10, 1873.

John Moyer married Euphemia, daughter of Benjamin Kriebel (page 135), in 1851. Children:
Benjamin.
Elizabeth. Died.
Lucy.
Milton.
John.
Jacob.
Ann, } twins. Mary died.
Mary, }
Abby. Died.
Abraham. Died.
Catharine. Died.
William. Died.

Jesse Beyer, son of Jacob Beyer (page 132), married Hannah Dettra in 1851. Children:
Louisa Ann, born November 19, 1853.

Mary Magdalene, born May 20, 1855.
William, born June 4, 1858.

John Mahlon Nuss, son of Michael Nuss (page 112), married Mary, daughter of Jesse Krauss (page 143), February 15, 1851. Children:
  Sarah Ann, born December 31, 1851. Died April 25, 1859.
  Priscilla, born June 25, 1853.
  Benjamin Franklin, born May 21, 1855. Died September 20, 1855.
Mary, wife of J. M. N., died June 6, 1855.
John M. Nuss married, second time, Leanna, daughter of David Andreas, January 24, 1860. Children:
  Levi A., born January 25, 1861.
  Sarah, born December 30, 1862.
  Oswin, born July 29, 1865. Died September 1, 1866.
  John Mahlon, born October 15, 1867.
  Leanna, born August 9, 1870.
  Mary, born February 2, 1874.
  Barbara, born March 20, 1877.
John M. Nuss resides in Stephenson County, Ill.

Ephraim Kriebel, son of Melchior Kriebel (page 126), married Anna, daughter of George Kriebel (page 137), February 20, 1851. Children:
  Leanna, born June 8, 1852.
  Abraham, born February 3, 1854.
  Amanda, born November 30, 1856.
  Emeline, born September 30, 1858.
  George, born May 29, 1861.
  Mary, born October 7, 1863. Died September 4, 1864.
  E. K. died September 2, 1864.

William W. Heydrick, son of Isaac Heydrick (page 139), married, first wife, Mary Brown, May 15, 1851. She died January 25, 1863.

He married, second time, Annie S. Cook, and had issue as follows:
    Lizzie Stone, born November 12, 1865.
    Ada McClintock, born October 30, 1871.
    Eva, born October 17, 1873.
    Florence Gurnsey, born January 26, 1876.
    William Jacob, born November 24, 1877.

Alexander F. Brown, son of Thomas J. Brown (page 130), married Caroline Kerr, in 1851. Children:
    Charles K., born March 17, 1852.
    Samuel K., born March 11, 1855. Died March 24, 1855.
    Thomas A., born July 11, 1870. Died October 8, 1876.

Jacob Shuh, born January 28, 1831, married Nancy, daughter of Isaac Master (page 107), September 14, 1851. Children:
    Adaline, born February 17, 1853.
    Mary A., born May 9, 1854.
    Allan, born November 13, 1855.
    Milton, born April 1, 1858. Died August 2, 1877.
    Henry, born October 26, 1860.
    Alice F., born October 6, 1872. Died July 27, 1876.
J. S. died March 23, 1875.

Septimus Kriebel, son of David Kriebel (page 111), married Elizabeth, daughter of George Schlotterer, September 23, 1851. Children:
    Henry, born August 7, 1852.

Emma, born July 25, 1854.
Franklin, born July 14, 1857.
Edwin, born January 27, 1860. Died April 14, 1860.
William, born February 5, 1861.
Mary Elizabeth, born May 30, 1864.
Septimus, born December 26, 1866.

Edward Schultz, son of Jeremiah Schultz (page 127), married Susanna, daughter of Daniel Yeakel (page 121), October 7, 1851. Children:
Morris, born August 17, 1853.
Emma, born January 28, 1856.
Mary, born August 27, 1859.
Daniel, born January 8, 1865.
Amelia, } twins, born September 23, 1868.
Elmira,

John Kriebel, son of Israel Kriebel (page 125), married Susanna S., daughter of Henry Y. Schultz (page 140), November 4, 1851. Children:
Henry S., born September 15, 1852.
Daniel, born September 24, 1854.
Sallie, born November 21, 1857.
Elizabeth, born December 4, 1859.
Mary, born June 26, 1862.
Susan, born December 28, 1864.
Joseph, born August 20, 1867.

Samuel G. Clemmer, born August 10, 1821, son of George Clemmer, married Judith, daughter of Andrew Gerhard (page 128), November 11, 1851. Children:
Andrew George, born December 11, 1853.
Catharine Ann, born November 30, 1854.
Daughter, born July 19, 1857. Died same day.

Sarah, born July 30, 1858. Died December 3, 1876.
Jonas, born June 30, 1860.
Joel, born August 9, 1864.
S. G. C. died February 16, 1870.

Thomas Schultz, son of Rev. Christopher Schultz (page 99), married Hannah, daughter of Jacob Kriebel (page 123), November 21, 1851. Children:
Horatio, born September 22, 1852.
Thamar, born February 17, 1858.
T. S. died April 13, 1873. He was a farmer, and lived in Hereford Township, Berks County, Pa.

Henry L. Heebner, son of Joseph R. Heebner (page 141), married Catharine K., daughter of Jacob Schult, December 7, 1851. Children:
Mary S., born January 7, 1854.
Martha S., born November 17, 1856.
Katie S., born March 2, 1861.
Jacob Wayne S., born March 1, 1865.

Adam Beyer, son of Jacob Beyer (page 132), married Mary Brunner, 1852. Had issue:
Amelia, born 1852. Died August 10, 1853.
Jackson, born December 28, 1853.
Jefferson, born August 2, 1855.
Wesley, born April 4, 1857.
Henry, born August 27, 1858.
Mary, wife of A. B., died December 19, 1866.
Adam Beyer married, second time, Elizabeth, daughter of Charles Hendricks, 1870. One child,
Irwin, born February 20, 1871.

Samuel Anson, born February 26, 1826, son of John

Anson, married Sarah Y., daughter of John Krieble (page 117), January 8, 1852. Children:
  Hannah Agnes.
  John K. Died young.
  Sarah Eliza. [Lillie.]
  Samuel K.
  Charles Matthew.
  Ida Mary.
  Horace K.
  A. Lincoln.
  Wilson K.
  Warren K. Died young.
  Alice K.

Abraham Dresher, son of Jacob Dresher (page 133), married Sarah, daughter of Rev. David Kriebel (page 120), January 13, 1852. Children:
  Daniel, born January 17, 1853. Died April 21, 1853.
  Amanda, born March 28, 1855. Died May 27, 1859.
  Emeline, born August 29, 1856.
  Abraham, born February 16, 1859.
  Lydia, born October 2, 1860.

Nathan Schultz, son of George Schultz (page 115), married Martha J. Mathers February 22, 1852. Wife born May 15, 1830. Children:
  Amos M., born April 24, 1855.
  Laura Jane, born August 24, 1857.
  George W., born March 21, 1860. Died October 18, 1865.
  Eveline S., born July 19, 1862.
  Anna Rebecca, born October 14, 1864.
  Hannah Elizabeth, born May 5, 1867.

Anthony H. Seipt, son of George Seipt (page 137), married Lydia, daughter of Abraham Detweiler, March 6, 1852. Children:
Mary Ann, born October 29, 1853. Died June 17, 1854.
Emma Jane, born February 10, 1855.
Manilus D., born May 31, 1860.
A. H. Seipt resides at Skippackville, and is President of the Perkiomen Railroad.

David W. Yeakel, son of Isaac Yeakel (page 91), married Sarah Lentz September 23, 1852. Wife born February 27, 1821. Children:
John L., born November 25, 1854.
George K., born August 2, 1857.
M. Lula, born April 29, 1863.

Joseph Anders, son of Joseph Anders (page 132), married Annie, daughter of Jacob Aleback, October 3, 1852. Wife born February 5, 1829. Children:
Isaiah, born March 14, 1854.
Martha, born February 1, 1860.
Joseph Wesley, born December 3, 1865.

Elias Kriebel, son of Israel Kriebel (page 125), married Sophia, daughter of Christopher Wiegner (page 150), October 20, 1852. Children:
William, born April 29, 1854.
Susanna, born July 3, 1856.
Mary Ann, born April 13, 1865.
Sophia, wife of E. K., died June 12, 1865.
E. K. died February 12, 1868.

Daniel Yeakel, son of Daniel Yeakel (page 121), married Sarah Landenschlager December 25, 1852. Wife born August 13, 1834. Had issue:

Henry, born December 18, 1853.
Allen, born November 4, 1856.
Mary, born December 18, 1860.
Horace, born September 10, 1864.
Annie, born August 16, 1870.

Rachel Schubert, daughter of David Schubert (page 106), married William Miller January 13, 1853, and had issue as follows:
Maria, born October 29, 1854.
Thomas, born February 13, 1857. Died August 29, 1857.
Elizabeth, born May 27, 1861.
Mandus, born August 22, 1868.
Levi, born June 1, 1870.

Christian Yeakel, son of Abraham Yeakel (page 90), married Frances Emma Carr in 1853. Had issue:
Mary Elizabeth, born January 29, 1854. Died May 29, 1854.
Samuel C., born August 14, 1855. Died September 4, 1862.
Frances Emma, wife of C. Y., died May 28, 1856.
Christian Yeakel married, second time, Leah Edel June 21, 1860. One child,
Kate Elizabeth, born January 22, 1862. Died September 16, 1863.

Daniel Beyer, son of Jacob Beyer (page 132), married Catharine Oberholzer in 1853. Children:
Ellen J., born December 21, 1856.
Elizabeth, born March 4, 1860. Died February 20, 1861.
William N., born December 20, 1862.
Emma K., born July 8, 1868.
Alvin D., born November 8, 1872.

Benjamin Gery, born August 20, 1826, married Lavina, daughter of Anthony Krauss (page 138), February 15, 1853. Children:
  James, born May 17, 1854. Died September 18, 1864.
  Nevin, born October 6, 1855.
  Sarah Catharine, born March 9, 1857. Died February 12, 1858.
  Hannah, born July 18, 1859.
  John Anthony, born December 30, 1861.
  Howard, born September 17, 1864.
  Benjamin Franklin, born September 22, 1866.
  Clement Ulysses, born December 2, 1868.
  Clara Lavina, born May 2, 1870.
  Charles Krauss, born July 13, 1872.
  Ella Maria, born November 6, 1874.

Benjamin A. Yoder, born January 17, 1825, son of George Yoder, married Sarah, daughter of Abraham Yeakel (page 118), February 27, 1853. Children:
  Audora, born October 10, 1854.
  Manoah, born June 18, 1859. Died May 4, 1866.
  George, born September 30, 1862. Died May 17, 1864.
  Hannah Amanda, born December 12, 1864. Died December 28, 1874.
  Daniel, born April 29, 1867.
  Franklin, born May 5, 1870.
  Charles, born February 21, 1873.

Samuel Gilbert, born November 20, 1826, married Catharine, daughter of Jesse Krauss (page 143), May 15, 1853. Children:
  Melaria, born June 17, 1854.
  Emma, born February 17, 1856.

Effinger, born May 1, 1859.
Alice, born June 29, 1867.

Charles Krauss, son of George Krauss (page 102), married Hannah, daughter of Daniel Yeakel (page 121), August 14, 1853. Children:
Levi, born February 24, 1855.
Edwin, born June 13, 1856. Died June 3, 1857.
Daniel, born March 9, 1858. Died April 4, 1859.
Horace, born February 8, 1860.
Milton, born October 18, 1862.
Daughter, born December 12, 1866. Died December 15, 1866.

David Kook married Elizabeth, daughter of Jacob Beyer (page 132), September 10, 1853. Children:
Franklin, born June 3, 1854.
Angeline, born August 31, 1857.
Jacob, born November 24, 1859.
Sarah Elizabeth, born July 15, 1863.
Catharine Ann, born May 15, 1867.

David Bieler, born November 12, 1828, married Amanda, daughter of Jacob Krauss (page 154), November 5, 1853. Children:
Son, born October 6, 1856. Died.
Emma, born December 25, 1857.
Allen, born November 10, 1862.
Elmira, born June 2, 1864.
Elmer, born August 14, 1867. Died.
Harrison, born December 27, 1868.

Jacob S. Yeakle, son of Augustus Yeakle (page 168), married Sarah Ann, daughter of Moses and Susanna Reeser. Wife born November 21, 1853. Children:

Minnie Elenora, born February 6, 1874. Died April 30, 1876.

Jennie Estella, born April 21, 1877.

Jesse Stout, born March 13, 1830, son of Jonathan Stout, married Amanda, daughter of Jacob S. Yeakel (page 152), December 1, 1853. Children:

    Albert Y., born November 29, 1854.

    Morris W., born August 17, 1858.

    Elva Amanda, born January 11, 1862. Died June 9, 1864.

    Emma C., born November 7, 1864.

    Edwin S., born January 28, 1870.

    Laura A., born June 24, 1876.

George Yeakel, son of Jacob Yeakle (page 106), married Amanda, daughter of Peter Streeper. Children:

    Walter, born July 22, 1855. Died February 14, 1864.

    Mary A., born May 14, 1858.

    Horace, born December 12, 1861.

Noah Yeakel, son of Abraham Yeakel (page 147), married Mary A., daughter of Cornelius Fleckenstein, January 1, 1854. Children:

    Irwin, born October 10, 1854. Died September 11, 1857.

    Martha, born September 28, 1857.

    Washington, born December 27, 1861. Died November 7, 1869.

    Henry, born May 18, 1866. Died February 22, 1869.

    N. Y. died October 23, 1866.

Edwin Weidner, born July 15, 1825, married Rebecca, daughter of Rev. Christopher Schultz (page 99), January 14, 1854. Children:
  Son, born June 18, 1855. Died in infancy.
  Myra, born October 3, 1856.
  Medora, born November 29, 1858.
  Susanna, born November 8, 1866.
  Sadie Leah, born May 3, 1875.
E. W. died October 25, 1877.

John Frederick Hartranft, son of Samuel E. Hartranft (page 115), married Sallie D. Sebring, daughter of William L. Sebring, of Easton, Pa., January 26, 1854. Children:
  Samuel Sebring, born October 30, 1855.
  Ada, born March 4, 1857. Died March 22, 1862.
  Wilson, born December 1, 1859. Died March 17, 1862.
  Linn, born June 28, 1862.
  Marion, born September 19, 1865.
  Annie, born February 7, 1867.
  Child. Not named.

John F. Hartranft was born in New Hanover Township, Montgomery County, Pa., December 16, 1830. He is the sixth in descent from Tobias Hartranft, whose record is given on page 2. In his seventeenth year he entered the preparatory department of Marshall College, Pa., where he remained two years, and then entered Union College, Schenectady, New York, where he graduated in 1853. In 1854 he was appointed Deputy Sheriff of Montgomery County by Sheriff Boyer, and again by Sheriff Rudy in 1855. Having read law with James Boyd, Esq., and Hon.

A. B. Longaker, he was admitted to practice law in 1859.

He was Colonel of the 1st Regiment Montgomery County Militia when President Lincoln issued his call for 75,000 men for the defence of the Government. Colonel Hartranft at once tendered the services of his regiment and was accepted; this was the 4th Pennsylvania Regiment, enlisted for ninety days. Colonel Hartranft, upon the expiration of the time of service of the 4th Regiment, served upon the staff of General Franklin at the battle of Bull Run. July 27, 1861, he was commissioned Colonel in the three years' service, and in the following September organized, at Camp Curtin, Harrisburg, the 51st Regiment Pennsylvania Volunteers. On the 18th of November the regiment left Camp Curtin, and was assigned to the corps of General Burnside, who was organizing the North Carolina expedition.

It is not intended to give an extended biography of General Hartranft in this work, as the active part he took in the suppression of the Rebellion would involve too large a space, but merely to note the chief incidents of his valuable and busy life.

He participated in the battles of Roanoke Island, Newbern, second Bull Run, Chantilly, South Mountain, Antietam, Fredericksburg, Vicksburg, Jackson, Campbell's Station, Knoxville, Wilderness, Spottsylvania, North Anna, Cold Harbor, Petersburg Mine, Weldon Railroad, Ream's Station, Poplar Spring Church, first and second Hatcher's Run, Fort Steadman, Petersburg, and Richmond. For his gallantry at Spottsylvania Court-house he was commissioned a Brigadier General, dating from May 12, 1864. For meritorious services he was breveted Major-General March 25, 1865.

This ended the military career of General Hartranft. In August, 1865, he was nominated Auditor-General, and elected in October of that year by 23,000 majority; in the fall of 1868 he was again elected to the same office by a handsome majority.

Upon the expiration of the second term of Governor Geary's administration, General Hartranft was placed in nomination for Governor of Pennsylvania by the Republican party, and after one of the most bitter political contests known in the history of this State, General Hartranft was elected by a triumphant majority of 35,000. On the 26th of May, 1875, Governor Hartranft was again nominated for the office of Chief Magistrate of his native State. This time he was unanimously placed in nomination by the Republican party, the only instance in which a Governor had no opposition in convention for a second term in the history of Pennsylvania. This time he was elected by a majority of over 12,000. Immediately upon his retirement from the Governorship of Pennsylvania President Hayes appointed him Postmaster of the city of Philadelphia, which position he now holds.

Governor Hartranft at present holds the position of Commanding General of the National Guard of Pennsylvania, by appointment of Governor Hoyt. President Johnson appointed him Colonel of the 34th Regiment of the U. S. Army, dating from the 28th of July, 1866, but as he intended to retire to civil life he declined the appointment by suitable acknowledgment.

In the Convention of the Republican party, held at Cincinnati, in the spring of 1876, for the purpose of nominating a candidate for President of the United States, Governor Hartranft's name was presented by his friends, but after several ballotings Governor Hayes, of Ohio, was placed in nomination.

Whatever position General Hartranft was called upon to fill, he always discharged its duties with distinguished ability, whether on the field of battle or as the Executive of the State of Pennsylvania. His modesty, firmness, and integrity won for him the confidence of all who had any business to transact with him.

Mahlon Erb, son of Jacob Erb (page 149), married Sarah, daughter of Abraham Heckler, September 3, 1854. Children:
    Abraham, born July 3, 1855.
    Susanna, born April 19, 1858.
    George, born June 21, 1861. Died May 6, 1869.
    Catharine, born January 2, 1864.
    Sarah, born March 13, 1866.
    Mary Jane, born October 8, 1870.
    Elizabeth, born August 16, 1873.
Sarah, wife of M. E., died January 15, 1879.

Nathaniel Krauss, son of Jesse Krauss (page 143), married Amanda Rowland October 1, 1854. Wife born August 8, 1836. Children:
    Mary C., born November 11, 1855. Died February 14, 1858.
    Rosa, born March 3, 1857.
    William, born October 27, 1858.
    Franklin Augustus, born August 8, 1860.
    Anna Riley, born September 2, 1862. Died January 22, 1873.

Reuben B. Scheffey, born May 12, 1831, married Catharine, daughter of Benjamin Beyer (page 157), October 28, 1854. Children:

    John B., born July 19, 1857. Died February 10, 1858.

    Martha Jane, born July 29, 1860.

    Emma Clara, born August 31, 1872.

Samuel Dresher, son of Oliver Dresher (page 151), married Susanna, daughter of George Scipt (page 137), November 9, 1854.

Andrew K. Kriebel, son of George Kriebel (page 137), married Regina, daughter of Israel Kriebel (page 125), November 16, 1854. Children:

    Isaiah, born December 28, 1855.

    Hiram, born March 31, 1858.

    Justice, born February 21, 1860. Died October 19, 1878.

    Hannah, born July 25, 1862.

    George, born November 7, 1864.

    Elmira, born March 8, 1867.

    Ambrose, born August 16, 1869.

    Irwin, born June 23, 1871.

    Andrew, Jr., born March 20, 1873. Died January 30, 1875.

A. K. Kriebel died January 22, 1878. He was a farmer, and lived at Locust Corner, in Towamencin Township, Montgomery County, Pa.

George D. Kriebel, son of Jacob Kriebel (page 144), married Susanna Strunk December 24, 1854. Had issue:

    Joel, born February 21, 1857.

    Mahlon, born December 4, 1860.

    Mary Ann, born July 18, 1864. Died January 15, 1865.

Emma, born August 25, 1866.
Hannah, born February 3, 1870.
Ellen Cora, born January 9, 1873.
This family resides in Hayesville, Sedgewick County, Kansas.

Joel Yeakel, son of Rev. Andrew Yeakel (page 114), married Mary Ann, daughter of Philip Heimbach, December 31, 1854. Wife born July 10, 1831. Children:
Amalia, born December 18, 1855.
John, born April 18, 1857.
Jonas, born October 24, 1858.
Philip, born January 20, 1861. Died September 11, 1862.
Susanna, born July 20, 1862.
William, born June 16, 1864.
Joel, born August 15, 1866.
Morris, born January 27, 1870. Died September 25, 1870.
Maria, born December 15, 1871.
Caroline, born March 22, 1872.

Enos Neuman, son of Samuel Neuman (page 128), married Augusta Walser. Children:
Oliver E., born May 12, 1856.
Edwin A., born April 30, 1861.
Alfred C., born June 29, 1863.
Christian M., born June 14, 1866.
Enos, born April 3, 1869.
Anna, born August 12, 1870.
Eva, born January 6, 1872. Died July 5, 1872.
Regina, born November 17, 1873.
Robert, born September 14, 1877.
E. Neuman lives in Virginia, near Richmond.

Joseph Nuss, son of Michael Nuss (page 112), married Ann Elizabeth Jacobs. Children:
- Mary Amanda, born June 22, 1856. Died August 1, 1875.
- Henry, born April 3, 1857.
- Calvin, born November 23, 1858.
- Emma Rebecca, born March 30, 1860.
- Daniel, born August 25, 1861.
- Sarah Catharine, born July 3, 1868.
- Cora Ellen, born May 1, 1871.

Joseph Nuss resides in Stephenson County, Illinois.

Charles Schubert, son of David Schubert (page 106), married Helena Fogel. Wife born October 18, 1834. Children:
- Anna, born November 1, 1856.
- Emma, born November 12, 1858.
- Louisa, born June 10, 1861.
- William, born September 12, 1863.
- George, born October 6, 1865.
- Rose, born May 29, 1867.
- Lisa, born April 14, 1875.

Jacob Beyer, son of Jacob Beyer (page 132), married Carolina Haas in 1855. Children:
- Amelia, born October 8, 1856. Died July 23, 1859.
- Abraham, born November 5, 1858.
- John, born July 26, 1860. Died March 11, 1878.
- Elizabeth, born September 23, 1862.
- Mary Ann, born July 15, 1865. Died December 28, 1865.

Samuel K. Master, son of John Master (page 98), married Nancy Burk January 25, 1855. Children:

Elizabeth Jane, born May 30, 1856. Died August 8, 1862.
William H., born November 1, 1858.
Mary L., born April 21, 1862.
Lewis Watson, born, February 23, 1864.

David C. Beyer, son of Andrew Beyer (page 104), married Elizabeth Swartz July 22, 1855. Children:
Wilamina, born August, 1856.
Justus, born February, 1858.
Douglass, born March, 1860.
Morris, born July 8, 1862.
D. C. Beyer died August 14, 1862.

Frederick B. Glase, born September 15, 1823, married Matilda, daughter of Augustus Yeakle (page 168), September 9, 1855. Children:
Sarah J., born March 17, 1856.
Elmira, born April 21, 1859.
Hiram, } twins, born November 23, 1861.
William, }
Elenora, born November 16, 1866.
Laura Rebecca, born February 4, 1876. Died September 1, 1877.

Tilghman Stahl, son of Jesse Stahl, married Susanna, daughter of Anthony Kriebel (page 126), November 6, 1855. Children:
Amelia, born November 11, 1856.
Mary, born November 13, 1858.
Franklin, born August 24, 1861.
John, born October 7, 1863.
Annie, born March 5, 1866.
Henry, born January 5, 1870.
Willie Harvey, born August 19, 1872.

Daniel Y. Urffer, son of David Urffer (page 109), married Susanna Wiegner November 17, 1855. Wife born November 12, 1833. Children:
Daniel W., born February 16, 1857.
Emma S., born February 18, 1859.
Sarah E., born March 23, 1861.
David W., born June 6, 1863.
Catharine, born January 26, 1865.
Hannah Manory, born April 17, 1867.
Ellen Maria, born September 12, 1870.
Agnes, born February 9, 1873.

Abraham A. Kriebel, son of Joseph Kriebel (page 151), married Catharine, daughter of Joseph R. Heebner (page 141), November 25, 1855. Children:
Ellwood H., born November 29, 1856. Died March 31, 1868.
Amos H., born July 27, 1859.
Susanna H., born April 26, 1863.
Joseph H., born August 14, 1865.
Anna Lurena, born December 21, 1873.
Horace H., born August 24, 1876.

Joseph S. Schultz, son of Henry Y. Schultz (page 140), married Ellemina, daughter of Joseph Stauffer, December 8, 1855. Children:
Horace, born November 4, 1856.
Susan, born November 17, 1858.
Emma, born February 2, 1861.
Elmira, born June 22, 1863.
William, born October 10, 1866.
Ellen, born October 28, 1869.

Peter D. Schell, son of Abraham Schell, married Ma-

tilda Y., daughter of Christopher K. Schultz (page 122), 1855. Children:
    Elmira S., born July 24, 1856.
    Emma S., born December 13, 1859.
    Horace S., born May 4, 1865.

Joel S. Schultz, son of Henry Y. Schultz (page 140), married Lydia Schlonecker December 22, 1855. Children:
    Lavina, born March 31, 1857.
    Henry S., born September 16, 1859.
Lydia, wife of J. S. S., died September 21, 1863.
Joel S. Schultz married, second time, Sarah Ziegenfus December 24, 1865. Children:
    Edwin, born October 6, 1867.
    Menda, born August 23, 1871.

Samuel Miller, born July 9, 1823, son of Jacob Miller, married Leah, daughter of Jacob Kriebel (page 123), December 27, 1855. No issue.
Leah, wife of S. M., died February 13, 1857.
Samuel Miller married, second time, Anna, widow of George Schultz (page 208), and daughter of Abraham Yeakel (page 118), February 5, 1859. Children:
    Asa, born February 13, 1860.
    Charles, born April 30, 1862.

John Stout, born September 10, 1828, son of Daniel Stout, married Hannah, daughter of David Kriebel (page 111), January 19, 1856. Children:
    Albert, born May 3, 1856.
    Septimus, born March 7, 1858.
    Allen, born March 19, 1860.

Adonia Schultz, son of Frederick Schultz (page 145), married Elizabeth, daughter of John Anders (page 169), in 1856. Children:
  Katie, born February 3, 1858. Died, 1859.
  Ambrose, born October 30, 1859.
  Mary Ann, born November 24, 1861.
  Lydia, born October 9, 1863.
  John, born December 20, 1865.

William Shaffer, born February 21, 1828, son of John Shaffer, married Carolina, daughter of Jacob S. Yeakel (page 152), February 24, 1856. Children:
  Milton Y., born May 19, 1860. Died August 5, 1860.
  George W., born July 31, 1861.
  Albert, born April 15, 1863.
  Anna C., born March 27, 1866.
  Mary A., born October 28, 1868.
  Lydia, born June 23, 1873. Died August 30, 1873.

Jacob H. Master, son of John Master (page 148), married Mary L., daughter of David Smith, March 19, 1856. Wife born December 11, 1830. Children:
  Mary J., born April 16, 1857.
  John L., born September 23, 1859.
  Charles L., born October 16, 1865.
  Rosa S., born March 31, 1870.
  Frank S., born May 5, 1872.

John W. Cheney, born October 5, 1830, married Jane, daughter of John Master (page 148), March 20, 1856. Children:
  Mary E., born December 29, 1856.
  Catharine, born May 22, 1861.

George M., born February 12, 1862.
Susanna, born June 25, 1863.
Laura, born August 1, 1865.
Homer F., born February 12, 1868.
Martha, born August 22, 1869.
Charles, born September 29, 1872.
Blanche, born February 23, 1878.

Samuel Levan, born November 15, 1835, married Mary, daughter of John Master (page 155), April 8, 1856. Had issue:
　Daniel M., born November 28, 1856.
　Julia Ann, born October 25, 1858.
　Levi, born April 7, 1861.
　Aaron, born April 27, 1864.
　Oliver, born December 14, 1866. Died July 6, 1867.

Horace Miller, born November 1, 1827, married Elmira Regina, daughter of Anthony Krauss (page 138), May 10, 1856. Children:
　Olivia Antoinette, born March 21, 1860. Died December 2, 1867.
　Emerson Franklin, born January 25, 1862.
　Emma Jane, born July 22, 1865. Died December 7, 1867.
　Carrie Krauss, born May 3, 1869. Died June 9, 1872.
　George Krauss, born October 17, 1871.

John Hiestand married Elizabeth, daughter of Israel Krichel (page 125), May 18, 1856. One child,
　Helena, born February 28, 1857. Died July 4, 1858.

J. H. died May 15, 1865, and his widow married, second time, Aaron Butz, March 3, 1867. No issue.

Peter Reichard, son of Henry Reichard, married Edith, daughter of Benjamin Kriebel (page 135), June 7, 1856. Children:
Job, born April 23, 1858.
Hannah, born May 18, 1864.

John S. Schultz, son of Jeremiah Schultz (page 127), married Sarah Ann, daughter of John Baus, July 5, 1856. Children:
Sarah, born July 8, 1857. Died July 10, 1857.
Howard, born September 23, 1858.
Clara, born March 27, 1860.
Irwin, born August 11, 1861.
Warren, born May 4, 1863.
Laura, born January 31, 1865.
Calvin, born July 4, 1866.
Edgar, born November 9, 1870.

Jacob S. Levan, born December 31, 1830, married Hannah, daughter of John Master (page 155), September 9, 1856. Children:
Isaac M., born June 30, 1857.
William E., born July 7, 1863. Died September 17, 1863.
Albert E., born September 12, 1869. Died September 12, 1872.
James S. L., born May 23, 1874.
J. S. L. died May 2, 1876. His widow married, second time, Edwin Roat, April 2, 1878.

Daniel Dresher, son of Samuel Dresher (page 94), married Elizabeth, daughter of Christopher Heebner (page 169), December 3, 1856. Children:

Ella, born September 23, 1857.
Blanche R., born August 7, 1859.
Mattie, born May 13, 1862.
D. D. died March 12, 1875, and his wife died November 2, 1878.

Isaac Kriebel, son of Samuel Kriebel (page 162), married Susanna, daughter of Adam Fisher (page 187), November 14, 1865. Had issue:
Mary, born January 21, 1868.
Abby, born April 3, 1873.

Henry Yeakel, son of Samuel S. Yeakel (page 174), married Sarah Rosenberger, December 13, 1856. Had issue:
Emeline, born December 22, 1857. Died December 5, 1861.
Susannah, born August 7, 1860. Died January 1, 1862.
Catharine, born October 6, 1862. Died November 2, 1863.
Sarah, first wife, died in 1863.
H. Y. married, second time, Sarah Holden May 27, 1865. Children:
Hannah, born June 26, 1866.
Milton M., born March 16, 1868.
Mary, born November 22, 1870.
Lucy, born December 13, 1872.
Henry H., born August 11, 1875.
Anna, born March 18, 1878.

Abraham H. Scipt, son of George Scipt (page 137), married Elizabeth, daughter of George Anders (page 139), September 27, 1856. Children:
Howard, born June 22, 1858.

Frank, born July 19, 1860. Died May 1, 1863.
Mary, born April 3, 1862.
Irene, born August 28, 1864.

Abraham H. Kriebel, son of Joseph Kriebel (page 160), married Susanna, daughter of Melchior Kriebel (page 126), October 23, 1856. Children:
   Salome, born January 10, 1859.
   Lavina, born September 23, 1860. Died April 22, 1873.
   Nathaniel, born August 15, 1862. Died January 6, 1864.
   Jeremiah, born February 19, 1865.
   Abraham, born November 29, 1867.
   Susanna, born December 27, 1871.

William S. Kriebel, son of Isaac S. Kriebel (page 158), married Sarah, daughter of Joseph Cassel (page 143), November 8, 1856. Children:
   Ann Rebecca, born October 15, 1857. Died October 12, 1860.
   Ellen, born September 29, 1859. Died May 2, 1862.
   Isaac, born September 26, 1862. Died April 11, 1875.
   Lawrence, born January 7, 1868.
   Sylvanus, born October 8, 1873. Died April 10, 1875.

Benjamin Erb, son of John Erb, married Angeline, daughter of Jesse Krauss (page 143), November 19, 1856. Children:
   Almer E., born April 1, 1866.
   John H., born November 12, 1867.
   Edgar A., born October 29, 1869.

Clement G., born November 6, 1871.
Ada J., born August 27, 1874.
Daniel W., born January 19, 1877.

Levi Yeakel, son of Abraham Yeakel (page 118), married Susanna, daughter of Jacob Ditloh, November 23, 1856. Wife born February 6, 1835. Children:
Asalina D., born April 8, 1857.
Caroline D., born February 24, 1860.
Ellen D., born November 28, 1863.
Mary D., born February 8, 1866.
Adaline D., born June 8, 1870.
Mira D., born July 26, 1872.
Levi G., born February 7, 1876.

Henry W. Snyder, son of Job Snyder (page 159), married Mary C., daughter of Enos Hagey, December 27, 1856. Wife born May 29, 1835. Children:
Annie H., born February 4, 1858.
Justus H., born February 23, 1861.
Josiah R. H., born July 3, 1865.
Susie H., born June 8, 1869.
Mary C., wife of H. W. S., died March 17, 1873.
Henry W. Snyder married, second time, Lavina, daughter of Jacob Schultz (page 195), 1878.

Henry Master, son of Isaac Master (page 107), married Alvira Haymaker December 31, 1856. Wife born February 22, 1840. Children:
Edward, born September 27, 1857.
Adoniam Judson, born November 23, 1859.
George M., born October 20, 1861.
Mary Jane, born September 14, 1863.
William Henry, born March 9, 1867. Died.

Isaac Master, son of John Master (page 155), married
Lydia Ann Freed. Children:
  Maria, born December 8, 1858.
  John Franklin, born October 5, 1860.
  Nancy, born March 24, 1862.
  Oliver, born June 17, 1864.
  Levi, born March 13, 1866.
  Irwin, born January 11, 1868.
  Albert Edward, born September 17, 1870.
  Elsie Jane, born October 17, 1872.
  Miranda, born January 31, 1875.
  William Austin, born March 5, 1877.

Thomas Yeakle, son of Augustus Yeakle (page 168), married Leanna Schock November 28, 1857. Had issue:
  Ida, born March 1, 1859.
  Hannah, born January 8, 1862.
  Franklin, born June 12, 1867.
  Alice Sophia, born March 25, 1870.

Jeremiah Meschter, son of Jeremiah Meschter (page 113), married Elizabeth, daughter of David Kriebel (page 111), February 7, 1857. Children:
  Henry, born November 25, 1857. Died December 30, 1857.
  Allen, born January 25, 1859.
Elizabeth, wife of J. M., died April 16, 1861.

Isaac Krauss, son of Jesse Krauss (page 143), married Catharine, daughter of James Fox, March 21, 1857. Wife born September 1, 1834. Had issue:
  Jefferson, born January 1, 1858.
  Sarah E., born August 1, 1867.

William M. Yeakel, son of John Yeakel (page 166), married Harriet D., daughter of Andrew Boyd, April 8, 1857. Children:
  Mary E., born June 22, 1858.
  John A., born February 24, 1860.
  Warren R., born May 15, 1862.
  Harry B., born December 9, 1863.
  L. Gertrude, born October 21, 1865.
  Harriet E., born March 11, 1867. Died August 7, 1867.
  William D., born November 16, 1868.
W. M. Y. died November 12, 1869. He was a printer by trade, and lived in Philadelphia.

Israel H. Urffer, son of Joshua K. Urffer (page 149), married Maria, daughter of Abraham Reinhard. Children:
  Charles W., born September 12, 1857.
  Albert H., born July 21, 1861.
  Sarah E., born February 6, 1864.

John Q. Master, son of John Master (page 148), married Rebecca, daughter of William C. Jones, September 18, 1857. Children:
  Alice Gertrude, born September 8, 1858.
  Emma Helen, born December 26, 1859.
  Elmer Watson, born August 31, 1861.
  Charles Edgar, born December 25, 1862. Died March 4, 1865.
  Mary Ettie, born May 21, 1866. Died September 7, 1866.
  Effie May, born February 11, 1868.
  Nellie Susan, born February 26, 1876.

Abraham H. Cassel, son of Isaac B. Cassel (page 161),

married Lydia, daughter of Abraham Kriebel (page 162), November 10, 1857. Children:
  Isaiah, born August 31, 1858.
  Mary Ann, born October 1, 1860.
  Abraham K., born September 30, 1862.
  Rebecca, born September 16, 1864. Died November 8, 1866.
  Sophia, born July 8, 1866.
  Emma, born December 25, 1868.
  Katie, born October 12, 1871.
  Lydia K., born January 13, 1874.

Joel Schultz, son of Henry H. Schultz (page 158), married Sarah K., daughter of Amos Schultz (page 168), November 21, 1857. Children:
  Emma, born January 27, 1859.
  Milton, born November 9, 1860.
  Isaac, born September 25, 1862.
  Henry, born February 16, 1865.
  Elizabeth, born September 12, 1867.
  William, born May 23, 1870.
  Susanna, born December 4, 1872.
  Lucina, born March 16, 1875.

Joseph Kriebel, son of Israel Kriebel (page 125), married Susanna Gehman March 13, 1858. One child, Horace, born July 30, 1859. Died April 10, 1860. J. K. died December 29, 1859.

James K. Master, son of Isaac Master (page 151), married Susanna Burns May 7, 1858. Wife born May 12, 1834. Children:
  Mary Elizabeth, born June 5, 1859.
  Martha Elzina, born December 16, 1860.
  James M., born November 3, 1862.

Isaac Sherman, born June 20, 1865.
Susanna Rosetta, born December 14, 1866.
Emily Jane, born December 13, 1868. Died September 2, 1870.
Nancy Elva, born September 2, 1871. Died August 22, 1873.
Thomas William, born April 27, 1874.
Susanna, wife of J. K. M., died October 8, 1874.

Elizabeth Yeakel, daughter of Samuel S. Yeakel (page 174), married David High in 1858. Had issue:
Addison,
John,   } all three dead.
Samuel,
Mary Ann, born 1862.
Elizabeth, wife of D. H., died January 3, 1866.

Charles Keller, born December 31, 1832, son of Samuel Keller, married Lydia, daughter of Jeremiah Anders (page 158), May 9, 1858. Children:
Catharine Elizabeth, born August 23, 1859. Died March 26, 1868.
Mary Amanda, born March 12, 1862. Died February 3, 1868.
Harry, born November 13, 1864.
Harvey, born June 7, 1866.
Elmer, born June 18, 1868. Died June 7, 1875.
Charles, born October 28, 1870. Died August 25, 1871.
Jeremiah, born July 29, 1872.
Anna, born December 9, 1874. Died September 8, 1875.

Henry Kriebel, son of Israel Kriebel (page 125), married Mary Ann, daughter of Jacob Wiegner. Children:

Howard, born July 6, 1859.
Ellen, born April 25, 1861. Died August 22, 1862.
Emerson, born December 20, 1862. Died April 15, 1863.

Mary Ann, wife of H. K., died.

Henry Kriebel married, second time, Elizabeth, daughter of Gabriel Griesemer (page 191), 1867. Issue:
Elmer, born July 27, 1867.
Lewis, born October 2, 1869.
Calvin, born July 6, 1870.
Regina, born May 24, 1872.
Owen, born February 2, 1874. Died February 25, 1874.
Sallie, born April 17, 1875.
Andrew, born September 4, 1877.

Jesse Yerger, born February 6, 1831, married Mary, daughter of Frederick Schultz (page 145), October 12, 1858. Children:
Selina, born May 23, 1859.
Josiah, born July 13, 1861.
Mary Ann, born October 19, 1862.
Isabella, born October 18, 1864.
John, born August 27, 1866.
Samuel, born September 23, 1869.
Irwin, born March 19, 1872.
Morris, born September 28, 1874.

Abraham K. Kriebel, son of George Kriebel (page 137), married Phœbe, daughter of Isaac S. Kriebel (page 158), October 14, 1858. Children:
Romanus, born February 6, 1860. Died April 7, 1875.

Sophia, born July 24, 1861.
Ellen, born March 2, 1864.
Charles, born June 17, 1865.
Emma, born June 8, 1868.
Christina, born November 8, 1871. Died February 24, 1875.
Amanda, born September 25, 1873.
Allen, born January 7, 1875.

Samuel K. Yeakel, son of Jacob Yeakel (page 155), married Sophia Reitz October 4, 1858. Children:
Mary Ella, born June 25, 1860.
Anna Martha, born October 18, 1861. Died April 3, 1864.
John Henry, born March 12, 1866.
Child, born August 21, 1867. Stillborn.
Samuel, born December 11, 1868.
Harvey, born October 22, 1871.
Sophia, wife of S. K. Y., was born May 30, 1831, in Dulach, Baden, Germany.

Benjamin L. Heebner, son of Joseph R. Heebner (page 141), married Susanna, daughter of Amos Godschall, December 12, 1858. Wife born September 23, 1837. Children:
Anna G., } twins, born January 27, 1860.
Amos G., }
Amos G. lived only 36 hours.
Mary Ellen G., born September 17, 1861.
Daniel G., born May 5, 1864.
Emma G., born April 19, 1867. Died May, 1867.

Joseph Wiegner, son of Abraham Wiegner (page 165), married Margaret, daughter of ———, December 25, 1858. Wife born January 15, 1832. Children:

GENEALOGICAL RECORD.   255

John B., born April 13, 1860.
Mary B., } twins, born May 9, 1869.
Lanie Lizzie,
 Lanie Lizzie died July 29, 1869.

Amos K. Krauss, son of Jacob Krauss (page 154), married Sophia Edelman February 4, 1858. Wife born January 17, 1840. Children:
 Cillia Amanda, born February 1, 1859.
 Ambrose, born August 5, 1860. Died August 12, 1860.
 Preston Percius, born July 31, 1861.
 Morris, born January 23, 1864.
 Percifer, born April 12, 1866.
 Puella, born March 17, 1869.
 Virginia, born January 27, 1871.
 Curtis, born December 13, 1872.
 Sylvia, born August 10, 1876.

Andrew A. Kriebel, son of Joseph Kriebel (page 151), married Lydia, daughter of Daniel K. Urffer (page 197), March 3, 1859. Children:
 Edwin U., born December 19, 1859.
 Sarah U., born October 11, 1861.
 George U., born September 9, 1863.
A. A. K. died of a broken leg in 1863.
Lydia, widow of A. A. K., died February 27, 1868.

Abraham Kriebel, son of Joseph Kriebel (page 166), married Rachel, daughter of David Anders (page 173), March 3, 1859. Children:
 Anna Katie, born December 26, 1859.
 Nathaniel, born September 30, 1862.
 Mary Jane, born December 1, 1866.

Moses Shuler, son of Joshua Shuler, married Sarah, daughter of Anthony Yeakel (page 184), August 9, 1859. Children:
  Albert, born October 28, 1861.
  Asa, born October 18, 1863.
  Ellen, born June 11, 1865.
  Wesley, born October 25, 1867.
  Elizabeth, born August 2, 1869.
  Morris, born October 21, 1872.

Mary Heydrick, daughter of Isaac Heydrick (page 139), married John Jacoby, May 5, 1859. Children:
  Widdifield, born May 8, 1861. Died in infancy.
  Russel Powel, born July 22, 1862.
  Emma Mary, born August 27, 1872. Died in infancy.
  Flora, born July 26, 1876.

David Heydrick, son of Isaac Heydrick (page 139), married Emily Hutchinson, of Easton, June 2, 1859. Children:
  Ella Francis, born August 1, 1861.
  Johnnie, born August 17, 1862. Died in infancy.
  Sarah Minnie, born March 27, 1863. Died in infancy.
  Mary Louisa, born October 26, 1866.
  Alfred Melville, born July 20, 1870.
  Charles Seymour, born June 4, 1872.

Henry K. Kindig, born October 29, 1839, married Sophia, daughter of Jeremiah Anders (page 158), September 10, 1859. Children:
  Mary, born June 24, 1860. Died February 5, 1861.
  Emma, born March 19, 1862.

Annie, born September 14, 1863.
John H., born February 20, 1866.
Katie, born February 23, 1868.
Lillie, born January 21, 1870.
Marvin, born August 12, 1872.
Carrie, born June 15, 1875.
Reside in Philadelphia.

Samuel K. Kriebel, son of Samuel Kriebel (page 133), married Rachel C., daughter of John Custer, October 15, 1859. Children:
Anna, born December 14, 1860.
Sarah Ella, born April 28, 1863.
Morris, born July 10, 1864.
Lizzie, born August 8, 1866.
Lydia, born January 10, 1868.
Susan, born December 27, 1871.
Samuel, born July 25, 1873.
John, born November 5, 1876.

Samuel K. Anders, son of George Anders (page 139), married Mary Ann, daughter of David S. Heebner (page 163), October 20, 1859. Children:
Horace, born July 23, 1860. Died August 22, 1860.
George H., born October 29, 1861.
David, born June 26, 1863. Died August 6, 1863.
Anna Laura, born April 24, 1866.

William A. Schultz, son of Samuel Schultz (page 179), married Maria, daughter of Anthony S. Heebner (page 135), October 18, 1859. Children:
Mary Ann, born August 26, 1860.
Harrison, born April 26, 1862. Died December 11, 1868.

Emma, born March 23, 1864.
Amanda, born May 23, 1866.
Amos, born February 28, 1870.
Katie, born September 23, 1872.
Samuel, born November 11, 1875.

Jesse Tyson, born January 23, 1835, son of John Tyson, married Sophia, daughter of Job Snyder (page 159), November 5, 1859. No issue.

William Schultz, son of George Schultz (page 115), married Catharine, daughter of Rev. George Meschter (page 154), November 8, 1859. Children:
George, born February 8, 1862.
Charles, born November 15, 1863.
Howard, born January 14, 1866.
Annie, born March 7, 1867.
Milton, born December 20, 1870.

John W. Master, son of Isaac Master (page 151), married Mary E. Burns November 24, 1859. Children:
Samuel W., born August 9, 1860. Died January 27, 1863.
James W., born November 29, 1861.
Rachel J., born August 19, 1863.
Nathan E., born September 27, 1865.
Jacob, born October 26, 1869.
Mary E., wife of J. W. M., born January 27, 1841, died July 28, 1871.
John W. Master married, second time, Mary A. Meley December 29, 1872. Children:
Mary M., born January 17, 1874.
Charles F., born January 15, 1875.
George W., } twins, born May 2, 1876.
Sarah C., }

George W. died May 19, 1876.
Sarah C. died May 3, 1876.
John E., born April 7, 1877.

Mary Yeakel, daughter of Samuel S. Yeakel (page 174), married Joseph A. Hendricks December 1, 1859. One child,
Emma, born February 11, 1865.
J. A. Hendricks lives at Perkasie, Bucks County, Pennsylvania, and is engaged in the mercantile business at that place.

Theodore W. Bean, son of William and Mary (Weber) Bean, married Hannah, daughter of John Heebner (page 145), January 4, 1860. Children:
William H., born July 25, 1861.
Mary L., born November 6, 1863.
Lane S., born June 27, 1878.
Colonel Bean enlisted August 23, 1862, in Company L, 17th Pennsylvania Cavalry, appointed 1st Sergeant; promoted to Second Lieutenant October 17, 1862, to First Lieutenant November 21, 1862, and to Captain of Company L, November 1, 1863. He was brevetted Major and Lieutenant-Colonel March 13, 1865, and discharged by General Orders June 20, 1865. He is a prominent member of the Norristown bar, having been admitted February 24, 1869. In 1876 he published "Washington at Valley Forge One Hundred Years Ago," etc., which was well received and had extensive circulation.

Nathan Kaufman, born December 12, 1819, married Rebecca, daughter of David Schubert (page 106). One child,
Franklin, born June 5, 1860.

William Hallman, born December 25, 1841, married Selina, daughter of Jacob Krauss (page 154), January 27, 1860. Children:
  Ellen, born May 22, 1861.
  Howard, born February 3, 1863. Died July 19, 1863.
  Samuel Franklin, born October 3, 1864. Died August 25, 1865.
  William Henry, born October 20, 1865.
  Emma Maria, born March 1, 1867.
  Lizzie, born November 12, 1868. Died June 22, 1869.
  Amanda Lydia, born January 23, 1870.

Joel S. Kriebel, son of Benjamin Kriebel (page 135), married Mary, daughter of Jacob Traut, May 5, 1860. Wife born December 20, 1840. Children:
  Benjamin F., born January 15, 1861.
  Jacob T., born December 11, 1863.
  Edwin Grant, born June 2, 1865.
  Linwood T., born June 8, 1869.
  Charles T., born June 17, 1872.
  Mary Ella, born March 6, 1878.

Christopher Heydrick, son of Charles H. Heydrick (page 141), married Frances Helen Irwin June 20, 1860. Children:
  Carl, born June 3, 1863.
  Harriet, Richard Irwin, } twins, born February 24, 1866.
    Richard Irwin died August 7, 1866.
  Eva D., born November 27, 1867. Died November 22, 1871.
  Frederick Paul, born October 23, 1869.

Helen, born May 30, 1876.

C. H. is an attorney-at-law, and resides in Franklin City, Pa.

John Henry Geisser, son of John Henry Geisser, married Catharine, daughter of John Yeakel (page 153), August 26, 1860. Children :
    Catharine, born August 31, 1861.
    Margaret, born April 8, 1863. Died January 18, 1864.
    Christina, born November 17, 1864. Died April 18, 1869.
    John Henry, born November 18, 1866.
    David, born September 16, 1868. Died December, 1869.
    Clara, born September 13, 1870.

Edwin S. Stahlnecker, son of George Stahlnecker, born October 1, 1836, married Anna Regina, daughter of Jacob S. Yeakel (page 152), August 30, 1860. Children :
    Lydia, born March 26, 1866. Died in infancy.
    Laura, born March 1, 1868. Died December 21, 1868.
    Alice, born July 29, 1871.
    Yeakle, born October 16, 1872. Died in infancy.
    Henry Wilson, born June 27, 1878.

Josephus Yeakel, son of John Yeakel (page 166), married Sophia M., daughter of John W. Harmar, September 17, 1860. Children:
    Amy M., born June 5, 1861.
    Marietta E., born June 1, 1864.
    Mary E., born March 24, 1867.
    Josephus Yeakel enlisted as a private in Company A,

150th Pennsylvania Volunteers (Bucktails), in 1862, and served during the years 1863, 1864, and 1865, until peace was declared. After returning home he worked at the printing business, which he had learned with Major Freas, of Germantown, and in 1867 commenced publishing the "Manayunk Sentinel." He represented the Twenty-first and Twenty-eighth wards in the Legislature of Pennsylvania during 1875, 1876, 1877, and 1878, and on January 1, 1879 was appointed an assessor of real estate and personal property in Philadelphia, for the term of five years.

Andrew Kriebel, son of Israel Kriebel (page 125), married Christina, daughter of Charles Schultz (page 181), October 17, 1860. Children:
  Allen, born June 28, 1861.
  Oscar, born September 10, 1863.
  Mary Alice, born June 3, 1866.
A. K. died October 10, 1876.

Anthony K. Heebner, son of Anthony S. Heebner (page 135), married Catharine S., daughter of John Anders (page 169), November 15, 1860. Children:
  Emanuel, born October 10, 1861.
  Jacob A., born November 1, 1868.

Matthias Lukens married Rebecca Ann, daughter of Joseph Wiegner (page 167), November 15, 1860. Children:
  Frankland, born January 20, 1862. Died August 9, 1862.
  William, born September 28, 1863.
  Frances, born October 18, 1867.
  Elizabeth, born October 14, 1875. Died November 28, 1875.

Michael Harris, son of Michael Harris, born December 11, 1810, married Catharine, daughter of Abraham Yeakel (page 90), December 17, 1860. No issue.

Samuel Wile, son of Samuel Wile, married Anna, daughter of Jesse Krauss (page 143). Children:
Emma, born August 8, 1862.
Charles, born August 21, 1864.
Oliver, born June 7, 1866. Died November 9, 1867.
Allen, born November 22, 1869. Died June 5, 1875.
Malaretta, born February 8, 1873.
Earlie, born April 1, 1877.

Levi Master, son of John Master (page 155), married Maria Fried January 1, 1861. Wife born January 24, 1840. Children:
William, born December 6, 1861. Died December 17, 1861.
Eliza Ann, born July 27, 1863.
Elsie Jane, born November 27, 1865. Died September 7, 1866.
Sheridan, born March 7, 1869.
Francis Barnes, born January 5, 1876.

Emily Yeakle, daughter of Joseph Yeakle (page 172), married Joseph Nash April 4, 1861. Husband born September 21, 1833. Children:
Elvie M., born April 4, 1862.
Joseph Y., born March 5, 1864.
Harry L., born October 30, 1866.
Annie, born December 27, 1870.
Daniel Irwin, born March 1, 1875.

Daniel Yeakel, son of Jacob Yeakel (page 181), married Mary, daughter of David Andrews, August 3, 1861. Children:
  Naomi, born November 11, 1862.
  George W., born January 10, 1866.
  Samuel A., born February 22, 1871.
  William A., born March 30, 1873. Died September 26, 1873.
  Susanna A., born May 5, 1874. Died September 22, 1874.
  Moses A., born March 23, 1876. Died April 8, 1876.
  Rosanna A., born April 7, 1877.

Solomon B. Yeakel, son of Benjamin Yeakel (page 170), married Emma D., daughter of John M. Reiter, September 3, 1861. Children:
  Mary M. L., born January 17, 1863.
  Morris A., born January 7, 1867. Died June 26, 1867.
  Elon J., born August 24, 1869.
  Ida E., born March 18, 1872.
  John B., } twins, born January 25, 1876.
  Solomon D., }
    Solomon D. died January 25, 1876.
  Emma D., wife of S. B. Y., born January 5, 1833.

Peter C. Heydrick, son of Charles H. and Mary Ann Heydrick (page 141), married Margaret Ann Doughty September 12, 1861. Children:
  William, born September 9, 1862. Died March 9, 1865.
  Charles, born August 17, 1864.
  James Doughty, born February 20, 1869.

Helen May, born July 21, 1871. Died April 3, 1872.

Kate Eliza, born May 26, 1873.

Isaac Y. Krauss, son of Anthony Krauss (page 138), married Theodora R., daughter of Rev. Frederick Waage, October 8, 1861. Children:

Elmer Frederick, born September 7, 1862.
Florence Sarah, born May 23, 1864.
Edgar Anthony, born May 24, 1867.
Charles Oswin, born May 14, 1869.
Walter Isaac, born January 23, 1878.

Theodora R., wife of I. Y. K., born November, 1839.

Joseph L. Heebner, son of Joseph R. Heebner (page 141), married Susanna, daughter of George Kriebel (page 137), October 17, 1861. Children:

Charles K., born August 10, 1862. Died same day.
George K., born July 5, 1863.
Ida Jane K., born December 28, 1864.
Elmira K., born July 11, 1867.
Susanna K., born March 30, 1870. Died next day.
Harrison K., born April 26, 1872.

Susanna, wife of J. L. H., died November 2, 1873.

Joseph L. Heebner married, second time, Mary Jane, daughter of James Hipple, March 16, 1875. Child,

James Warren, born July 25, 1877.

William Yeakel, son of Joseph Yeakel (page 128), married Lucinda, daughter of John Backenstos, November 24, 1861. Children:

Cora Jane, born May 8, 1868.
Ellen Jane, born May 8, 1871.
Rosa Margaret, born October 20, 1872.
William Alfred, born February 9, 1875.

W. Y. resides near Zionsville, Lehigh County, Pa., and is a farmer.

Charles Kriebel, son of George Kriebel (page 137), married Mary, daughter of Abraham Reiff, February 14, 1862. Children:
George R., born November 7, 1862. Died January 30, 1863.
Sarah Jane, born August 16, 1864.
Laura, born June 21, 1868. Died August 14, 1868.
Katie R., born September 19, 1869.
Lillie, born October 20, 1878.
Mary, wife of C. K., born March 30, 1843.

Amos R. Freyer, born January 20, 1838, married Mary Ann, daughter of David Meschter (page 189), March 7, 1862. Children:
Ambrose, born August 22, 1863.
Ammon, born December 7, 1864.
Alfred, born December 27, 1866.
Amie, born August 27, 1872.
Elizabeth, born November 13, 1873.

Anna Wiegner, daughter of Joel Wiegner (page 167), married John F. Fisher, born December 22, 1831, son of Jacob Fisher, in 1862. Children:
Sarah, born October 10, 1862.
Son, born December 1, 1864. Died aged 7 days.
Susanna, born December 8, 1865.

William Schultz, son of Henry Y. Schultz (page 140), married Dinah Haugen May 1, 1862. Children:
Anna, born July 30, 1862.
Olivia, born September 30, 1864. Died February 19, 1870.

Amanda, born May 22, 1868.
Sarah, born July 4, 1871.
James, born June 17, 1874.

Jacob Hoffman married Anna, daughter of Anthony Yeakel (page 184), May 8, 1862. Children:
Emma, born March 8, 1863.
Franklin, born February 4, 1865.
Harrison, born September 15, 1866.
Calvin, born July 23, 1874.
Ellwood, born May 31, 1876.

Henry M. Beideman, born August 1835, married Hannah, daughter of Jacob B. Beyer (page 175), May 31, 1862. Children:
Isaac B., born March 25, 1863.
Daniel B., born May 29, 1864.

John Anders, son of Jeremiah Anders (page 158), married Susanna, daughter of Abraham Clemens, June 17, 1862. Children:
Maria, born January 26, 1863.
Abraham, born October 21, 1864. Lived only one day.
Jeremiah, born May 27, 1866.
Catharina, born February 29, 1868.
Anna, born September 15, 1869.
John, born August 4, 1871. Died May 1, 1875.
Horace, born January 23, 1873.
Sue, born May 10, 1875.
Clara, born February 1, 1877.

Manoah Meschter, son of Henry Meschter (page 150), married Sarah Ann, daughter of Reuben Rothenberger, August 9, 1862. Children:

Sally Ann, born January 1, 1863.
Mary Etta, born May 8, 1864. Died June 7, 1865.
Reuben Henry, born October 14, 1866.
Alice, born August 27, 1868.
Emeline, born August 7, 1870.
James, born May 19, 1873.
John, born October 29, 1874.
Charles Alfred, born July 24, 1876.
William Franklin, born August 23, 1878.
Sarah Ann, wife of M. M., born November 18, 1841.

Henry H. Keck, son of George Keck, born January 24, 1837, married Susanna M., daughter of Benjamin Yeakel (page 170), October 14, 1862. Children:
Arabella, born 1863.
Irene E., born June 21, 1869.

Maria Yeakle, daughter of George Yeakle (page 190), married Manassa De Long December 13, 1862, by whom she had three children, two sons and a daughter, all still living.
Maria, wife of M. De L., died December 5, 1872.

George Krauss, son of Henry Krauss (page 175), married Sarah, daughter of Christopher Wiegner (page 150), November 4, 1862. Children:
Ellen, born February 5, 1864.
Dinah, born September 4, 1865.
Samuel, born October 13, 1867.
Andrew, born November 24, 1869.
Manuel, born October 16, 1871.
Amanda, born November 25, 1873.
Anatta, born July 5, 1876.

Samuel Heydrick, son of George Heydrick (page 87),

married Maria, daughter of Abraham Kriebel (page 162), November 11, 1862. Children:
   Daniel, born November 15, 1863.
   George, born January 28, 1865.
   Susanna, born March 19, 1867.
   Mary, born March 23, 1868.
   Anna, born February 26, 1870.
   Regina, born January 12, 1872.
   Sarah, born October 17, 1873.
Maria, wife of S. H., died November 16, 1873.

William Dennis, son of William Dennis, born November 16, 1833, married Elizabeth, daughter of Christopher Wiegner (page 150), December 25, 1862. Children:
   Oswin, born August 24, 1863.
   William, born June 21, 1865.
   Susanna, born July 18, 1867. Died March 29, 1868.
   Horace, born January 7, 1869.
   Sarah Agnes, born January 27, 1871.
   Abraham, born February 3, 1874.
   Samuel, born February 24, 1877.

Charles W. Beyer, son of Samuel B. Beyer (page 179), married Sallie Ann De Haven December 25, 1862. Wife born September 17, 1842. Children:
   George W. J., born February 5, 1866. Died August 9, 1867.
   Mary Alice, born August 17, 1867.
   Walter M., born June 18, 1870.

Christina Kriebel, daughter of George Kriebel (page 137), married Abraham Rittenhouse, born June 13,

1842, son of Samuel Rittenhouse, January 20, 1863.
Children:
  Sophia, born January 3, 1864.
  Maria, born January 10, 1867.
  Samuel K., born November 12, 1870. Died August 5, 1871.
  Charles, born July 25, 1873.
  Susan, born April 6, 1876. Died April 8, 1876.
  John, born May 28, 1877.

Samuel Wiegner, son of Christopher Wiegner (page 150), married Susanna, daughter of James Fox, born March 26, 1844. Children:
  Adelaide, born November 27, 1864.
  James Alvin, born August 8, 1868. Died December 28, 1869.
  Lenora, born September 17, 1871.
  Laura, born February 20, 1874.

George Biles married Harriet, daughter of John Master (page 155). Children:
  Alice, born December 30, 1864.
  George Frederick, born February 14, 1866.
  Oscar P., born September 23, 1867.
  John Master, born October 6, 1869.
  William J., born June 24, 1871.
  Harriet Eliza, born April 1, 1873. Died April 26, 1874.
  Mary Ann, born January 25, 1875.
  Frances Maud, born November 25, 1877.

Abraham K. Anders, son of George Anders (page 139), married Mary Ann, daughter of John Hendricks, January 27, 1863. Wife born March 4, 1836. Children:

Fransanna, born September 8, 1864. Died August 22, 1865.

Franklin H., born August 9, 1866.

Charles Heydrick, son of Isaac Heydrick (page 139), married Sallie P. Cannon, daughter of Governor Cannon, of Delaware, January 21, 1863. Children:
Margaret C., born April 14, 1867.
Ellie Buckalew, born July 18, 1870. Died July 5, 1871.
Ray, born November 16, 1871.

William L. Heebner, son of Joseph R. Heebner (page 141), married Edith, daughter of Anthony Anders (page 173), February 6, 1863. Children:
Anna Elizabeth, born January 24, 1864. Died January 13, 1865.
Anthony A., born September 7, 1865.
Hannah Louisa A., born May 22, 1868. Died March 7, 1873.
Susanna A., born December 26, 1873.
Amanda A., born August 4, 1875.

Isaac C. Beyer, son of Jacob B. Beyer (page 175), married Sarah Elizabeth Gross, April 25, 1863. Wife born August 15, 1844. Children:
Elizabeth G., born January 29, 1866.
Wilson G., born February 7, 1868.

Sarah Elizabeth, wife of I. C. B., died August 14, 1870.

Isaac C. Beyer married, second time, Sophia Swartz, June 8, 1872. Wife born June 29, 1850. Children:
Howard S., born December 17, 1874.
Jacob Abner S., born July 9, 1877.

Edwin B. Krauss, son of George S. Krauss (page 175), married Hannah, daughter of Anthony Krauss (page 138), May 23, 1863. One child,
 Albert, born April 28, 1866.

Abraham A. Yeakle, son of Samuel Yeakle (page 134), married Anna Eliza, daughter of Jesse Sheppard (page 183), September 15, 1863. Children:
 Frank S., born June 16, 1864.
 J. Morris, born June 23, 1867.
 Hattie May, born July 2, 1870.

Jacob Stahlnecker, son of George Stahlnecker, born March 14, 1838, married Elamina, daughter of Jacob S. Yeakel (page 152), September 17, 1863. Children:
 Franklin Y., born October 27, 1868.
 Edwin S., born December 23, 1870.
 Mary Y., born May 9, 1873.

Henry K. Urffer, son of Daniel K. Urffer (page 197), married Mary, daughter of Rev. Joshua Schultz (page 172), 1863. Children:
 Edwin, born December 22, 1863.
 Elmira, born March 19, 1865.
 Adam, born October 1, 1868.
 Allen, born February 15, 1870.
 George, born November 8, 1871.
 Laura, born July 23, 1873.
 Samuel, born August 13, 1875.
 Daniel, born September 10, 1877.

David M. Cassel, son of Joseph Cassel, born October 24, 1839, married Amanda, daughter of Joseph B. Kriebel (page 199), October 17, 1863. Children:
 Ida K., born September 3, 1864.

Milton K., born March 2, 1867.
Joseph K., born August 24, 1870.
Margaret K., born September 9, 1874.

Anna Yeakel, daughter of Samuel S. Yeakel (page 174), married Samuel Bishop July 10, 1863. One child, Amanda, born November 29, 1864.

Samuel Carl, son of George Carl, born May 10, 1825, married Elizabeth, daughter of Jesse Krauss (page 143), October 17, 1863. Children:
George Morris.
Elijah James, born April 24, 1866.
Elizabeth Catharine, born April 4, 1869.
Ellen Amanda, born March 30, 1871.
Joshua Albert, born February 28, 1875.

Nathaniel Beyer, son of Benjamin Beyer (page 157), married Mary Jane Keyser November 7, 1863. Wife born July 28, 1844. Children:
Vienna, born August 11, 1864.
Nathan Montgomery, born September 24, 1870.

Abraham S. Krauss, son of Henry Krauss (page 175), married Sarah, daughter of Enoch Schultz (page 194), October 15, 1863. Children:
Allen, born March 2, 1865.
William, born January 23, 1867. Died August 20, 1868.
Laura, born July 19, 1868.
Annie, born May 1, 1870.
Harvey, born November 20, 1872.
Charles, born July 17, 1875.
Emma Jane, born October 29, 1877.

Henry Master, son of Jacob Master (page 152), married Phœbe P., daughter of David Dubois, October 29, 1864. Had issue:
Rosetta Edna, born December 12, 1864.
Lent, born October 5, 1866.
Josephine, born April 21, 1872. Died February 20, 1875.
Roy, born September 5, 1875.
Bertie, } twins, born October 14, 1876.
Myrtie, }
Bertie died October 29, 1876.
Myrtie died November 6, 1876.

Jacob Wiegner, son of John Wiegner (page 179), married Sophia, daughter of Henry Krauss (page 175), February 2, 1864. Children:
Priscilla, born December 21, 1864. Died.
John, born September 25, 1866.
Christianna, born December 31, 1867.
Marian, born April 25, 1870. Died.
Ida, born October 1, 1871.
Laura, born August 8, 1873.
Carolina, born March 18, 1875.
Sophia, born June 23, 1877.

John Wiegner, son of Ezra Wiegner (page 199), married Adeline, daughter of Daniel Wiegner, March 12, 1864. Children:
Amalia Sarah, born October 12, 1864.
Mary Jane, born December 5, 1866.
Malinda, born May 14, 1869.
Alvin W., born October 17, 1871.
Ephraim, born May 15, 1874.
Emma Maria, born November 14, 1877.

Martin Keel, born May 26, 1841, married Barbara A., daughter of Jacob Meschter (page 129), April 19, 1864. Children:
  Catharine Elizabeth, born June 25, 1865.
  Andrew Howard, born March 7, 1867. Died July 15, 1868.
  Harry Thompson, born November 11, 1869.
  Maggie Cole, born October 23, 1871.
  Emma List, born October 8, 1875.
  Martin Keel resides in Chester City, Pa.

Jesse A. Heydrick, son of Charles H. and Mary Ann Heydrick (page 141), married Lizzie W. Nellis May 5, 1864. Children:
  Florence T., born October 8, 1865. Died August 10, 1866.
  James C., born March 1, 1869.
  William H., born February 22, 1871.
  Thomas G., born August 23, 1873.
  Lawrence C., born May 5, 1875.
  Annie Mabel, born January 22, 1877.

Nathaniel H. Anders, son of Frederick Anders (page 142), married Regina G., daughter of Joseph Schultz (page 180), May 19, 1864. Children:
  Howard S., born November 12, 1866.
  Alsenia S., born July 20, 1868. Died April 10, 1870.
  Ada May S., born May 29, 1873.
  D. Webster S., born June 10, 1877.

Joel H. Krauss, son of Aaron Krauss (page 174), married Mary E. Sunderman June 16, 1864. Had issue:
  Granville Moody, born March 8, 1865.
  Thaddeus Stevens, born February 5, 1867.

Mattie Cora, born November 5, 1869.
Francis Gurney, born February 28, 1873. Died July 5, 1874.

William H. H. Master, son of Isaac Master (page 151), married Carolina Kitchart August 22, 1864. Issue:
Ellsworth, born October 17, 1865. Died April 23, 1877.
Ida Viola, born March 7, 1867.
Rhoda Dell, born June 15, 1869.
Minnie May, born September 18, 1872.
Christopher L., born February 23, 1875.
Carolina, wife of W. H. H. M., born March 31, 1840.

James Beyer, son of Jacob Beyer (page 132), married Elizabeth Dettra in 1864. Children:
James Irwin, born November 28, 1869.
May Ella, born January 3, 1872.
Vernon, born July 29, 1874.

Joseph K. Schultz, son of Frederick Schultz (page 145), married Sarah S., daughter of Isaac S. Kriebel (page 158), October 18, 1864. Children:
Sarah Ellen, born June 15, 1865. Died January 6, 1867.
Eugene, born February 4, 1867.
Allen, born October 21, 1868.
Amanda, born December 29, 1870.
Mary, born June 30, 1873. Died August 24, 1874.
Elmer, born January 15, 1875.
Isaac, born April 7, 1876.
Emma Jane, born December 1, 1877.

John S. Anders, son of David Anders (page 173), married Mary S., daughter of Joseph Boorse, October 22, 1864. Wife born October 28, 1844. Children:

David B., born April 25, 1866.
Joseph B., born May 8, 1868.
John B., born April 14, 1870.
Mary Alice, born May 16, 1872. Died May 11, 1873.
Louisa B., born July 25, 1874.
Walter B., born October 17, 1877.

Enos Schultz, son of Henry H. Schultz (page 158), married Lydia N., daughter of Enoch Schultz (page 194), November 5, 1864. No issue.

Abraham G. Oberholzer, son of Abraham K. Oberholzer, born April 16, 1841, married Regina, daughter of Joseph Kriebel (page 166), November 19, 1864. Children:
Mary Ann K., born August 17, 1865.
Katie Lizzie K., born August 26, 1869.

David Krauss, son of Andrew Krauss (page 84), married Sophia, daughter of John B. Miller, December 4, 1864. Wife born February 10, 1835. Children:
Victor, born February 25, 1867.
Louis, born March 27, 1871. Died January 8, 1878.

Job Kriebel, son of Benjamin Kriebel (page 135), married Sarah Ann, daughter of Jacob Trout, December 17, 1864. Wife born August 10, 1843. Children:
Emeline, born May 26, 1869.
Sylvanus, born January 3, 1875.

George Pennick married Mary Ann, daughter of Samuel Beyer (page 204). Children:
Ellwood, born May, 1866.

Horace Edgar, born December, 1868. Died November 17, 1877.
Irwin, born April, 1873.
Bertha, born December, 1876.

John M. Baker married Emma, daughter of Samuel Beyer (page 204). One child,
Anna, born November 25, 1866.

Jacob Wean, son of Jacob Wean, born August 25, 1836, married Sophia S., daughter of John Anders (page 169). Children:
Mary, born November 21, 1866. Died November 14, 1868.
Laura, born February 18, 1874.

James U. Bean married Sarah, daughter of Jacob Beyer (page 132), January 28, 1865. Children:
Ida Jane, born November 26, 1865.
James Wilson, born October 16, 1867.
Mary Catharine, born April 24, 1870.
Sarah Elizabeth, born September 14, 1872.
Charles Nelson, born July 24, 1878.

John E. Brecht, son of John Brecht, married Sarah, daughter of George Kriebel (page 137), February 18, 1865. Children:
Emma K., born January 21, 1866.
George K., born October 7, 1867.
Samuel K., born December 14, 1869.
Katie K., born October 19, 1874.

Solomon Kriebel son of Jacob Kriebel (page 123), married Anna Maria Schlicher December 14, 1866. Wife born June 12, 1846. Children:

Samuel, born February 21, 1869.
Ella Amanda, born October 25, 1870.
Hannah, born February 20, 1873.
Charles Franklin, born September 19, 1875.
William, born February 20, 1878.

Charles William Heydrick, son of Charles H. and Mary Ann Heydrick (page 141), married Mary Clark Ten Broeck May 4, 1865. Children:
Mary Ten Broeck, born September 3, 1867.
Christopher, born September 20, 1869. Died October 13, 1871.
Benjamin Alexander, Sophia, } born December 17, 1871.
Sophia died December 27, 1871.
Josephine Jacquelin, born December 26, 1873.
Louis Clare, born May 20, 1875.
Charles Francis, born February 2, 1877.
Anna Amanda, born February 7, 1879.

Solomon Krauss, son of Henry Krauss (page 175), married Elizabeth, daughter of Henry Huber, May 18, 1865. Children:
Ellen, born October 4, 1865.
Henry, born January 22, 1867.
William, born April 26, 1869.
Emma, born November 4, 1874.

Joseph Snyder, son of Job Snyder (page 159), married Amanda, daughter of Samuel Sterner, June 16, 1865. Wife born October 19, 1825. Children:
Job S., born November 5, 1867.
Salome S., born March 2, 1869.
Samuel S., born March 20, 1870.

Isaac Snyder, son of Isaac Snyder (page 165), married Elizabeth, daughter of Enos Hagey, September 2, 1865. Children:
  Amanda, born July 19, 1867.
  Edwin, born November 8, 1869.
  Isaac, born December 25, 1871.
  Nathaniel, born July 25, 1873.
  Joseph, born May 30, 1875.
  Lizzie Ann, born June 29, 1878.

Simon Cassel, son of Daniel Cassel, married Esther, daughter of Bernard B. Freyerd (page 188), September 5, 1865. Children:
  Allen F., born December 4, 1866.
  Katie F., born November 25, 1868.
  Jacob F., born November 6, 1870.
  Charles F., born October 3, 1872.
  Annie F., born August 10, 1874.
  Edith F., born July 20, 1876.

Andrew Kriebel, son of Abraham Kriebel (page 162), married Elizabeth, daughter of Jacob Alderfer, September 12, 1865. Wife born March 30, 1840. Children:
  Jacob, born June 24, 1866.
  Anna, born August 17, 1868.
  Howard, born February 1, 1871.
  Henry, born May 20, 1873.
  Andrew, born January 10, 1879.

George Weikert, son of Jacob Weikert, born October 29, 1826, married Sarah, daughter of Jacob Yeakel (page 181), October 21, 1865. Children:
  Emeline, born September 21, 1868.
  William, born May 7, 1872.

Isaac D. Heebner, son of David S. Heebner (page 163), married Catharine, daughter of Jacob Grater, October 26, 1865. Children:
  Mary Jane, born March 7, 1870.
  Charles G., born October 18, 1874.

Joseph K. Schultz, son of Amos Schultz (page 168), married Susan B., daughter of George S. Krauss (page 175), November 9, 1865. Children:
  Elmer K., born April 20, 1867.
  Hannah K., born March 11, 1870.
  Amos K., born November 12, 1871.
  Olivia K., born January 17, 1876.

Anna Schultz, daughter of George Schultz (page 153), married Christian Stahl December 19, 1865. Children:
  George, born February 8, 1867.
  Flora, born November 23, 1868
  Isaac, born February 1, 1871.
  Albert, born December 20, 1872.
  Levi, born August 14, 1874.
  Ida, born April 23, 1878.

Solomon Schell, son of Jonathan Schell, born January 22, 1833, married Anna, daughter of Christopher Wiegner (page 150), 1865. Children:
  Elias, born April 20, 1866.
  Susanna, born February 16, 1868.
  Amandus, born May 6, 1874.

William H. Bachman married Anna, daughter of Jacob Kriebel (page 144). Children:
  Morris Piper, born April 18, 1867.
  Charles Henry, born August 25, 1871.
  Olivia, born January 21, 1876.

Thomas R. Gerhard, son of Solomon Gerhard (page 155), married Annie Shelton January 20, 1866. One child,
Walton W., born October 30, 1866.
T. R. Gerhard resides in New Jersey.

George H. Seipt, son of George Seipt (page 137), married Sarah M., daughter of Samuel Anders (page 183), January 25, 1866. Children:
Mary Ann, born July 10, 1867.
Samuel A., born September 19, 1869.
George A., born July 6, 1871.
Allen A., born October 23, 1874.
Howard A., born April 29, 1878.

Mary Yeakel, daughter of Jacob Yeakel (page 155), married Henry S. Moyer January 28, 1866. Children:
Ella, born January 17, 1867.
Hannah, born March 5, 1870.
Harry, born August 15, 1872.
Irwin, born November 30, 1875.

George S. Anders, son of Anthony Anders (page 173), married Amanda, daughter of John S. Heebner (page 208), January 27, 1866. One child,
Anthony H., born December 22, 1866.

William Hoffman, married Sarah, daughter of Samuel H. Schultz (page 202), February 3, 1866.

Harrison Y. Krauss, son of Anthony Krauss (page 138), married Mary Oberholzer February 10, 1866. Wife born August 21, 1844. One child,
Emma R., born May 2, 1869.

Charles W. Eberhard, born August 27, 1845, married Emma R., daughter of Anthony Krauss (page 138), March 18, 1866. No issue.

Solomon Yeakel, son of Abraham Yeakel (page 118), married Amanda, daughter of John Albright, June 23, 1866. Children:
  Laura Ann, born January 24, 1868.
  Asher A., born February 1, 1870.

Isaac B. Yeakel, son of Samuel Yeakel (page 184), married Maria K., daughter of Charles Wiand, 1866. Children:
  Charles Frederick, born January 25, 1867.
  Hannah B., born July 26, 1868.
  Susan L., born February 14, 1872.
  Asher Christopher, born January 20, 1874.
  I. B. Yeakel is a practicing physician near Schultzville, Berks County, Pa.

Allen O. Bieler, son of Henry Bieler, born July 18, 1845, married Caroline, daughter of Henry H. Schultz (page 158), December 29, 1866. Children:
  Oswin, born October 2, 1868.
  Clinton, born February 3, 1870. Died May 3, 1870.
  Susanna, born October 3, 1871. Died July 14, 1872.
  Rosanna, born December 22, 1873.

George W. Fisher, son of Jacob Fisher, married Susanna, daughter of Jacob Yeakel (page 161), December 30, 1866. Children:
  Ida, born February 18, 1868.
  Jacob Edward, born June 18, 1870.

James Beard married Martha Jane, daughter of Samuel Beyer (page 204). Children:
  William Walker, born March 20, 1868.
  Harry, born November 8, 1869.
  Lillie, born March 18, 1872.

Franklin, born July 1, 1874.
Hannah, born August 6, 1876.

William K. Anders, son of George Anders (page 139), married Mary A., daughter of Benjamin and Barbara Kugler, January 20, 1867. No issue.

Michael Hienerschitz, born September 27, 1840, married Catharine, daughter of Jacob Krauss (page 154), March 24, 1867. Children:
Emma K., born July 15, 1870.
Katie Laura K., born December 16, 1874.

Hiram Schultz, son of Michael Schultz (page 191), married Catharine B. Hackman May 27, 1867. Children:
Matilda, born July 25, 1868.
Ida, born March 30, 1872.
Alvin, born October 14, 1874.
Morris, born March 27, 1877.

Jacob K. Freyer, son of Bernard B. Freyer (page 188), married Mary D., daughter of James Kerr, September 10, 1867. No issue.

Samuel Z. Kriebel, son of William Kriebel (page 192), married Sarah, daughter of Henry Stong, October 12, 1867. Children:
Mary Emma, born December 26, 1870. Died January 16, 1871.
Sallie Amanda, born April 4, 1874.
Alvin, born November 28, 1875. Died December 8, 1875.

Addison Schultz, son of Daniel S. Schultz (page 193), married Sarah, daughter of Charles Gerhard (page 171), October 17, 1867. One child,

Adelaide, born April 14, 1869.
Sarah, wife of A. S., died November 19, 1875.
A. S. died April 9, 1876. This was Dr. Schultz, formerly of Schultzville, Berks County, Pa.

John W. Master, son of Jacob Master (page 152), married Mary G., daughter of William Harris, August 3, 1867. Had issue:
Lorretta, born August 15, 1868.
Edna May, born June 28, 1874.

Henry H. Heebner, son of Abraham Heebner (page 149), married Susanna, daughter of Joseph Krauss (page 183), October 26, 1867. Children:
Abraham, born November 20, 1869. Died April 9, 1872.
John, born January 9, 1871.
Ellen, born April 2, 1872.
Flora, born December 26, 1874.
Harvey, born February 18, 1877.

William F. Harpst married Emma R., daughter of Edward Yeakel (page 195), October 30, 1867. Had issue:
Henry E., born July 25, 1868. Died March 16, 1869.
Frederick M., born May 30, 1870.
Sarah B., born May 27, 1875.

John B. Kriebel, son of Abraham Kriebel (page 162), married Rebecca, daughter of Isaac Cassel (page 161), November 7, 1867. Children:
Martha, born December 17, 1868.
Alvin, born May 3, 1870.
Mary, born November 30, 1871.
Sarah, born August 4, 1873.

J. B. Kriebel is a minister of the Society of Schwenkfelders, and resides near Kulpsville, Pa.

Josiah D. Heebner, son of David S. Heebner (page 163), married Susan S., daughter of Abraham Anders (page 185), November 21, 1867. Children:
  Horace A., born June 7, 1870.
  Ann Rebecca, born July 17, 1873. Died June 17, 1875

George K. Meschter, son of Rev. George Meschter (page 154), married Mary Ann, daughter of Charles Krieble (page 190), November 21, 1867. Children:
  Cyrus, born March 14, 1869.
  Charles, born September 19, 1871.
  Nora, born August 14, 1874.
  Irene, born April 24, 1876.
G. K. Meschter is a physician, and lives near Centre Point, in Worcester Township.

Isaac S. Yeakle, son of Augustus Yeakle (page 168), married Amanda, daughter of Solomon Schultz (page 206), November 30, 1867. Children:
  Mary Ann, born September 17, 1868.
  Laura Jane, born February 25, 1872.
  Samuel Newton, born January 9, 1874.
  Martha Ellen, born March 22, 1876.
  Howard, born October 19, 1879.

Michael Gehman, son of Samuel Gehman, born November 30, 1831, married Hannah, daughter of Samuel Krauss (page 170), December 24, 1867. Children:
  Flora, born September 1, 1868.
  Kate, born June 11, 1870.
  Charles, born December 29, 1871.
  Matilda, born December 1, 1877.

George Wiegner, son of John Wiegner (page 179), married Emma, daughter of Henry Cassel, December 28, 1867. Children:
  Horace, born September 10, 1868.
  Howard, born September 7, 1869. Died July 17, 1870.
  Henry F., born November 29, 1872.
  George R., born May 18, 1877.

Mahlon Krauss, son of Jesse Krauss (page 143), married Diana, daughter of Reuben Schantz, January 18, 1868. Wife born June 7, 1844. Children:
  Edwin, born May 18, 1869.
  Allen, born May 7, 1872. Died February 7, 1877.
  Harry Eugene, born May 13, 1874.
  Milton, born July 29, 1876.
  M. K. died April 12, 1877.

Sarah Yeakel, daughter of Samuel S. Yeakel (page 174), married William Barringer May 30, 1868. Children:
  Irwin, born May 9, 1870.
  Anna, born March 18, 1872.
  Sarah, wife of W. B., died November 19, 1875.

Jacob F. Fischer, son of Jacob Fischer, born December 25, 1838, married Anna, widow of Ephraim Kriebel (page 223), and daughter of George Kriebel (page 137), January 25, 1868. Children:
  Sophia, born January 24, 1869.
  Laura, born April 28, 1871.

Mahlon H. Cassel, son of Joseph Cassel (page 143), married Lydia K., daughter of Rev. George Meschter (page 154), January 25, 1868. Children:
  Minnie M., born November 27, 1868.

Flora, born March 26, 1870.
Alice, born July 12, 1871.
Martha, born May 8, 1873.

William S. Anders, son of Abraham Anders (page 185), married Susanna, daughter of Aaron Krauss (page 174), February 1, 1868.

This is the Rev. W. S. Anders, a minister of the Society of Schwenkfelders.

Joseph S. Anders, Jr., son of Anthony Anders (page 173), married Hannah, daughter of Abraham Kriebel (page 162), February 4, 1868. Children:
Anna, born July 8, 1870.
Araminta, born January 31, 1871.
Hannah, born October 1, 1873. Died February 2, 1874.
Margaret, born June 9, 1875. Died November 28, 1875.
George, born March 10, 1878.

Charles Heydrick, son of Abraham Heydrick (page 97), married Mira, widow of Samuel Yeakel (page 177), and daughter of George Rex, February 22, 1868. No issue.

Benjamin S. Kriebel, son of Benjamin Kriebel (page 135), married Emeline, daughter of Hezekiah Zieber, March 14, 1868. Wife born September 18, 1849. Children:
Sybilla G., born February 18, 1869.
Catharine Ann, born September 15, 1870.
Roger G., born January 18, 1874.
Hezekiah G., born November 30, 1875.

Manoah Schultz, son of Rev. Joshua Schultz (page 172),

married Annetta, daughter of John Trump, April 25, 1868. Wife born July 23, 1848. Children:
 Katura, born February 13, 1869.
 Ambrose, born April 25, 1872.
 Sallie, born September 9, 1873.
 Anna Amanda, born November 3, 1875. Died same day.
Annetta, wife of M. S., died November 6, 1875, and he married, second time, Mary Wiand, in 1878.

Enos Benner, son of Samuel Benner, married Mary, daughter of Ezra Wiegner (page 199), May 2, 1868. Children:
 Sarah Ann, born September 26, 1869.
 Margaret, born August 11, 1872.
 Lavina, born August 18, 1874.
 Matilda, born March 11, 1876.
 Elmer, born February 6, 1878.

Charles Fluck married Sarah H., daughter of Reuben Schultz (page 187), May 23, 1868. One child,
 Albert Franklin, born November 19, 1873.

Septimus Kriebel, son of Henry Kriebel (page 188), married Harriet Wood June 10, 1868.

Amos A. Yeakel, son of Edward Yeakel (page 195), married Virginia A. Jones June 17, 1868. Children:
 Edward H., born March 18, 1872.
 Elmer Allen, born June 2, 1875.
A. A. Yeakel is editor of a paper in West Greenville, Mercer County, Pa.

Jacob K. Meschter, son of Rev. George Meschter (page

154), married Hannah, daughter of Joseph Cassel (page 143), July 3, 1868. One child,
Nellie, born June 25, 1874.

Lewis E. Master, son of George C. Master (page 189), married Minerva Hanford July 6, 1868. Wife born May 24, 1850. Children:
Mary Roberts, born April 28, 1869.
Emma Maud, born December 11, 1871.
Alice B., born July 31, 1874. Died November 21, 1874.
Minerva, wife of L. E. M., died November 7, 1874.

John Van Karnel, born October 17, 1842, married Elizabeth, daughter of Samuel Master (page 218), August 16, 1868. Children:
Anna S., born April 16, 1869.
Amelia, born April 27, 1871. Died September 3, 1872.
Ida, born March 8, 1875.
Charles, born February 16, 1877.

William H. Younts, born June 20, 1841, married Mary K., daughter of Aaron Master (page 192), September 17, 1868. Children:
Phœbe B., born September 10, 1869.
Lewis A., born March 5, 1872.
Quincy A., born February 1, 1874.
Jasper F., born October 4, 1876.

Charles Meschter, son of. Rev. Jacob Meschter (page 202), married Catharine, daughter of Benjamin Linsenbiegler, September 26, 1868. Children:
Andrew Howard, born October 13, 1869.
Samuel Ellwood, born June 14, 1873. Died July 9, 1875.

Joseph H. Anders, son of Frederick Anders (page 142), married Susanna, daughter of Abraham Kriebel (page 162), November 19, 1868. Children:
Harvey, born September 1, 1869.
Emerson, born January 4, 1873.
Susanna, wife of J. H. A., died January 10, 1879.

Hiram A. Krieble, son of Charles Krieble (page 190), married Susanna, daughter of Rev. Jacob Meschter (page 202), November 26, 1868. Children:
Alan, born March 7, 1871. Died May 15, 1875.
May, born May 7, 1875.
Charles, born December 14, 1877.

Henry S. Keely, born February 25, 1844, married Sarah, daughter of Frederick W. Schultz (page 145), November 28, 1868. Children:
Mary S., born October 11, 1869.
Clara S., born October 24, 1872.
Harvey S., born April 12, 1875.
Harry S., born July 20, 1877.

Jacob D. Heebner, son of David S. Heebner (page 163), married Lydia, daughter of Jacob Kriebel (page 200), November 28, 1868. Children:
Alvin K., born July 16, 1870.
David K., born July 9, 1871.
Wilson K., born January 18, 1874.

Charles Hiestand married Mary, daughter of Israel Kriebel (page 125), December 19, 1868. Children:
Ida, born December 24, 1869.
Louisa, born October 22, 1872.
Emma, born September 16, 1875.
Mary, born November 24, 1877.

Elijah Kriebel, son of Levi Kriebel (page 193), married Margaret E., daughter of James Kane, December, 1868. Wife born June 18, 1847. Children:
Frank, born February, 1870. Died October, 1873.
Agnes E., born July, 1874.

Samuel Schultz, son of Henry H. Schultz (page 158), married Mira, daughter of Reuben Schantz, in 1869. Wife born November 29, 1847. Children:
Amanda, born November 1, 1869.
Ellen, born November 24, 1870. Died February 26, 1871.
Wilson, born March 12, 1872. Died September 20, 1872.
Charles, born September 21, 1873. Died June 4, 1874.
Caroline, born January 31, 1876.
Emanuel, born February 27, 1877.

Isaac B. Schultz, son of Anthony Schultz (page 185), married Magdalena S., daughter of John Anders (page 169), January 16, 1869. One child,
Howard A., born August 4, 1870.

John Snyder, son of Jesse Snyder (page 176), married Elizabeth Ann, daughter of Silas Kolb, January 23, 1869.

David D. Kriebel, son of Jacob Kriebel (page 200), married Susanna, daughter of Samuel Schultz (page 179), January 23, 1869. Children:
Son, born April 25, 1870. Died same day.
Mary Ann, born April 28, 1871.
Harrison, born July 4, 1872. Died July 18, 1872,

Laura, born April 14, 1874. Died August 18, 1874.

Wilson, born September 6, 1875. Died October 15, 1875.

Ellena, born March 13, 1877. Died August 8, 1877.

Joseph Z. Yeakel, son of Joseph Yeakel (page 128), married Susanna E., daughter of Nathan Carl, January 30, 1869. Children:
Corwin J., born 1869.
Sarah A., born September 16, 1874. Died August 8, 1875.
Sarah Jane, born December 15, 1876.

Daniel W. Yeakle, son of Joseph Yeakle (page 172), married Mary E. Thompson April 14, 1869. Wife born February 3, 1849. Had issue as follows:
Mary Theresa, born September 3, 1870.
Emily, born April 23, 1873.

George Schultz, son of Samuel Schultz (page 164), married —— Rhoads May 15, 1869. Children:
Henry, born October 25, 1870.
Maria, born January 26, 1878.

Jacob Yeakle, son of Joseph Yeakle (page 172), married Emma J., daughter of Dr. Charles Bolton, January 21, 1869. Wife born January 21, 1846. Children:
Lucy B., born October 31, 1869.
Joseph H., born January 7, 1871.
Sarah Elizabeth, born April 18, 1874.

Samuel Gerhard, son of Solomon Gerhard (page 155), married Mary E. Starr March 28, 1869. Children:

Elmer S., born December 20, 1869.
Katie R., born July 23, 1872.
Samuel B., born May 28, 1875. Died July 17, 1875.
S. Gerhard resides in the State of New Jersey.

John Schultz, son of Henry Y. Schultz (page 140), married Catharine Blank September 25, 1869. One child,
  Charles Henry, born March 13, 1870.
Catharine, wife of J. S., died April 18, 1875.

Ambrose Gerhard, son of Daniel Y. Gerhard (page 201), married Regina K., daughter of Anthony Schultz (page 205), October 14, 1869. Children:
  Elmer, born January 21, 1871.
  Agnes, born March 28, 1872.
  Mary, born August 19, 1873.
  Horace, born July 3, 1877.

Nathaniel Hallman, son of Jacob Hallman, married Helena, daughter of Anthony Yeakel (page 184), October 30, 1869. One child,
  Harvey, born August 9, 1870.

Abraham Schultz, son of David Schultz (page 198), married Mary Ann, daughter of Joel Yeakel (page 197), October 30, 1869. Children:
  William H., born April 7, 1873.
  Ellen Jane, born November 13, 1875.

Jacob Weierman, son of Michael Weierman, born November 22, 1839, married Susanna, daughter of Job Snyder (page 159), November 15, 1869. Children:
  Henry S., born November 1, 1870.

Susanna S., born November 23, 1871.
Jesse S., born December 24, 1874.
Sophia S., born February 12, 1875.

Enoch M. Heebner, son of Joseph R. Heebner (page 141), married Deborah, daughter of Samuel Rittenhouse, December 11, 1869. Children:
Mary Ann, born December 17, 1870.
Samuel, born December 12, 1872.
Joseph, born July 3, 1876.
John, born April 19, 1878.

Joseph S. Anders, son of Abraham Anders (page 185), married Sarah F., daughter of Levi Weaver, January 28, 1870. One child,
Ellwood W., born May 3, 1871.

Reuben D. Kriebel, son of Jacob Kriebel (page 200), married Mary S., daughter of David Anders (page 173), February 5, 1870. Children:
Jacob, born February 3, 1871.
Ellen, born July 24, 1873.
David, born October 2, 1877.

Jacob F. Wood, born May 18, 1848, married Lydia, daughter of Augustus Yeakle (page 168), March 5, 1870. Children:
Harry, born December 23, 1871.
William, born September 15, 1874. Died January 12, 1877.

Samuel Urffer, son of Samuel Urffer (page 152), married Caroline, daughter of Henry Weiss, May 12, 1870. Wife born December 6, 1848. Children:
Alice M., born December 31, 1871. Died July 19, 1872.

William H., born November 30, 1873. Died July 20, 1877.
Lizzie A., born October 3, 1875.
Edward J., born July 29, 1877.

Allen F. D. Johnson, born May 9, 1845, married Susanna, daughter of Amos Schultz (page 168), June 4, 1870. Children:
Elmer Ellsworth, born June 26, 1872.
Jacob Paris, born November 8, 1874.

Edward Ellis Master, son of George C. Master (page 198), married Carrie A. Barnum June 9, 1870. One child,
Edward Henry, born November 29, 1873. Died February 2, 1875.

Peter Schultz, son of Henry Y. Schultz (page 140), married Susan B. Stauffer July 11, 1870. Children:
Manoah, born November 27, 1873.
Nora, born January 1, 1878.

Levi Kerling Master, son of John Master (page 148), married Mary A., daughter of Lemuel Smith, September 8, 1870. Children:
Leoni C., born October 25, 1871.
Susie L., born May 2, 1873.
Oren P., born December 30, 1874.
Maurice M., born May 17, 1877.

Henry Ackerman, son of Jacob Ackerman, born December 28, 1848, married Sarah Ann, daughter of Joseph Krauss (page 183), September 10, 1870. Children:
Arthur Wilson, born July 12, 1873.
Emma Jane, born June 12, 1876.

Edward S. Krauss, son of Jonathan Krauss (page 196), married Sarah, daughter of John S. Heebner (page 208), November 12, 1870. Children:
    Warren, born June 29, 1872.
    Morris, born September 17, 1874.
    Susanna, born May 19, 1877.

Cornelius Beyer, son of Henry F. Beyer (page 208), married Caroline Keyser January 1, 1871. Issue:
    Ida, born October 26, 1871.
    Edda, born February 27, 1873.
    Kate, born October 18, 1874.
    Henry, born February 21, 1876.

Jesse S. Kriebel, son of Isaac S. Kriebel (page 158), married Susanna, daughter of William Kriebel (page 192), February 4, 1871. Child,
    Malinda, born March 4, 1878.

Noah Snyder, son of George Snyder (page 182), married Catharine Ann, daughter of Levi Henge, 1871. Children:
    Wilemina, born November 23, 1871.
    Mary Amanda, born March 23, 1873.
    Sarah Minerva, born August 6, 1874. Died May 4, 1876.
    Catharine Ann, wife of N. S., died February 25, 1876.

George Simpson, son of William Simpson, born February 22, 1847, married Lucianna, daughter of George Schultz (page 208), February 23, 1871. One child,
    Anna, born October 8, 1872.

John Beck married Katie, daughter of Henry F. Beyer (page 208), June 4, 1871. Children:

Lewis, born December 23, 1872.
Addie, born September 13, 1875.
Franklin, born April 1, 1878.

Isaiah Burgstresser, son of John Burgstresser, born March 5, 1840, married Sophia, daughter of Abraham Kriebel (page 162), July 25, 1871. Children:
Anna, born February 16, 1872.
Mary, born October 3, 1873.
Emma, born January 21, 1875.
Lizzie, born January 19, 1877.
George, born February 9, 1879.

Henry S. Kriebel, son of Septimus Kriebel (page 224), married Lizzie Ann, daughter of Elias Cassel, July 22, 1871. Wife born March 24, 1850. Children:
Septimus, born September 23, 1874.
Elias Wilbur, born December 25, 1877.

Edwin Weber, son of Martin Weber, born August 3, 1845, married Anna, daughter of Daniel Seibert (page 159), July 22, 1871. One child,
Lily Elizabeth, born June 18, 1875.

Simon H. Yeakel, son of Benjamin Yeakel (page 170), married Emeline, daughter of George Haines, September 12, 1871. Wife born November 14, 1845. One child,
George B., born November 3, 1875.

Samuel B. Master, son of John Master (page 148), married Loretta J., daughter of William Roberts, September 21, 1871. Wife born August 15, 1853. Children:
Ora R., born November 8, 1873.
Thomas W., born January 29, 1876.
Ada B., born December 28, 1877.

John K. Kriebel, son of George A. Kriebel (page 207), married Katie L., daughter of Abraham Reiff, November 18, 1871. Wife born March 31, 1849. Children:
    Abraham R., born December 21, 1872.
    Susan Helen, born July 28, 1874.
    Charles, } twins, born March 5, 1877.
    Mary,

Henry S. Kriebel, son of John Kriebel (page 225), married Catharine, daughter of John Wiegner (page 179), November 18, 1871. Children:
    Mary Emma, born August 18, 1872.
    Clara, born November 15, 1874.
    Erwin, born May 11, 1877.

William Scipt, son of George Scipt (page 137), married Amanda, daughter of Samuel Schultz (page 179), November 25, 1871. Children:
    Irene, born November 3, 1873.
    Ella, born October 31, 1876.

Hosea K. Kriebel, son of Reuben Kriebel (page 214), married Amanda, daughter of Isaac Zimmerman, November 30, 1871. Wife born May 6, 1853. Children:
    Isaac Clarence, born August 7, 1872.
    Reuben Owen, born June 17, 1874.
    Charles Wesley, born September 3, 1876.
    Frederick Light, born December 23, 1878.

Oswin Hillegass, son of William Hillegass, married Sarah, daughter of Anthony Schultz (page 185), 1872. One child,
    Warren, born January 22, 1873.
Sarah, wife of O. H., died August 9, 1873.

Enos Kriebel, son of George A. Kriebel (page 207), married Magdalena, daughter of Abraham Wiegner (page 165), January 20, 1872. Children:
  Warren, born November 3, 1872.
  Mary, born March 6, 1874.
  Edwin, born September 19, 1875.
  Ida, born January 7, 1878. Died March 10, 1878.

Samuel A. Schultz, son of Samuel Schultz (page 179), married Matilda, daughter of John Anders (page 169), February 10, 1872. Children:
  Twins, sons, born April 3, 1874. Died same day.
S. A. S. died May 13, 1875.

Elvie E. Yeakle, daughter of Joseph Yeakle (page 172), married Cleaver R. Supplee February 14, 1872. Husband born August 6, 1847. Children:
  Percy E., born November 27, 1872.
  John P., born November 1, 1875.
  Emma E., born December 20, 1877.

Jared K. Master, son of George C. Master (page 189), married Magdalena Fellman May 9, 1872. Wife born February 13, 1851. Children:
  Charles Adsett, born July 10, 1873. Died October 14, 1874.
  Walter, born November 23, 1874.
  Albert, born December 12, 1876.

Chester K. Schultz, son of Solomon Schultz (page 206), married Maggie H., daughter of Jacob Crater, March 29, 1872. Wife born June 28, 1854. Children:
  Isaac Linnwood, born July 7, 1873.
  Mary Alice, born March 9, 1875.
  Sophia G., born July 6, 1877.

James Brown, son of Thomas J. Brown (page 130), married Mary E. Byles June 27, 1872. Children:
Aton Wick, born September 9, 1873.
Anna, born May 14, 1875.

James M. Beyer, son of Jacob C. Beyer (page 214), married Sallie Mirkil September 16, 1872. Wife born September 30, 1852. Children:
James Walter, born March 14, 1874.
Lidey Bainbridge, born August 12, 1877. Died September 22, 1877.
Franklin G., born November 25, 1878.
Resides in Philadelphia.

Solomon S. Schultz, son of Jeremiah Schultz (page 127), married Hannah L. Magill September 27, 1872. Children:
Edward M., born July 22, 1873.
William M., born February 15, 1878.
S. S. S. is a physician, and received a thorough medical education in the best schools of Europe, and at present holds the position of Superintendent of the State Insane Asylum at Danville, Pa.

Edwin K. Schultz, son of Amos Schultz (page 168), married Amanda, daughter of Andrew K. Schultz (page 196), October 19, 1872.

Edward Berger married Ann, daughter of Henry F. Beyer (page 208), October 22, 1872. Children:
Henry, born October 15, 1873.
George A., born August 1, 1876.

Jeremiah Kriebel, son of Jeremiah Kriebel (page 200),

married Isabella Shelly August 10, 1872. Wife born February 21, 1855. Children:
Charles, born January 17, 1874.
Jacob, born April 7, 1876.
William, born April 19, 1878.

William D. Heebner, son of David. S. Heebner (page 163), married Emma L., daughter of Jesse Frantz, November 6, 1872. Children:
Clarella, born August 27, 1873.
Carrie Blanche, born April, 1876.

Elias Snyder, son of Jesse Snyder (page 176), married Lydia, daughter of Abraham Wiegner (page 204) November 9, 1872. Children:
Mary Ann, born November 24, 1873.
Abraham, born February 23, 1876. Died August 14, 1876.

Josiah Hunsberger, son of Jesse Hunsberger, born September 2, 1847, married Sarah S., daughter of Jonathan Krauss (page 196), November 23, 1872. Children:
Hannah K., born July 2, 1873.
Susanna K., born February 22, 1875.
Henry Sylvanus K., born June 12, 1876.
Mary Anna K., born October 1, 1877.

Adam Krauss, son of John Krauss (page 190), married Anna Stauffer. One child,
Nora, born August 18, 1874.

Eli D. Wiegner, son of Joseph Wiegner (page 167), married Emma, daughter of Solomon Griesmer. Children:
Charles O., born April 8, 1874.
Olive C., born March 17, 1876.

Samuel Yeakel, son of John Yeakel (page 217), married Savilla M. A. Harper February 8, 1873. Issue:
Warren H., born December 1, 1873.
Eva L., born December 31, 1875.

Lizzie S. Kriebel, daughter of Joseph B. Kriebel (page 199), married Jonas B. Moyer, born March 1, 1847, son of Samuel L. Moyer, March 2, 1873. Children:
Elmer K., born April 18, 1874. Died August 20, 1875.
Irwin K., born May 12, 1876.

David Krauss, son of Aaron Krauss (page 174), married Emma, daughter of Jacob Kneedler, March 5, 1873.

Franklin Scipt, son of Abraham Scipt (page 221), married Lizzie, daughter of Henry Bean, April 12, 1873. Children:
Mary Alice, born January 29, 1874.
Kate Minerva, born August 30, 1876.

Peter Brown married Angeline, daughter of Samuel Master (page 218), April 16, 1873. Children:
Elizabeth A., born December 26, 1873.
Agnes M., born March 8, 1876.

Isaac W. Yeakel, son of Jacob Yeakel (page 181), married Miranda, daughter of Moses Wolfgang, May 20, 1873. Wife born January 31, 1857. One child,
Lilie Jane, born September 19, 1875.
I. W. Y. is a clergyman of the Evangelical Association. Resides in Schuylkill County, Pa.

Joseph Y. Schultz, son of Samuel Schultz (page 164),

married Angeline, daughter of John Leister, May 31, 1873. Child,
Franklin, born February 19, 1876.

Levi Schultz, son of George Schultz (page 208), married Elizabeth, daughter of Israel Stauffer, September 27, 1873. Wife born December 29, 1855. Children:
Harrietta, born April 27, 1875.
Sada, born August 28, 1877.

Quincy Fretz married Catharine, daughter of Jacob Yeakel (page 155), October 10, 1873. One child,
Alice, born August 9, 1874. Died August 30, 1874.

Henry S. Krauss, son of Henry Krauss (page 175), married Amanda, daughter of Joseph Hofman, October 25, 1873. Children:
Howard, born March 7, 1876.
Amelia, born September 24, 1877.

William Z. Kriebel, son of William Kriebel (page 192), married Kate H., daughter of Elias Swartley, September 13, 1873. Wife born July 1, 1852. Children:
Elmer, born May 11, 1874. Died September 25, 1874.
Mamie, born October 1, 1875.

Philip K. Schultz, son of Jacob Schultz (page 195), married Amanda, daughter of Aaron Krauss (page 174), November 1, 1873. Children:
Calvin, born September 19, 1875.
Jacob, born February 3, 1877.

Michael Z. Kriebel, son of William Kriebel (page 192), married Mary, daughter of Abraham Cassel, November 1, 1873. Issue:
William, born September 28, 1874.

Charles B. Keenly married Julian A., daughter of Jacob Yeakel (page 181), November 1, 1873. Issue:
Ella G., born December 3, 1874.
Robert E., born February 21, 1877.

William H. Anders, son of Andrew Anders (page 217), married Susanna M., daughter of Samuel Anders, (page 183), November 15, 1873. Children:
Emma Jane, born September 25, 1874.
Andrew, born July 6, 1877.

Ambrose Yeakel, son of Anthony Yeakel (page 184), married Elizabeth, daughter of Joel Yeakel (page 197), November 22, 1873. Children:
Clara, born April 18, 1875.
James, born December 28, 1876.

James M. Beyer, son of Samuel B. Beyer (page 179), married Ellie M. Bean December 24, 1873. Child,
Frank, born November 7, 1875.

Charles Meschter, son of Rev. Jacob Meschter (page 202), married Matilda, daughter of David Clemmer, 1873. Children:
Nora, born April 24, 1874.
Harvey, born July 24, 1876.

John Newman married Lydia, daughter of Samuel Beyer (page 204). Children:
Cyrus, born May, 1874.
Eliza, born September, 1877.

Daniel H. Schultz, son of Reuben Schultz (page 187), married Katie Geary January 31, 1874. Children:
Matilda, born ———, 1874.
Amanda, born October 4, 1877.

George Hayman, son of Israel Hayman, married Sarah, daughter of John Yeakel (page 153), January 14, 1874. Children:
 Ida May, born January 24, 1875.
 John Y., born March 16, 1878.

William Krauss son of Aaron Krauss (page 174), married Isabella Bean, January 31, 1874. Issue:
 Ellwood, born December 15, 1874.
 Howard, born December 31, 1875.
 Emma, born July 26, 1877.

George E. Long married Mary E., daughter of William C. Beyer (page 214), February 4, 1874. Issue:
 Henry E., born January 1, 1875.
 Lilian E., born January 20, 1878.

Abraham Schultz, son of Michael Schultz (page 191), married Anna B. Meyer March 7, 1874. Child,
 Parker, born November 1, 1875.

Jacob K. Master, son of Jacob Master (page 152) married Laura, daughter of James Hutson, February 1, 1874. Issue:
 Luther Benson, born May 13, 1876.

Willoughby Seibert, son of Daniel Seibert (page 159), married Mary, daughter of Solomon Kemmerer, March 28, 1874. Children:
 Kate Elizabeth, born March 13, 1875.
 Laura Jane, born June 21, 1878.

John Hey, born June 7, 1842, married Melissa, daughter of George C. Master (page 189), July 7, 1874. Issue:
 Mary Thornton, born October 18, 1877.

Abraham Erb, son of Mahlon Erb (page 236), married Mary, daughter of John Leister, September 12, 1874. Children:
Howard, born April 22, 1875.
Mary Ann, born ———, 1878.

Charles S. Anders, son of Abraham Anders (page 185), married Kate B., daughter of George Detwiler, October 3, 1874.

Francis Z. Kriebel, son of William Kriebel (page 192), married Mary, daughter of Elias Swartly, October 17, 1874. Children:
Minnie Minerva, born April 21, 1876.
William Sebastus, born December 4, 1877.

Susan K. Freyer, daughter of Bernard Freyer (page 188), married Charles H. Johnson, born March 17, 1849, son of William Johnson, October 24, 1874. One child,
Marcus F., born June 6, 1876.

Aaron B. Kriebel, son of Abraham Kriebel (page 162), married Eliza, daughter of Jesse Snyder (page 176), October 30, 1874. Children:
Mary Ann, born January 8, 1876.
Abraham S., born April 13, 1878.

John Jones, son of Samuel Jones, born September 8, 1824, married Lydia, daughter of Abraham Wampole, November 21, 1874. Wife born December 27, 1837. No issue.

Charles M. Urffer, son of Samuel Urffer (page 152), married Catharine Ann, daughter of George Werst,

November 26, 1874. Wife born June 10, 1857. Children:
   Anna Maria, born May 14, 1875. Died August 14, 1875.
   Samuel, born June 8, 1877.

Samuel Kriebel, son of Joseph B. Kriebel (page 199), married Emma, daughter of Abraham Ziegler, December 9, 1874. Children:
   Ella May Z., born October 23, 1876.
   Child, born 1878.

John Bergey married Susanna, daughter of Elias Kriebel (page 228), December 12, 1874. Children:
   Elmer K., born November 8, 1875.
   Annie K., born September 6, 1877.

Frederick G. Shepps married Isabella, daughter of Elias Beyer (page 215), December 19, 1874. One child,
   Ida Mary, born June 5, 1878.

Daniel S. Kriebel, son of Isaac S. Kriebel (page 158), married Mary A., daughter of Chauncey Abbey, December 21, 1874. Wife born December 21, 1853. One child,
   Clarence, born January 28, 1876.

Daniel Longacre married Mary Ann, daughter of Andrew K. Schultz (page 196), December 23, 1874. One child,
   Emma, born May 1, 1877.

Horace Brinton, son of Samuel Brinton, married Priscilla, daughter of Levi Heebner (page 220), December 24, 1874. One child,
   Mabel, born November 10, 1875.

Lewis Beyer, son of Benjamin Beyer (page 257), married Sallie R. Smoyer in 1875. Wife born November 16, 1852. One child,
    Allen S., born 1875.

Cyrus Beyer, son of Samuel Beyer (page 204), married Susan Miller in 1875. Children:
    Jane, born June, 1876. Died March, 1878.
    Samuel, born December 25, 1877. Died May, 1878.

Franklin Stauffer married Sarah, daughter of Joel Yeakel (page 197), March 28, 1874. One child,
    Anna, born June 23, 1876.

John Mahlon Krauss, son of Henry Krauss (page 175), married Sarah, daughter of Jonathan Christman, January 2, 1875.

Abraham Yeakel, son of Samuel S. Yeakel (page 174), married Sarah Lewis January 9, 1875. Children:
    Joseph L., born January 9, 1876.
    Anna A., born July 8, 1877.

Hiram M. Anders, son of Samuel Anders (page 183), married Araminta Zimmerman February 7, 1875. Children:
    Warren, born October 20, 1875.
    Ella, born February 3, 1877.

Henry Yeakel, son of Daniel Yeakel (page 228), married Diana Berndt February 13, 1875. One child,
    Harry Alvin, born April 9, 1876.

Elias U. Moyer, born February 4, 1850, married Lydia Ann, daughter of Elias Beyer (page 215), March 11, 1875. Children:

Anna Bell, born December 17, 1875.
William U., born June 3, 1877.

Anthony B. Schultz, son of Anthony Schultz (page 185), married Hannah, daughter of Israel Place, March 13, 1875. Children:
Mary Ella, born February 5, 1876.
Idella P., born June 26, 1878.

George B. Dresher, son of Eli Dresher (page 214), married Cecilia E. Roset April 8, 1875. One child,
Cecilia R., born June 28, 1877.

Charles Snyder, son of Job Snyder (page 159), married Deborah, daughter of John Nice, June 12, 1875. Wife born July 17, 1850.

David W. Cassel, born January 16, 1856, married Anna R., daughter of Joseph B. Beyer (page 186), September 11, 1875. Children:
Mary Ann B., born July 11, 1876.
John B., born May 30, 1878.

John Harrey, born June 19, 1856, married Sarah, daughter of Henry Kriebel (page 188), October 18, 1875.

Atwood Yeakle, son of William Yeakle (page 219), married Caddie, daughter of Samuel H. Aiman, November 10, 1875. One child,
Willie L., born November 8, 1876.

Levi Y. Meschter, son of Rev. Jacob Meschter (page 202), married Elizabeth, daughter of Frank Shelly, November 13, 1875. One child,
Agnes, born April 18, 1877.

Addison Bookheimer, son of Frederick Bookheimer (page 213), married Susanna, daughter of Adam Kriebel (page 221), November 16, 1875.

Levi N. Schultz, son of Enoch Schultz (page 194), married Sallie L., daughter of Abraham Reiff, January 1, 1876. Wife born May 17, 1853. One child,
    Abraham R., born November 28, 1876. Died February 19, 1877.

Josephus Gerhard, son of Daniel Y. Gerhard (page 201), married Elizabeth K., daughter of Amos Schultz (page 168), January 8, 1876. One child,
    Son, born February 9, 1878.

Jonas S. Kriebel, son of Abraham Kriebel (page 206), married Annie, daughter of Aaron Krauss (page 174), January 8, 1876. One child,
    Harvey, born May 29, 1878.

Willoughby K. Heinly, born October 1, 1847, married Maria K., daughter of Jacob Krauss (page 154), January 29, 1876. One child,
    Emma, born May 12, 1877. Died.

Samuel S. Schultz, son of Rev. Joshua Schultz (page 172), married Amanda L., daughter of James Roberts, February 19, 1876. Wife born August 24, 1858. Children:
    Ida, born 1876.
    Allen, born January 12, 1878.

Levi R. Beyer, son of Joseph B. Beyer (page 186), married Mary L. Kindy March 30, 1876. Wife born April 1, 1843. One child,
    Elon K., born August 17, 1877.

Christian Bieler, son of Henry Bieler, born August, 1846, married Rosina, daughter of George Schultz (page 208), April 8, 1876. Children:
Kora, born October 4, 1876.
Oliver, born April 5, 1878.

George Scipt, son of Abraham Scipt (page 221), married Elizabeth K., daughter of Frederick Bookheimer (page 213), April 29, 1876. One child,
Berthie Regina, born April 16, 1877.

John Yeakel, son of Joel Yeakel (page 238), married Emeline E., daughter of John Bear, ——— 1876. Wife born December 20, 1858. Child,
Charles H., born September 25, 1877.

Henry Gehman, born March 15, 1844, married Mary, daughter of Jacob Yeakel (page 215), July 29, 1876. Child,
Frederick Charles, born November 5, 1877.

Daniel C. Kratz, son of ——— Kratz, married Amanda, daughter of George Snyder (page 199), 1876. Child,
George, born January 5, 1877.

John Jacob, son of Henry Jacob, married Susanna, daughter of Henry Krauss (page 175), October 19, 1876.

Aaron Snyder, son of Jesse Snyder (page 176), married Emeline, daughter of Abraham Dresher (page 227), October 21, 1876.

Jeremiah K. Anders, son of Jeremiah Anders (page 158),

married Mary, daughter of Abraham Anders (page 185), November 4, 1876. Child,
Eugene, born December 22, 1877.

Jackson Beyer, son of Adam Beyer (page 226), married Elizabeth Queal November 30, 1876. Child,
Lucy J., born April 11, 1878.

Abraham C. Wiegner, son of Abraham Wiegner (page 165), married Ella Cordelia, daughter of ———— ————, December 25, 1876. Wife born February 8, 1856. Child,
Henry James, born January 25, 1878.

Noah Seibert, son of Jonas Seibert (page 216), married Amanda S., daughter of Isaac S. Kriebel (page 158), December 30, 1876.

Horatio Schultz, son of Thomas Schultz (page 226), married Magdalena, daughter of Andrew K. Schultz (page 196), January 20, 1877. Child,
Elenora, born May 19, 1878.

Abraham K. Meschter, son of Rev. George Meschter (page 154), married Hannah, daughter of Joseph Cassel, March 31, 1877. Wife born March 26, 1846. Hannah, wife of A. M., died August 2, 1878.

Lewis Kuntz married Lydia E., daughter of Benjamin Yeakel (page 170), April 1, 1877.

George G. Mann married Isabella, daughter of William C. Beyer (page 214), May 3, 1877. Reside in Philadelphia.

David Master, son of Samuel Master (page 218), married Maria Gable June 4, 1877. Wife born September 29, 1855.

William H. Stoner married Susanna, daughter of John Yeakel (page 217), June 4, 1877.

Edwin K. Kriebel son of George A. Kriebel (page 207), married Amelia, daughter of Mahlon Souder, in 1877.
Child,
 Emma, born December 26, 1877.

Isaiah A. Anders, son of Joseph Anders (page 228), married Annie, daughter of John Kuhn, June 27, 1877.

Abraham Seipt, son of Abraham Seipt (page 221), married Lydia, daughter of Frederick Bookheimer (page 213), October 13, 1877.

Addison Schultz, son of Michael Schultz (page 191), married Susanna, daughter of Jonas Seibert (page 216), November 3, 1877.

Edwin N. Schultz, son of Enoch Schultz (page 194), married Susanna, daughter of Rev. Joshua Schultz, (page 172), November 10, 1877.
 Child born December, 1878. Died same day.

Joseph Hunsberger, son of John Hunsberger, married Martha, daughter of Henry L. Heebner (page 226), November 17, 1877.

William Yeakel, son of Jacob Yeakel (page 161), married Jennie A., daughter of Hezekiah Coats, December 8, 1877. Wife born August 15, 1847.

Daniel K. Anders, son of George Anders (page 139), married Edith, daughter of Dr. Hassenplug, December 18, 1877.

Benjamin Krauss, son of Jonathan Krauss (page 196), married Hannah, daughter of Andrew Anders (page 217), November 3, 1877.

William Sies married Lydia, daughter of Henry Y. Schultz (page 140), December 27, 1877.

Samuel Wolf, son of Samuel Wolf, married Emma Jane, daughter of Anthony H. Seipt (page 228), December 27, 1877.
This is Dr. Wolf, of Skippackville, Pa.

Allen Yeakel, son of Daniel Yeakel (page 228), married Caroline, daughter of George Schultz (page 208), January 17, 1878.

Charles S. Kriebel, son of Abraham Kriebel (page 206), married Lydia, daughter of Jonas Seibert (page 216), February 9, 1878.

George Cain married Mary J., daughter of Jacob H. Master (page 243), February 21, 1878.

Jacob K. Schultz, son of Jacob Schultz (page 195), married Minerva Rothermel February 21, 1878. Wife born December 21, 1854.

Wilson S. Krauss, son of Jesse Krauss (page 143), married Susanna, daughter of Charles Wiand, May 23, 1878.

Milton Yeakel, son of Joel Yeakel (page 197), married Carolina Schiffert August 31, 1878.

Jacob Yeakel son of Jacob Yeakel (page 161), married Lizzie Shaffer, September 5, 1878.

Sarah Jane Beyer, daughter of John Beyer (page 219), married Edwin Bean, son of John Bean, November 24, 1878.

Martha A. Anders, daughter of Joseph Anders (page 228), married Luther, son of Norris Dowlin, December 25, 1878.

Samuel S. Kriebel, son of Jonas Kriebel (page 211), married Anna, daughter of James Currier, December 31, 1878.
Wife born August 10, 1858.

Edwin Z. Kriebel, son of William Kriebel (page 192), married Kate, daughter of John Bean, February 1, 1879.

Amanda Kriebel, daughter of Ephraim Kriebel (page 223), married Edwin Rodenberger February 8, 1879.

Margaret Master, daughter of Christopher Master (page 92), married William Nelson. Children:
  James.
  Margaret.
  Josephine.
  Elizabeth.

Mary Master, daughter of Christopher Master (page 92), married Nimrod Kerrick. Children:
  Josephine.
  William.
  Phœbe Ann.
  Leonades.
  Thomas.

Hannah Master, daughter of Christopher Master (page 92), married John Ross. Children:
  Mary.
  Elenor.
  Frank.
  Christopher.
  Thomas.
  John W.
  Margaret, } twins.
  Sarah,
  Rachel.

Ann Master, daughter of Christopher Master (page 92), married Joseph Speer. Children:
  Margaret.
  Mary.
  John.
  Samuel..
  Catharine.
  Matilda.
  Emma.
. Reside in Kansas.

Samuel Master, son of Christopher Master (page 92), married Angeline, daughter of William Gorden. Children:
  Mary.
  William.
  Leonades.

APPENDIX TO THE RECORD.

Abraham Hartranft, on page 31, married, second time, Susannah Seidel, and by her left no issue. She died December 29, 1779, in Philadelphia, with her stepson John.

Anna Warmer came to Pennsylvania in 1734, with her brother Andreas Warmer (page 17), was never married, and died December 30, 1750.

Barbara Reinewald, recorded on page 15, was a sister of Christoph Reinewald (page 12).

Maria, wife of George Anders (page 4), was a sister of George Reinewald (page 12).

The maiden name of George Dresher's wife (page 4) was Byer or Baer.

Frederick Schœpps (page 10) was 80 years of age when he died.

Abraham Heydrick, brother of George and Caspar Heydrick (recorded on page 11), came to Pennsylvania at the same time, and died single from injuries received by falling from a cart October 16th, 1767, in his 48th year. He was a tailor by trade. His father, whose name was Abraham, died before his sons came to this country.

Eve, wife of Caspar Heydrick (page 11), was a sister of Balthasar Heydrick (page 9).

Judith, wife of David Scipt (page 15), was a sister of Christoph Reinewald (page 12), and of Barbara (page 15).

Christoph Reinewald (page 12) was born in Silesia in 1703. His wife was Susanna Scipt.

George Heebner (page 21), was a brother of Hans (page 14).

Hans Heebner (recorded on page 14), while assisting his son in taking in the second crop of hay, fell from the wagon, and of the injuries received he died September 17, 1754. This occurred at his son Melchior's, in Worcester Township, then the County of Philadelphia.

Susanna Beyer, daughter of Abraham Beyer (page 17), married Turk or Dirk Casselberger November 1, 1762, and had issue:
    Dirk, born October 24, 1763. Died March 11, 1841.
    Paul, born 1765.
    Andrew, born.
No record of either of these parents.

George Hoffman and his wife, Barbara Scipt, came to Pennsylvania in 1734, with one son,
    Balthasar, Jr., who died December 20, 1754.
    George H. died June 29, 1765, in the 81st year of his age, and his wife died November 29, 1760.

The maiden name of Susanna, widow of Adam Wiegner, was Heydrick (see page 17).

Melchior Schultz, son of George Schultz (page 3), married and had children:
  Anna, born October, 1757.
  David, born April 29, 1759. Died April 2, 1764.
  1 Catharine, born October 5, 1760. Died February 16, 1761.
  2 Catharine, born December, 1761.
M. S. came to an untimely death by falling from his horse, on the 24th of February, 1764, from the injuries of which he died the 3d of March following.

George Wiegner, son of Melchior Wiegner (page 17), married, to whom unknown, May 22, 1764, and died January 25, 1776, aged 38 years.

Maria Wiegner (Heebner), the mother of Melchior Wiegner (page 17), was half-sister to David Heebner (page 9), Christopher (page 18), and Regina Yeakle (page 5). She died February 6, 1765, aged 86 years.

Susanna, wife of Caspar Kriebel (page 11), maiden name was Wiegner.

Matthias Gerhard (page 58) died August 20, 1803, and his second wife died April 7, 1838, aged 85 years, 10 months, and 23 days.

Regina, daughter of Christopher Reinewald (page 43), married John Garner, and died September 1, 1818, in the 46th year of her age.

Anna Krauss, mother of Balthasar (page 3), when she came to Pennsylvania in 1733, had at least two daughters besides her son Balthasar: Maria, who married Leonard Knopf and left issue, and Susanna, who married —— Neis, and died July 28, 1794, and another son, Melchior, who was of unsound mind, died September 16th, 1779.

Reuben Yeakel, son of Carl Yeakel (page 120), is the Rev. Reuben Yeakel, Bishop of the Evangelical Association, and resides in Norristown, Pa. His jurisdiction as Bishop of the Church embraces the Middle and Western States of the Union.

Christopher Heebner (page 74) was a farmer, and lived and died on the farm now owned by Governor Hartranft, in Norriton Township, north of the Borough of Norristown, Pa.

Hans Heebner (page 14) had a son Melchior, who married, February 11, 1752, and had two daughters:
Elizabeth, born April 11, 1753.
Margaret, born October 16, 1755.
This is all of the record we have of this family.

Maria, daughter of Gregorius Meschter (page 15), married December 20, 1762, to whom unknown.

George Yeakel came to Pennsylvania in 1734. He lived with Dr. Wagner (page 33), in Worcester Township, and died single, September 11, 1764, aged 68 years. He was possibly a relative of Dr. Wagner.

Anna, daughter of Melchior Schubert (page 56), married a man by the name of Ebbert, and died February 21, 1845.

Maria, daughter of Christopher Reinewald (page 43), married Godfried Bostan, and died February 3, 1826, aged 55 years.

Maria Krauss, daughter of David Krauss (page 85), married Joseph Bitting, and whose daughter married Anthony Schultz (page 185). Maria Bitting died October 18, 1837.

Maria Krauss (page 18) was sister to Ursula, wife of the Rev. Balthasar Hoffman (page 5).

Caspar Yeakel, son of David Yeakel (page 9), arrived in Pennsylvania in 1734 with his father and brothers. Married and left one daughter,
  Susanna.
C. Yeakel died some time previous to 1784. In a letter written by Jacob Yeakel (page 61) in 1784, to a cousin, he mentions this Caspar as his uncle, and brother of his father Christopher.

Eve Meschter (page 16) came to Pennsylvania. Her husband was Melchior Meschter, and died in Germany, previous to her emigration to this country with her children.

It appears that Abraham Beyer (page 17) had a son George, who died September 19, 1744, and a daughter, who was the youngest child, named Susanna. MSS. in possession of Reuben Schultz, of Upper Hanover.

Rosina Beyer, wife of Abraham Beyer (page 17), was a sister of Anna Wagner (page 17), and Maria, wife of Christopher Heebner, Sr. (page 18).

Christopher Kriebel, recorded on page 32, was a minister of the Society of Schwenkfelders, and lived in Lower Salford Township, Montgomery County, Pa. George Kriebel, on page 22, was his brother.

Ursula, wife of the Rev. Balthasar Hoffman (page 5), was sister of Abraham Beyer (page 17), and of Maria Krauss, widow (page 18).

The following list contains all the ministers of the Society of Schwenkfelders since the arrival in Pennsylvania:

George Weiss, Balthasar Hoffman, Christopher Schultz, Sr., Christopher Kriebel, George Kriebel, Christopher Hoffman, Melchior Kriebel, Melchior Schultz, Andrew Kriebel, Andrew Yeakel, John Schultz, Christopher Schultz, Jr., Balthasar Heebner, David Kriebel, Daniel Kriebel, Joshua Schultz, William Schultz, George Meschter, Reuben Kriebel, Abraham Heebner, Jacob Meschter, William S. Anders, and John B. Kriebel.

ERRATA.

In George Kriebel's record, on page 22, in the third line, it should read page 10, instead of page 5.

In Melchior Schultz's record, on page 22, in the third line, it should read Eve Meschter, page 16, instead of Melchior Meschter, page 9.

In the record of Rev. Christopher Schultz, in the third line from the beginning, it should read page 10, instead of page 5.

In the record of Edward Dowers, on page 80, it is stated that he was born in 1796, it should be 1769.

In the record of Rev. Joshua Schultz, page 172, in the second line, it should read page 108, instead of page 102.

In Charles Meschter's record, on page 290, in the first line, it should read Jacob Meschter, page 129, instead of Rev. Jacob Meschter, page 202.

In the record of Governor Hartranft, page 233, in the second line, read page 150, instead of page 115, and in the sixteenth line, read page 5, instead of page 2.

In the record of Andrew Anders, page 217, in the first line, read page 133, instead of page 132.

In the records of the children of Anthony S. Heebner, read page 136, instead of page 135.

In the records of the children of George Anders, on page 140, read page 140, instead of page 139.

In the record of Abraham A. Kriebel, on page 241, in the third line, read page 141, instead of page 110.

In the record of Levi Heebner, on page 220, read page 128, instead of page 97.

INDEX.

A.

Ackerman, Henry, 296
Althouse, Henry, 112
Anders, Abraham, 46
" Abraham, 67
" Abraham, 95
" Abraham, 185
" Abraham, 211
" Abraham K., 270
" Andrew, 69
" Andrew, 217
" Anthony, 173
" Balthasar, 4
" Benjamin, 83
" Charles S., 307
" David, 173
" Daniel K., 314
" Frederick, 142
" George, 4
" George, 4
" George, 38
" George, 76
" George, 140
" George, 142
" George S., 282
" Hiram M., 309
" Isaiah A., 314
" Jacob, 140
" John, 91

Anders, John, 169
" John, 267
" John H., 219
" John S., 276
" Jeremiah, 158
" Jeremiah K., 312
" Joseph, 133
" Joseph, 228
" Joseph H., 291
" Joseph S., 295
" Joseph S., Jr., 288
" Martha A., 316
" Nathaniel H., 275
" Samuel, 183
" Samuel K., 257
" William H., 305
" William K., 284
" Rev. William S., 288
Anson, Samuel, 226

B.

Bachman, William H., 281
Baker, John M., 278
Barnit, Jacob, 209
Barnes, William, 138
Bates, Thomas L., 180
Bean, Jacob, 90
Bean, James U., 278
Bean, Theodore W., 259

Beard, James, 283
Bechtel, Joseph, 190
Beck, John, 297
Beideman, Henry M., 267
Benner, Enos, 289
Bergy, John, 308
Beyer, Abraham, 17
" Abraham, 35
" Abraham, 60
" Adam, 226
" Andrew, 40
" Andrew, 104
" Benjamin, 157
" Charles W., 269
" Cornelius, 297
" Cyrus, 309
" Daniel, 229
" David C., 240
" Elias, 215
" Henry C., 194
" Henry F., 208
" Isaac C., 271
" Jackson, 313
" Jacob, 65
" Jacob, 132
" Jacob, 239
" Jacob B., 175
" Jacob C., 214
" James, 276
" James M., 301
" James M., 305
" Jesse, 222
" John, 133
" John, 219
" Joseph, 114
" Joseph C., 209
" Joseph B., 186
" Lewis, 309
" Levi R., 311
" Nathaniel, 273
" Samuel, 204

Beyer, Samuel B., 179
" Sarah Jane, 316
" William, 180
" William C., 214
Berger, Edward, 301
Bieler, Allen O., 283
" Christian, 312
" David, 231
Biles, George, 270
Bookheimer, Addison, 311
" Frederick, 213
Boyer, Charles E., 164
Brecht, John E., 278
Brinton, Horace, 308
Brown, Alexander F., 224
" Harriet H., 212
" James, 301
" Peter, 303
Burgstresser, Isaiah, 298

C.

Cain, George, 315
Carl, Samuel, 273
Cassel, Abraham H., 250
" Benjamin, 113
" David M., 272
" David W., 310
" Isaac B., 161
" Joseph, 143
" Mahlon H., 287
" Simon, 280
Cheney, John W., 243
Clemens, Jacob, 189
Clemmer, Samuel G., 225
Cole, Nathan, 222
Corson, Amos, 177
Cress, Jacob, 84

D.

Dennis, William, 269
Detweiler, Christian, 134
" Joseph, 201

Detwiler, George R., 182
Dowers, Edward, 80
Dresher, Abraham, 60
" Abraham, 227
" Christopher, 24
" Christopher, 89
" Daniel, 245
" Eli, 214
" George, 4
" George, 50
" George B., 310
" Jacob, 133
" Jacob, 217
" Oliver, 151
" Samuel, 94
" Samuel, 237

E.

Eberhard, Charles W., 282
Erb, Abraham, 307
" Benjamin, 247
" Jacob, 149
" John, 94
" Mahlon, 236
Evans, Andrew, 219
" David Z., 218

F.

Fisher, Adam, 187
" George W., 288
" Jacob F., 287
Flinn, Edmund, 73
Fluck, Charles, 289
Fretz, Quincy, 304
Frey, Jacob, 74
Freyer, Amos R., 266
" Bernard B., 188
" Jacob K., 284
" Susan B., 307

G.

Gehman, Henry, 312

Gehman, Michael, 286
Gehoe, Matthias, 80
Geisser, John Henry, 261
Gerhard, Ambrose, 294
" Andrew, 128
" Charles, 171
" Daniel Y., 201
" Jacob, 81
" Josephus, 311
" Matthias, 58
" Matthias, 96
" Peter, 40
" Peter, 85
" Samuel, 185
" Samuel, 293
" Solomon, 155
" Thomas R., 282
Gerry, Benjamin, 230
Gilbert, Samuel, 230
Glaze, Frederick B., 240
Griesmer, Gabriel, 191

H.

Hagy, Samuel, 182
Hallman, Nathaniel, 294
" William, 260
Harpst, William F., 285
Harris, Michael, 263
Harrey, John, 310
Hartman Jacob H., 188
Hartranft, Abraham, 31
" Barbara, 32
" George, 38
" John F., 233
" Leonard, 61
" Leonard, 101
" Melchior, 36
" Samuel E., 150
" Tobias, 5
Hayman, George, 306

Heebner, Abraham, 72
" Abraham, 73
" Abraham, 134
" Abraham, 149
" Anthony K., 262
" Anthony S., 136
" Ann, 156
" Rev. Balthasar, 77
" Benjamin L., 254
" Christoph, 18
" Christopher, 39
" Christopher, 74
" Christopher, 169
" David, 9
" David, 136
" David S., 163
" Enoch M., 295
" George, 21
" George, 49
" George, 178
" Hans, 14
" Hans Christopher, 31
" Hannah, 118
" Henry, 104
" Henry H., 285
" Henry L., 226
" Isaac D., 281
" Jacob, 201
" Jacob D., 291
" John, 145
" John S., 208
" Joseph L., 265
" Joseph R., 141
" Josiah D., 286
" Joshua, 165
" Levi, 220
" Margaret, 121
" Myra, 178
" Sarah, 124
" Susanna, 178
" William D., 302

Heebner, William L., 271
Heinley, Willoughby H., 311
Hey, John, 306
Heydrick, Abraham, 47
" Abraham, 97
" Balthasar, 9
" Balthasar, 70
" Caroline M., 130
" Caleb, 174
" Caspar, 11
" Charles, 271
" Charles, 288
" Charles H., 141
" Charles William, 279
" Dr. Christopher, 74
" Christopher, 260
" David, 256
" George, 11
" George, 41
" George, 87
" George N., 171
" Harriet E., 221
" Isaac, 139
" Jesse A., 275
" Mary, 256
" Peter C., 264
" Samuel, 142
" Samuel, 268
" William W., 224
Hierneshitz, Michael, 284
Hiestand, Charles, 291
" John, 244
Hillegass, Oswin, 299
Hoffman, Rev. Balthasar, 5
" Christopher, 37
" Jacob, 267
" William, 282
Huber, Charles, 170
Hunsberger, Joseph, 314
" Josiah, 302

INDEX. 331

J.

Jacob, John, 312
John, Caspar, 14
Jones, John, 307
Johnson, Allen F. D., 296

K.

Kaufman, Nathan, 259
Keck, Henry H., 268
Keel, Martin, 275
Keely Henry S., 291
Keenly, Charles B., 305
Keiser, Paul, 206
Keller, Charles, 252
Kile, Jacob, 171
Kindig, Henry K., 256
Kline, Samuel, 116
Kook, David, 231
Kratz, Daniel C., 312
Krauss, Aaron, 174
" Abraham S., 273
" Adam, 302
" Amos K., 255
" Andrew, 84
" Anna, 3
" Anthony, 138
" Balthasar, 19
" Balthasar, 49
" Benjamin, 315
" Charles, 231
" Christopher, 34
" Daniel, 214
" David, 85
" David, 277
" David, 303
" Edward S., 297
" Edwin B., 272
" George, 102
" George S., 175
" George, 268

Krauss, Harrison Y., 282
" Henry, 175
" Henry S., 304
" Isaac, 249
" Isaac Y., 265
" Jacob, 154
" Jeremiah, 78
" Jesse, 143
" Joel, 181
" Joel H., 275
" John, 79
" John, 190
" John Mahlon, 309
" Jonathan, 196
" Joseph, 183
" Joseph, 203
" Mahlon, 287
" Maria, 18
" Nathaniel, 236
" Samuel, 170
" Solomon, 279
" Susanna, 168
" William, 306
" Wilson S., 315
Kriebel, Aaron, 208
" Aaron B., 307
" Abraham, 44
" Abraham, 61
" Abraham, 66
" Abraham, 71
" Abraham, 93
" Abraham, 126
" Abraham, 162
" Abraham, 206
" Abraham A., 241
" Abraham H., 247
" Abraham K., 253
" Abraham, 255
" Adam, 221
" Amanda, 316
" Andrew, 52

Kriebel, Andrew, 76
" Andrew, 262
" Andrew, 280
" Andrew A., 255
" Andrew K., 237
" Anthony, 126
" Benjamin, 103
" Benjamin, 116
" Benjamin, 135
" Benjamin S., 288
" Caspar, 11
" Charles, 190
" Charles, 266
" Charles S., 315
" Christina, 269
" Christoph, 11
" Christopher, 32
" Christopher, 67
" Christopher, 106
" Daniel S., 308
" David, 42
" David, 111
" David (Rev.), 120
" David D., 292
" Edwin K., 314
" Elias, 228
" Elijah, 292
" Edwin Z., 316
" Ephraim, 223
" Francis Z., 307
" Enos, 300
" George, 22
" George (Rev.), 41
" George, 54
" George, 137
" George, 164
" George A., 207
" George D., 237
" Henry, 188
" Henry, 252
" Henry S., 298

Kriebel, Henry S., 299
" Hiram A., 291
" Hosea K., 299
" Isaac, 100
" Isaac, 146
" Isaac, 209
" Isaac, 246
" Isaac S., 158
" Israel, 125
" Jacob, 71
" Jacob, 123
" Jacob, 144
" Jacob, 200
" Jeremiah, 62
" Jeremiah, 200
" Jeremiah, 301
" Jesse S., 297
" Job, 122
" Job, 277
" Joel S., 260
" John, 117
" John, 225
" John B. (Rev.), 285
" John K., 299
" Jonas S., 311
" Jonas, 211
" Jonathan, 127
" Joseph, 151
" Joseph, 160
" Joseph, 166
" Joseph, 251
" Joseph B., 199
" Levi, 193
" Lizzie S., 303
" Melchior, 11
" Melchior (Rev.), 55
" Melchior, 126
" Michael Z., 304
" Reuben, 214
" Reuben D., 295
" Rosina, 188

Kriebel, Samuel, 94
" Samuel, 124
" Samuel, 133
" Samuel, 162
" Samuel, 194
" Samuel, 308
" Samuel B., 210
" Samuel K., 257
" Samuel S., 316
" Samuel Y., 205
" Samuel Z., 284
" Septimus, 224
" Septimus, 289
" Solomon, 109
" Solomon, 278
" William, 192
" William S., 247
" William Z., 304
Krupp, Eli, 176
Kuntz, Lewis, 313

L.

Levan, Jacob S., 245
" Samuel, 244
Long George E., 306
Longacre, Daniel, 308
Lukens, Matthias, 262

M.

Mann, George G., 313
Master, Aaron, 192
" Ann, 317
" Christopher, 92
" David, 313
" Edward Ellis, 296
" George C., 189
" Hannah, 317
" Henry, 248
" Henry, 274
" Isaac, 107
" Isaac, 151
" Isaac, 249

Master, Jacob, 152
" Jacob, 221
" Jacob H., 243
" Jacob K., 306
" James K., 251
" Jared K., 300
" John, 98
" John, 148
" John, 155
" John Q., 250
" John W., 258
" John W., 285
" Levi, 263
" Levi Kerlin, 296
" Lewis E., 290
" Margaret, 316
" Mary, 316
" Rachel, 135
" Samuel, 218
" Samuel, 317
" Samuel B., 298
" Samuel K., 239
" William H. H., 276
Mentzel, George, 16
" Melchior, 16
Meschter, Abraham K., 313
" Balthasar, 57
" Charles, 290
" Charles, 305
" Christopher, 46
" Christopher, 56
" Christopher, 105
" David, 19
" David, 189
" Eve, 16
" George, 81
" Rev. George, 154
" Dr. George K., 286
" Gregorius, 15
" Henry, 150
" Jacob, 129

Meschter, Rev. Jacob, 202
" Jacob K., 289
" Jeremiah, 113
" Jeremiah, 249
" Levi Y., 310
" Manoah, 267
" Maria, 9
" Melchior, 12
" Melchior, 56
Metz, John, 147
" Joseph, 131
Miller, Horace, 244
" Levi, 216
" Samuel, 242
Moyer, Abraham S., 200
" John, 222
" Solomon S., 198
" William, 211
" Elias U., 309

N.

Nase, John, 161
Neuman, Christoph, 16
" Christopher, 69
" David, 39
" Enos, 238
" Melchior, 16
" Samuel, 128
Newman, John, 305
Nuss, John Mahlon, 223
" Joseph, 239
" Michael, 112
" Nathan, 187

O.

Overholtzer, Abraham G., 277
" John, 107

P.

Pennick, George, 277
Peters, John, 109

R.

Randenbush, Jacob, 198
Reed, John, 155
Reichard, Peter, 245
Reinewald, Balthasar, 46
" Barbara, 15
" Barbara, 15
" Christoph, 12
" Christopher, 40
" Christopher, 43
" Christopher, 98
" George, 12
" Jonas, 139
" Melchior, 48
Rittenhouse, Daniel, 127
Robinson, John, 124
Rodenberger, Jacob, 216
Rose, Isaac, 195
" Uriah, 203

S.

Scheffey, Reuben B., 236
Schell, Peter D., 241
" Solomon, 281
Schiffert, Daniel, 147
Schlicher, John, 110
Schubert, Charles, 239
" Christopher, 14
" Christopher, 116
" David, 21
" David, 106
" Lewis, 185
" Melchior, 56
" Rachel, 229
" Timothy, 210
Schœps, Frederick, 10
Schultz, Abraham, 52
" Abraham, 172
" Abraham, 203
" Abraham, 294

INDEX. 335

Schultz, Abraham, 306
" Adam, 92
" Dr. Addison, 284
" Addison, 314
" Adonia, 243
" Amos, 168
" Andrew, 59
" Andrew, 102
" Andrew, 108
" Andrew, 206
" Andrew K., 196
" Anna, 281
" Anthony, 185
" Anthony, 205
" Anthony, 207
" Anthony B., 310
" Balthasar, 48
" Caspar, 111
" Charles, 163
" Charles, 181
" Chester K., 300
" Rev. Christopher, 24
" Christopher, 51
" Rev. Christopher, 99
" Christopher K., 122
" Daniel, 117
" Daniel, 191
" Daniel II., 305
" Daniel S., 193
" Daniel S., 213
" David, 30
" David, 54
" David, 64
" David, 105
" David, 187
" David, 198
" Edward, 225
" Edwin K., 301
" Edwin N., 314
" Enoch, 194
" Enos, 277

Schultz, Frederick W., 145
" Gabriel, 115
" George, 3
" George, 20
" George, 23
" George, 90
" George, 115
" George, 153
" George, 208
" George, 293
" Gregorius, 13
" Gregory, 59
" Hannah, 205
" Henry, 220
" Henry, 195
" Henry II., 158
" Henry S., 192
" Henry W., 119
" Henry Y., 140
" Hiram, 284
" Horatio, 313
" Isaac, 100
" Isaac B., 292
" Israel, 146
" Jacob, 86
" Jacob, 177
" Jacob, 195
" Jacob K., 315
" Jeremiah, 127
" Joel, 207
" Joel, 251
" Joel S., 242
" John (Rev.), 82
" John, 188
" John, 294
" John S., 245
" Jonathan, 156
" Joseph, 115
" Joseph, 180
" Joseph, 191
" Joseph K., 276

Schultz, Joseph K., 281
" Joseph S., 241
" Joshua (Rev.), 172
" Joseph Y., 303
" Levi, 304
" Levi N., 311
" Manoah, 288
" Matthias, 96
" Melchior, 22
" Melchior (Rev.), 64
" Melchior, 119
" Michael, 191
" Nathan, 227
" Peter, 296
" Philip K., 304
" Reuben, 187
" Samuel, 101
" Samuel, 164
" Samuel, 179
" Samuel, 292
" Samuel A., 300
" Samuel H., 202
" Samuel S., 311
" Solomon, 206
" Solomon S., 301
" Susanna, 14
" Thomas, 197
" Thomas, 226
" William, 113
" William, 258
" William, 266
" William A., 257
Seibert, Daniel, 159
" David, 130
" Jacob, 63
" Jonas, 216
" Noah, 313
" Willoughby, 306
Seipt, Abraham, 89
" Abraham, 221
" Abraham, 314

Seipt, Abraham H., 246
" Anthony H., 228
" Caspar, 35
" Christopher, 22
" David, 15
" Franklin, 303
" George, 137
" George, 312
" George H., 282
" William, 299
Shaffer, William, 243
Shepard, Jesse, 183
Shepps, Frederick G., 308
Shuh, Jacob, 224
Shuler, George, 129
" Moses, 256
Shupe, Jacob, 215
Sies, William, 315
Simpson, George, 297
Smith, Richard F., 209
Snyder, Aaron, 312
" Abraham, 119
" Amos, 205
" Amos, 211
" Charles, 310
" Christian, 72
" Christopher, 65
" Daniel, 207
" Elias, 302
" George, 63
" George, 182
" George, 199
" Heinrich, 38
" Henry, 68
" Henry W., 248
" Isaac, 165
" Isaac, 280
" Jacob, 88
" Jesse, 176
" Job, 159
" John, 292

Snyder, Joseph, 112
" Joseph, 279
" Noah, 297
Spencer, Roderick R., 220
Springer, John, 149
Stahl, Tilghman, 240
Stahlnecker, Edwin S., 261
" Jacob, 272
Stauffer, Franklin, 309
Stout, Jesse, 232
" John, 242
Stoner, William H., 314
Stroh, Peter, 178

T.

Tyson, Jesse, 258

U.

Urffer, Balthasar, 103
" Charles M., 307
" Daniel K., 197
" Daniel Y., 241
" David, 109
" George, 51
" Henry K., 272
" Israel H., 250
" Joshua K., 149
" Michael, 89
" Samuel, 152
" Samuel, 295

V.

Van Fossen, Michael, 107
Van Karnel, John, 290

W.

Wagener, Anna, 18
" Daniel, 68
" David, 36

Wagener, David, 83
" David D., 131
" Jacob, 123
Wagner, Dr. Abraham, 33
" Anna, 17
" Christopher, 37
" Melchior, 33
Warmer, Andreas, 17
Wean, Jacob, 278
Weber, Edwin, 298
Weikert, George, 280
Weiss, Rev. George, 1
White, Dr. Humphrey, 120
Wiand, Daniel, 196
" Henry, 98
Wiedner, Edwin, 233
Wiegner, Abraham, 34
" Abraham, 76
" Abraham, 165
" Abraham, 204
" Abraham C., 313
" Anna, 266
" Christoph, 21
" Christopher, 150
" Daniel, 167
" Eli D., 302
" Ezra, 199
" George, 33
" George, 287
" Hans, 16
" Jacob, 274
" Joel, 167
" John, 80
" John, 179
" John, 274
" Joseph, 167
" Joseph, 254
" Melchior, 17
" Samuel, 270
" Susanna, 15
" Susanna, 17

Wierman, Jacob, 294
Wile, Samuel, 263
Wolf, Joel, 156
Wolf, Dr. Samuel, 315
Wood, Jacob F., 295

Y.

Yeakel, Abraham, 10
" Abraham, 32
" Abraham, 90
" Abraham, 118
" Abraham, 147
" Abraham, 309
" Allen, 315
" Ambrose, 305
" Amos A., 289
" Andrew, 85
" Rev. Andrew, 114
" Anna, 32
" Anna, 144
" Anna, 151
" Anna, 273
" Anthony, 184
" Balthasar, 20
" Balthasar, 42
" Balthasar, 43
" Benjamin, 170
" Carl, 120
" Caspar, 57
" Christopher, 36
" Christopher, 105
" Christopher, 110
" Christian, 95
" Christian, 229
" Daniel, 121
" Daniel, 212
" Daniel, 228
" Daniel, 264
" Daniel S., 210

Yeakel, David, 9
" David, 69
" David, 97
" David W., 228
" Edward, 195
" Elizabeth, 145
" Elizabeth, 252
" George, 22
" George, 48
" George, 104
" George, 190
" George, 232
" Hans Heinrich, 18
" Hans or John, 45
" Henry, 246
" Henry, 309
" Isaac, 91
" Dr. Isaac B., 283
" Rev. Isaac W., 303
" Jacob, 61
" Jacob, 81
" Jacob, 136
" Jacob, 155
" Jacob, 161
" Jacob, 181
" Jacob, 215
" Jacob, 315
" Jacob S., 152
" Jeremiah, 37
" Jeremiah, 103
" Rev. Jesse, 201
" Joel, 197
" Joel, 238
" John, 86
" John, 153
" John, 166
" John, 217
" John, 312
" Joseph, 153
" Joseph, 128
" Joseph, 213

Yeakel, Joseph Z., 293
" Josephus, 261
" Levi, 248
" Magdalena, 144
" Mary, 125
" Mary, 259
" Mary, 282
" Melchior, 50
" Milton, 315
" Noah, 232
" Regina, 10
" Samuel, 158
" Samuel, 177
" Samuel, 184
" Samuel, 303
" Samuel K., 254
" Samuel S., 174
" Sarah, 287
" Simon H., 298
" Solomon, 110
" Solomon, 283
" Solomon B., 264
" William, 265
" William, 314
" William M., 250
Yeakle, Abraham, 58
" Abraham, 77

Yeakle, Abraham A., 272
" Atwood, 310
" Augustus, 168
" Charles, 199
" Christopher, 23
" Christopher, 66
" Daniel W., 293
" Elvie, 300
" Emily, 263
" George, 172
" Isaac, 71
" Isaac S., 286
" Jacob, 106
" Jacob, 293
" Jacob S., 231
" Jeremiah, 45
" Joseph, 172
" Maria, 268
" Matthias, 13
" Regina, 5
" Samuel, 134
" Thomas, 249
" William, 219
" William A., 216
Yerger, Jesse, 253
Yoder, Benjamin A., 230
Younts, William H., 290

www.ingramcontent.com/pod-product-compliance
Lightning Source LLC
Chambersburg PA
CBHW020220240426
43672CB00006B/366